This is Not a Sad Story

HOW GOD TOOK MY BAD NEWS AND MADE IT BETTER

HAYDEN CREBBIN PALM

https://www.thepeoplemender.com

ISBN: 978-0-578-58957-2

Printed and bound in the United States of America
Maverick Publications • Bend, Oregon

What we've heard from you!

I just wanted to contact you to say what a difference Hayden's book is making in my life. I bought the book on Monday. As soon as I got home, I began reading. I bawled like a baby reading the diagnosis. I received very similar information, just a different type of rare aggressive cancer. I have been a ball of knots and so afraid or worried to tell people what I am going through. As I read Hayden's book, I am finding comfort in the feelings I have been having, and today for the first time since being diagnosed, I woke up with a sense of calm I haven't felt in some time. I just wanted to let you and your family know the impact your amazing, beautiful daughter and her words of strength and honesty have had on me. I find solace in Hayden's book. Thank you for sharing this with so many! —*Sherese*

I had a conversation with a coworker whose mom was recently diagnosed with cancer, and they have been struggling to understand why God has allowed this to happen. My first thoughts were about Hayden and all of the wise perspectives she shared in her blog. I pointed them toward her writings and found myself re-reading her entries until very late last night. After recovering from a rollercoaster of thoughts, prayers, and reflections, I am feeling motivated to become bolder in my faith. Hayden was so wonderful to me, and watching the way her faith persisted through cancer will have an impact on my walk the rest of my life, and I will be sharing her book in my old age. So, thanks for raising such a gem, she'll be changing lives and pointing others to Christ for years to come. —*Meredith*

Hayden had a God-given gift of expressing her thoughts and feelings in such a raw and authentic way. Even though I never met Hayden, I felt connected to her. Every time I might be having a small pity-party kind of day, here would come one of Hayden's new blogs, and wow, her words would bring me back to reality and gratitude! —*Maureen*

In the Ethiopian culture, where I grew up, it is very unusual to deal with the fact that you are dying and even more, planning your own funeral service. As a Christian, I grew up being taught that God is always good to us, and in our journey with Jesus, bad things will barely happen to you—which is far from the teaching of the Bible. It's encouraging and comforting personally for me that there is a beautiful life with Jesus in his kingdom with his father where there shall be no tears, death, nor sorrows. My sister Hayden understood this and gave her life to Jesus with joy, not with sadness. This is the greatest mystery that only a born-again Christian could understand. Thank you, Hayden, for teaching me this and sharing your faith, and I can't wait to see you in the kingdom of God. —*Nathan*

This year my own son died, and I am realizing how much pain you must have experienced and endured since Hayden passed away. I thought I knew, but I didn't. There is no possible way to understand the grief from a comfortable distance. I've read Hayden's words with new eyes. I'm new in my grief, and it is so painful right now. I was blindsided by it, but so thankful for having Hayden's words for myself and others. —Lisa

I came to know your daughter Hayden when I was in Seattle. I did not personally meet her. I met her blog. My best friend discovered he had cancer, and when I started to search the internet for hope, I found Hayden. I've always wanted to thank you for your kid. For her heart. For her words. For her belief. Thank you for raising such a wonderful woman that touched my heart so immensely when I needed it most. —Jaime

My dad is at home on hospice care now, and my family is really struggling. I was trying to figure out what to buy my dad because he is unable to do most things now. A friend suggested I get Hayden's book so my mom can read it to him, and it'll be a gift to both of them. I just want to say that I am always blown away by Hayden's strength and your faith. —Tessa

I'm about 2/3 done with the book. It is beautiful, inspiring, and the greatest example of selflessness, integrity, honesty and courage. I'm so glad I got the book and will be passing it to a few friends. Thank you, and to see the lives touched by Hayden is such a beautiful blessing. —Sarah

Hayden made such a difference in my au pair life here in Germany; she will never be forgotten. We have been bringing up so many great memories about Hayden, and we wanted to let you know how she continues to bless our lives. We talked about you and your family and how we hope you are getting stronger every day. Her words continue to help our lives. Thank you. —Gesyca

My grandparents got their package with Hayden's book today! My grandma called me right away to tell me how touched they were that both Adam and Elise signed it for them. Thank you for helping me make it extra special. It means so very much to me to give them something so meaningful. —Jennifer

I am enjoying the book so much! It's brought back some cancer memories of my own, but I appreciated Hayden's positive attitude while I was walking through my own battle. Her battle was so much more difficult than mine, but the emotional battle was still there. —Lisa

Dedication

This book is dedicated to you. The person who cared enough to pick up this book, whether for yourself or to care for someone else. Thank you. For what good are words if they are not read?

Foreword

"I can't stop this suffering, but I can control my perspective and focus on what I learn on the journey."

—Hayden Crebbin Palm (2017+)

For the reader who has been so fortunate to open this remarkable book, you are invited to join an extraordinarily brave young woman on a journey not of her choosing but one which she nonetheless unflinchingly accepted. Diagnosed with a rare and aggressive form of skin cancer, in her blog Hayden made the commitment to describe with absolute honesty the full rollercoaster of emotions she experienced: doubts, fears, intense sorrows as well as hopes and joys of a life transformed by cancer. In her willingness to share her story, she invites her readers to witness and learn from her suffering—a suffering that she accepted as her unique cross (cf. Matt. 16:24) while also recognizing it as an invitation to intimate communion with Christ in His suffering.

Here is a poignant account of her patient endurance while her medical team worked tirelessly to cure the cancer through multiple operations, radiation, and chemotherapy. Although curtailed by the cancer, hers was a life lived fully and with profound gratitude—a very powerful witness to the truth that quality takes ultimate precedence over quantity. As the cancer progressed and her treatment options narrowed, she endured increasing amounts of physical pain and suffering. Ultimately, her deep Christian faith sustained her through it all.

Cicely Saunders (+2005), the founder of the modern hospice movement, committed her life's work as a devout Christian physician, nurse, and social worker to relieving the suffering of persons struggling with progressive cancer. From close bedside observation of her patients, she realized that suffering affects at least four dimensions of the person: the physical, psychological, social and spiritual. She coined the term, "Total Pain," to capture this holistic vision of the person who suffers.

Palliative care represents an extension of hospice philosophy to the care of any person with a life-threatening illness who experiences suffering, including cancer survivors as well as others living with chronic illnesses. The World Health Organization has defined palliative care as "...an approach that improves the quality of life of patients and their families facing the problems associated with life-threatening illness, through the prevention and relief of suffering by means of early identification and impeccable assessment and treatment of pain and other problems, physical, psychosocial and spiritual. Palliative care uses a multidisciplinary team approach to address the needs and distress of patients and their families, including bereavement counseling, if needed; enhances quality of life, and may also positively influence the course of illness; and is applicable early in the course of illness, in conjunction with other therapies that are intended to prolong life, such as chemotherapy or radiation therapy, and includes those investigations needed to better understand and manage distressing clinical complications."

Careful attention to relieving pain and other forms of distress associated with life-threatening illnesses in no way compromises survival. Indeed, introduction of palliative care at the time of diagnosis of advanced cancer has actually been shown to improve quality of life, reduce the incidence of depression and extend survival. Hayden's patient endurance through all her suffering was a profound witness to the power of her Christian faith. Introduction of palliative care earlier in the course of her illness would likely have provided additional valuable support that could have helped to ease the suffering she and her family shared as she transitioned from hoping for a cure to her ultimate healing encounter with Christ in death.

Daniel B. Hinshaw, M.D.
Consultant in Palliative Medicine &
Professor Emeritus of Surgery,
University of Michigan Medical School

Introduction:

When Hayden and Chandler were little kids, they loved to cuddle up on the couch and have me tell them stories. It wasn't long before they were gifted storytellers themselves. Sometimes through words, other times through photography and videography. When Hayden was 16, she got her first job working as a courtesy clerk at Albertson's grocery store. Every day when she returned home, we would clap our hands together and start to chant, "Story time, story time!" Hayden would sit and tell us of the hilarious mishaps that happened to her during the workday. She always made us laugh and giggle at her many over-the-top adventures. It wasn't long before she started writing a blog on her Myspace. Now that's a blast from the past, isn't it!

When Hayden returned from living in Germany, she attended college at Moody Bible Institute in Spokane, Washington, where she started a photography blog called "Humans of Moody." Of the 700 students attending, she interviewed and photographed 300 of them. Oh, how Hade loved photography and writing, but she especially loved to tell other people's stories. People were her passion. She never met a stranger.

"I really loved the community there, and when I started Humans of Moody I really got to know it. I got to know a ton of people. You're just in your element, and you just feel really comfortable. I love community."

It was in Spokane that Hayden noticed a tiny bump on her cheek in April of 2015. On June 26th of that same year, she was diagnosed with a rare and aggressive form of skin cancer called Merkel Cell Carcinoma, a deadly cancer usually found in elderly white males. She was 21.

"The first thought that I had was, 'Seriously? Merkel? That's what it's called? That's the ugliest name I've ever, ever heard...."

By this time Hayden was working in Santa Cruz, California at Camp Redwood Glen with Chandler and three of her cousins. This camp will forever hold a special place in our hearts and play a major role in our lives. Camp is the place we experienced the first of God's blessings, starting with the camp nurse, Traci Clark, who just happened to have a background in oncology and working with newly diagnosed cancer patients. Oh, the providence of our great God.

"Here I was, thinking I would be treating bee stings and ended up being able to continue to work in my passion, in the woods, at summer camp. When I first met Hade, I never in my wildest dreams would have imagined that she had cancer. Her diagnosis and treatment were fast and furious. In a matter of two weeks, she went from painting spaceships and worrying about what to do on break day to fighting for her life."

From day one, Hayden decided she would write about her experiences with cancer and take us along on her journey. Open, honest, real, and raw. All of it. The good, the bald, and the ugly.

"I remember my mom telling me, 'You need to journal this, but I hate journaling because what's the point? For me, I don't have the motivation to do something just for me...I remember feeling like all I ever saw with the cancer patients that I knew was just the happy side. So here I am about to go through it, and I felt like I knew nothing about it. So I wanted to share my story openly from the beginning so that other people would know what it's actually like."

So, here we are. The next pages are Hayden's words. We have worked hard to preserve her voice in her writing. We have taken out a few "so's" and "you guys," added a few commas and some quotation marks to help make the blog easier to read, but the goal has always been for you to hear from Hayden's heart and her wisdom. Her story. So, grab a Kleenex and a cup of coffee and get to know my amazing daughter, a new friend for you, Hayden Sajl MayLynn Crebbin-Palm—a current resident of Heaven.

(Quotes are from Hayden's interview with Hannah Steinkopf-Frank, Herald & News)

Diagnosed

June 26, 2015

Today, I was diagnosed with cancer. "I have cancer," is something I never anticipated saying or even thinking about, but the doctor's report is in. You know, as she was explaining that it was Merkel Cell cancer and it is rare and has never been seen in someone my age, I just had to chuckle to myself a little. You see, ever since I was a kid and the doctor would tell my mom, "There's like a one percent chance of this happening," I was usually in that one percent. So, my family started calling me the one percent girl. *Of course*, I have been diagnosed with a super rare form of cancer—the one percent girl is at it again! The fear and uncertainty of what lies ahead comes and goes in waves. Initially, I was so shocked that I nearly fell to the ground. Cancer was just something that happened to other people, not here, not me, not now. But as I cried out to God and sought out my answers, He gave me everything I could ever need. Let me tell you about how God took my bad news and made it better.

Let me introduce you to my cousin Angelica, who we lovingly call JB. When she was a toddler, my mom started calling her Jelly Bean which my dad eventually shortened to Jabes which morphed into JB. She is one year older than me and we are more like sisters than cousins. I have never known life without her. Sleepovers, dress up, tea parties, boys, and traveling. We have done it all together. JB is the girl that does it all. She will drive 5 hours to put on a fab baby shower for a friend on Friday, leave at the crack of dawn the next morning to attend another friend's birthday party in another city, and drive 5 more hours to watch one of the cousins' football game. She is creative, and a mover and shaker. Everyone needs the support of a JB in their life!

So, four years ago, my cousin JB took a job with the Salvation Army at "Camp Redwood Glen" as a camp counselor. She loves kids, but didn't know why she took the job as a counselor, and she even tried to avoid the job, but God continued to call her back as a counselor for several summers. Fast forward four years to February of 2015, and JB had just accepted a job, not as a camp counselor this time, but as the camp director of that same Camp Redwood Glen. As camp director, she had miraculously convinced myself, my sister, and two of my cousins to join her for the summer. The most significant selling point for us was that Camp Redwood Glen was located just 15 minutes from the beautiful beaches of Santa Cruz, California.

It was during this time I had noticed a small bump on my left cheek. My sister Chandler and I were living in Spokane and were attending Moody Bible Institute. The bump was nothing too big or noticeable; I just dabbed a bit of makeup on it and moved on. As the weeks passed by, the bump started to get a little bigger, but still wasn't anything that I was worried about.

Our college classes were finished so we packed up our belongings and headed back to our home town of Klamath Falls.

We didn't have much time to spend in Klamath before we left for camp and the bump was now quite big (about the size of a blueberry) and was making my face numb. While at home, my mom had a doctor friend at church take a quick look at the bump after our church service. He told us it was nothing to worry about and was just a sebaceous cyst, but since it was on my cheek, he suggested I have it removed by a plastic surgeon.

So, my sister Chandler and I packed my little white, Honda CRV with as many suitcases and tote bags as it could possibly hold and hit the road Santa Cruz bound.

After being at camp for a couple of weeks, my mom found a plastic surgeon in Scotts Valley not far from camp, and I went to her to have the bump removed. After a quick check-up Dr. Pletsch told me it was a sebaceous cyst and nothing to worry about, and it would just be a simple removal. I was given a shot of local anesthetic and the surgery commenced. What was supposed to be a simple 20-minute procedure quickly turned into an intense, hour-long surgery. I passed out twice from the sounds of clipping and the smell of burning flesh being cauterized! Finally, the doctor stitched me up and told me that in 30 years of

But as I cried out to God and sought out my answers, He gave me everything I could ever need. Let me tell you about how God took my bad news and made it better.

practice, she had never seen anything like that and she had no idea what the foreign specimen she removed from my face was or if it's even benign. Talk about a traumatizing experience and not what I expected at all.

Moving forward the specimen was sent to the pathologist whom later reported inconclusive results. More waiting and recovering from surgery which wasn't too bad! Praise God.

When the pathologist got back to me he said he thought it was a rare form of cancer and he wanted to send it to Stanford to get tested. I was in shock for sure, because like I mentioned earlier, cancer was not even a word that I entertained in my thoughts. The Lord answered my prayers and the biopsy results from Stanford got back to me the next day!

Unfortunately, that's when they told me that I had Merkel Cell Cancer.

Now, this has been a lot of bad news and a lot of back story detail. But I want to celebrate the intricate detail in which God showed His mighty hand. If JB hadn't been called to this camp, and wouldn't have asked us to come, then I wouldn't have been able to go to Dr. Pletsch, and if I hadn't gone to Dr. Pletsch then the specimen wouldn't have been checked by Stanford, and I most likely would have been misdiagnosed. That already just overwhelms me!

Dr. Pletsch then made a phone call to her oncologist friend Dr. Yen who got me in to see him in a few hours on a Friday. He then got me connected to the hospital for labs and got me a PET scan for Monday. He is also a graduate of Stanford, and was able to text the doctors there directly about my case.

Later, as I came home from the craziness of the day, I found out that our camp nurse, Traci, used to work as a cancer nurse navigator helping cancer patients walk through the entire cancer treatment process. She told me that she had no idea why God called her to the middle of the woods at a camp to be a nurse. I know why! God sent her to help me, and how blessed I am because of it.

I was sitting quietly that evening after the doctors, labs, information, and people came to a calm, and I got scared. I decided to research Merkel Cell Carcinoma and educate myself. As my brain flooded with stats and medical terms, my computer froze. I just started weeping, and crying out to the Lord in fear. It was one of those guttural cries that you just need. After a few minutes I decided to distract myself, so I turned the computer back on. It turned on but the screen was black, and all of a sudden, this song by Kari Jobe started to play called "Love Came Down", and the lyrics blew me away.

If my heart is overwhelmed
And I cannot hear your voice
I hold on to what is true
Though I cannot see

Through the words of that song, the Lord gave me a taste of peace and allowed me to bask in His hope and presence. I was reassured by those lyrics and by the song that He sent me, and I was reminded that He is in control and He is my strength, He makes me brave.

Later that night I felt called to speak at the campfire. I felt like God wanted me to see that He is going to use this cancer trial to further His kingdom. I told the kids at the campfire gathering that I have cancer. I told them I was scared, and that it's okay to be afraid. But I also told them that although I am so afraid, I have joy and peace. I can find strength in God's promise that He began a good work in me and will see it through to the end. That He works all things together for our good and His glory. That although I may not see it right now, God is going to use this, and good will come from it. And because of this, I have been blessed to have hope. Hope is the most amazing gift the Lord has given us. Without Christ, I would be hopeless, and I would not be able to make it. He is my strength, and He absolutely makes me brave. After I was done speaking, the kids just embraced me. They surrounded me with love and comfort and just held me. God let me see His work the first day of my battle with cancer.

On a lighter note, I have to share this. As kids are embracing me around the campfire, and people are crying, Teralee, this small, 6-year-old redhead on crutches, who reminded me of my foster sister Lesley, tugs on my sweatshirt and says, "Well, maybe you'll be one of them who ACTUALLY makes it!" I'm going to let that sink in for a minute. It was so unfiltered that I couldn't even be offended; instead, I burst out in laughter, and she's right, maybe I will be.

Fellowship

June 27, 2015

My parents Rob and Alisha, arrived safely at camp today. My dad is a teacher, and my mom is a housewife so praise God they have the summer off and have been able to be with me. The Lord showed His blessings today as Ed, the director of Camp Redwood Glen, was so generous and had the resources to host them and set them up with a room—at no charge. Camp has saved my life so far, kind of literally!

When I woke up, I laid on the pillow and played the day over and over in my head. It felt like a distant dream or a movie I had watched. As reality sunk in, I had another moment of fear and hurt, and I had a great bawl sesh. It has been a lot harder today because there aren't doctors or people or information or labs or tests or kids. Just silence and stillness. I feel like that is when the real testing of your faith comes; if you can lean on God and find peace in the stillness when there is nothing to distract you from your thoughts.

It's so comforting to have my parents here, and they are the best support I could ever dream of. They are my rocks outside of Christ, and they love and care about me unconditionally. It's hard to see them in pain. I know they genuinely want to be strong and show me that, but everyone has their moments. It comes and goes in waves. I hate seeing them cry, and it breaks my heart.

I got some really encouraging words today from people. Ty, a friend from Moody, wrote me a charming post on Facebook and Michelle wrote me a card that made me cry, but in a good way.

I feel like that is when the real testing of your faith comes, if you can lean on God and find peace in the stillness when there is nothing to distract you from your thoughts.

Mom and I were talking today about what is helpful to say and what is not. For example: "At least it's curable!" "Hang in there!" "It's not a death sentence!" "You're one tough son of a bitch!" We had a good laugh at that one, "you're one tough son of a bitch." It definitely brought me zero comfort, so if that's what they were going for they missed the mark, but I have to give them some credit because it made for a good laugh!

I will never again underestimate the power of words. The fact that people take the time to comfort me and send me encouragement has made a considerable impact on the way I have traveled down this road so far. Sometimes you want to say something but insecurity holds you back, sometimes time holds you back. Things get in the way, I understand, but make the time. Every single message, card, text, phone call, comment, and like on Facebook and my blog has given me strength and courage in my cancer battle. Every time I start to get scared the Lord has sent an encouraging word through my friends and family, and I feel brave.

The Lord showed me today the importance of community, fellowship, and the gift He has given us with the power of words.

Transparency

June 28, 2015.

I know it may seem cliché to say, but now that I have cancer, I take notice of the things that I took for granted before, but I don't care, it's true. I stood in the middle of camp and stared at the trees and up at the sky. Redwood trees just have this majestic feel about them, tall and strong, not swayed by much, and they are an example to me of how I want to be throughout this battle. I want to be tall, and strong, and I want to have a faith that is not swayed by this. Instead, I want a faith that can grow stronger because of these trials. I also have taken the time to listen. To sit and listen to the people I love laugh and share memories, to listen to a room full of people praise God, to listen and absorb all the beauty that the Lord created for us.

It's okay to be scared. I have to remind myself because sometimes I feel like I should be brave all the time—to show people that I'm okay. Just because I'm scared doesn't mean I don't have faith. Just because you are a Christian doesn't mean your life is going to be easy and perfect. James 1:2-4 says:

> "Consider it pure joy my brothers and sisters, when you face trials of many kinds, because you know the testing of your faith produces perseverance. Let perseverance finish its work so that you may be mature and complete, not lacking anything."

My Mom prayed a prayer earlier, and it served as an excellent reminder to me. She said, "Lord help me in my unbelief, help me see that we are so blessed that you have chosen us to suffer for you." Or something like that. When I was younger, I never understood that idea. The idea that we should find joy in suffering. I used to think, "Why do bad things happen to good people?" or "Why does a loving God want us to suffer?" or "This isn't fair, why me?" And although those are normal questions, I haven't asked them. The Lord has prepared me and shown me that trials are to be celebrated. That something bigger and better is coming and that He never gives us anything that we can't handle with Him.

I'm not mad at God. I was thinking about the scene from *A Walk to Remember* earlier, where Jamie is crying and tells Landon, "It's okay to be mad at God," and I thought to myself, I'm not mad at Him. He has given me so much peace and He has given me reasons to find and seek joy in Him.

It's okay to be scared. I have to remind myself because sometimes I feel like I should be brave all the time—to show people that I'm okay. Just because I'm scared doesn't mean I don't have faith. Just because you are a Christian doesn't mean your life is going to be easy and perfect.

I love the song "You Make Me Brave" by Amanda Cook. The song talks about how God makes us brave and He gives us the courage to step out from the shore and into the waves without fear. I first heard it sung by Courtney, a worship leader at Moody Bible Institute in Spokane, and oh the passion in which she sings that song rings over and over in my head. Songs are amazing. The lyrics have the power to move you and comfort you. What a blessing music is, and I appreciate it so much.

One last thing from today, the Lord taught me the importance of transparency. Everyone always tries to hide their struggles, hide their flaws, and make it seem like they have it all together. I wonder how far that gets people. I know for me the times when I've been honest about my life I find that others can join me in my struggle and support me, encourage me, relate to me, and just love me. You can help others by being transparent, and it's biblical to do so. God didn't give us trials to walk them alone. I've been blessed by being open about my battle with cancer. The response to the blog has been so encouraging and awesome! Please continue to let me know how you are feeling and please be challenged to share your struggles and allow others to learn from you or be there for you.

Merkel Miracle

June 29, 2015

Last night I told my mom that the worst thing about having cancer was the fact that she made me eat a whole bowl of kale. Blah, tastes like the smell of mowing the lawn! I told her that if she squeezed the kale into pill form, then I'd eat it.

Even though I threw a 3-year-old tantrum, I really am grateful to have parents that care enough about me to make me do things that they know are best for me even if I don't like to do them. That's a hard position to be in, and a lot of parents choose smooth sailing over doing the right thing for their children. So, thank you, Mom and Dad.

I got my PET scan done today. Geeze, they sure don't warn you that it is one of the most boring things of your life! It was sort of how I imagine being trapped in a dungeon would be. Two hours of sitting still, no talking, no reading, no music, just you and your thoughts. I was thinking while I moved in and out of the tube machine, why would they want cancer patients to sit alone with their thoughts for two hours?! Good thing I'm not normal. Instead of thinking about the trials ahead or the what-ifs that come with cancer, instead I sang songs, blogged, replayed baby VHS tapes from my childhood, thought about all of the messages I've received from you guys, I even watched YouTube—yes, all in my head. I also fell asleep, that was awkward. I guess if I can fall asleep during a PET scan it's safe to say I can sleep anywhere.

Oh, you probably want the update on the results. That's important! So, I have to get another surgery on my cheek to make sure the doctors clear the margins (around the tumor to get all the cancer cells). The doctors also saw some active spots lower in my neck that we will discuss. There is a small lesion on my lungs that we have to keep an eye on and there are several nodes in my abdomen that are larger than normal but weren't hot (active) on the PET scan. This is all information given to me by Dr. Yen but he is not the specialist in this area. He has referred me to Stanford to see the experts. They will look at my PET scan and be able to discuss treatment options as well as tell me if the nodes in my abdomen are cancerous. I don't want to say too much until after my appointment on Wednesday!

"Do not be anxious about anything, but in every situation, by prayer and petition, with thanksgiving, present your requests to God. And the peace of God, which transcends all understanding, will guard your hearts and your minds in Christ Jesus" (Philippians 4:6-7).

Can I tell you how baffled and humbled I am by you all! I mean for starters I have been blessed by an abundance of encouraging words, texts, likes, comments, shares, calls, you name it and it has been done.

It has challenged me to make sure that I say what's on my mind (good things). I thought about how many times I look at someone and think "Wow what an awesome servant's heart they have" or "She has beautiful eyes!" These things seem so simple, and we think these thoughts all the time, but how many times do we actually let that person know? Most of the time less than half! What holds us back? Time, insecurity, awkwardness, shyness, etc. There have been so many people who have said so many awesome things to me, and I never want to forget the way it has made me feel.

I want others to experience the joy received from a kind word. I challenge you, and myself to say the things you're thinking. Let the girl you work with know that you love how she is always willing to do the odd job that you hate, or let the guy at the bank know that he has impeccable taste in ties!

I want to give a quick shout out to my nurse navigator, Traci. She has the most caring spirit, and she has sacrificed her time and work to help me as a friend. She is so awesome and puts up with so many questions! I literally texted her at 1:00 AM this morning freaking out because I ate two cherries at midnight and I had my PET scan today. I had a nightmare that the cherries showed up on the PET scan as stomach cancer because I didn't want to admit to the doctors that I ate them! What a funny text to receive at one in the morning, "I ate two cherries at midnight! Crap! Am I going to have to reschedule my test!?" I should start #cancerprobs.

I challenge you and myself to say the things you're thinking. Let the girl you work with know that you love how she is always willing to do the odd job that you hate, or let the guy at the bank know that he has impeccable taste in ties!

I was thinking about Merkel Cell cancer. "Merkel." I mean come on you guys, cancer is already a horrible and disgusting thing to go through, can't you give us the pleasure of naming it something nice sounding?

"I'm sorry to inform you Ms. Crebbin, but you have a rare form of cancer known as Unicorn Cell Cancer." At least I can wear that name proud! But, since I have Merkel Cell Cancer, I found a way to enjoy the name a little. You know how there is that guy who says "'Murica!" in that weird slurred voice? I don't actually know what that's from, but a kid in my high school used to say it all the time. Well if you use that same voice and slur it in the same way, "Merkel" sounds like "Muricle." "MIRACLE" for those of you who didn't catch that! I'm determined to be the Merkel Miracle!

Battle Scars

June 30, 2015

I have a scar on my face from the first surgery. In the past, I would have cringed, and my insecurities would have overwhelmed me. I would have dabbed makeup on it every day, and I would have tried to hide it from the world in fear that they would judge me. Not today my friends, not now. I think of cancer like a war I'm fighting. When you go to war, you fight for what you love. Well, I love my life, and I am willing to do what it takes to fight this war with everything I have. So, consider the first battle won, and I have a cool battle scar that I can wear with pride!

I am going to teach you a life lesson for free, and you don't even have to go through cancer to learn it! Don't waste your time worrying about what people think. You will always make one person so happy, and at the same time, you will make the other person furious. You will have the perfect hair, but you will have the worst body. The list can and will go on for the rest of your life. So my suggestion, embrace and CELEBRATE who you are and how God made you.

Comparison is the thief of joy, people! The moment you let go of your insecurities, you will be astounded by the amount of peace that will overflow your life. You don't realize how deep those things dictate you. I never did. I used to be so controlled by my insecurities that I would turn down KLOVE when I was at the drive-thru so the people handing me my meal wouldn't judge me for listening to Christian music. How sad is that? But that used to be my reality, I was completely controlled by insecurity, and I never knew peace.

Insecurity means you don't trust God. Think about it. If you trusted Him and His plan, then it wouldn't matter who thinks you aren't pretty or who gets mad at you for having faith because the Lord doesn't want them in your life! All you can do is live your life, and do the best to glorify God through it. The Lord has changed me so, so much. I mean, now He has given me so much peace that I can fight this cancer.

I had a really wonderful day today. No doctors, tears, or worries, and I wasn't as exhausted as I usually am! I got to spend the day enjoying the beauty of downtown Santa Cruz, and I got to spend some quality time with my cousin Jessica whom I love with all my heart. Several people told me that they'd shave their head if I end up having to shave mine. Geeze, talk about humbling! I just about crumbled hearing that. Actually, I did, on the inside, and if that were a thing, I'd be all crumbly... yeah...anyway, I've said it a million times (ok like 10), and I'll say it a million more times, the love and support I've received throughout all of this is SO AMAZING AND WONDERFUL. You all and God are going to save my life. So, thank you.

I am going to teach you a life lesson for free, and you don't even have to go through cancer to learn it! Don't waste your time worrying about what people think.

I have my appointment with Stanford tomorrow at 1:30. Basically, I am meeting with Dr. Sunwoo, and with a last name like that, I know he's going to know exactly what to do. He is an ENT (ears, nose, and throat) surgeon, so he'll most likely be doing my biopsies. Those are the two upcoming battles, the two biopsies. The war will continue after that, but I find that it's much easier to take it one step at a time. You don't try to shove a whole hamburger down your throat, well, unless you're a drunk frat boy doing a dare; otherwise you take one bite at a time. I encourage those of you who want tons of answers to do the same!

Dad heard a sermon by Paul Washer today where he says something like, "When God says *our good* He means He is going to conform us to Christ, not a good life by human standards." That is such an excellent reminder to me when we as Christians read that in the Bible, "our good," and "His glory," we often think *our good,* as in a good life.

Most people would think that having cancer doesn't seem like a good life; I'd say you're right. By human standards cancer sucks, and it's not what I'd define a good life as. But when I look at it from God's perspective, it's such a good life, you guys. Why? Because he is conforming me to be like Christ. My life is changing for the better right in front of my eyes, and I can see Him molding and forming me to be more Christ-like, and that is exactly what "for our good" means.

I am just so blessed that God has allowed me to see the fruit of my trial. Not only in my own life but in the things you all share with me. God is doing His work. A dear friend of mine, Kelsey, described it as, "You are the needle contributing your stitch to God's masterpiece, and he is the hand that is moving you." Well Lord, you just keep on stitching!

Frankenstein

July 1, 2015

I haven't cried in two days. I mean, I tear up at the wonderful words and blessings that people have given me, but I haven't cried that intense, guttural cry. I was thinking about why I cry. The thing is, I haven't cried because I'm mad. My cry hasn't been for injustice; my cry hasn't been pain. I had a hard time pinpointing what my cry was for. I determined it was just a cry to God. A cry to God showing Him that I am helpless and hopeless in this without Him, that I genuinely need Him and I am letting go and lifting it all up to Him. Don't get me wrong, I have cried because I'm scared, and I have cried for the ones I love. Seeing them hurt is painful, but I think the times in which I talked about having those gut-wrenching cries, they were me letting go of the things I can't control and trusting that God has a more excellent plan than I could ever even fathom.

I went to Stanford today. Praise God that traffic was clear and we got there on time. Dr. Sunwoo is one of the best, so I felt very confident in his advice and treatment plan for the nodes. I hate that doctors are required to list off every potential risk factor.

It was like watching one of those ads for medication where you are almost better off skipping the medication because of the horrible side effects. Like, "Call if you experience suicidal thoughts, nausea, vomiting, heart failure, pain in the abdomen, headaches, dry mouth, an obnoxious mother-in-law..." After that was said and done he had a special surprise for me lol.

"So now what we want to do is what's called a fine needle biopsy. Basically, we want to sample the tumor on your neck to confirm that it is indeed cancer so we can plan the surgery." A fine needle biopsy was the ONE thing I didn't want to happen. So, we walked into a different room with white walls and creepy posters of people with half their skin removed. Once you're an adult, it's like the doctors don't care if you feel happy or not. What happened to Dr. Seuss themed rooms with toys and suckers and decent reading material?

Anyway, they sat me down, gave me the risk spiel, and then they gave me the numbing shot in my neck. That shot though, OW! I would rather skip the numbing shot because that's always been the most painful part! Then they jabbed a giant needle right into the tumor, like I was Frankenstein's Monster. Now as most of you know, I am a total drama queen, but it makes for good stories! So, they take the first sample, and it came back negative. Then they took a second, and to my dismay, a third. After the third biopsy, they got what they were looking for - cancer. I can't say that I'm surprised, Dr. Yen prepared me for that.

Now a shout out to my prayer warriors, I need surgery ASAP, but it's hard to come by an appointment. Dr. Sunwoo is pushing for next Friday, maybe Monday, so please pray that a spot opens up! Please don't pray that the person in surgery before me gets hit by a car or catches the plague. But pray that God opens a spot for me.

Time for a perspective check. Do you realize I have only known about my cancer for 6 days, you guys? And while the appointments and doctors and procedures can be overwhelming at times, I have to stop and thank God for how blessed I have been! I could be sitting here for two weeks just waiting, worrying that my cancer is spreading, but instead everyone has been proactive, and I am getting a move on it. The Lord has been opening doors like crazy and Dr. Sunwoo will be clearing the margins on my face and doing a neck dissection. It will be pretty gnarly but whatever it takes.

I determined it was just a cry to God. A cry to God showing Him that I am helpless and hopeless in this without Him, that I genuinely need Him and I am letting go and lifting it all up to Him.

It's my beautiful sister's birthday tomorrow. I have to catch myself because I feel guilty that our family is going through this on her birthday. I want to make tomorrow about her and not about my cancer! Please help me do that by wishing her a happy birthday. She is one of the most important people in my life, and she truly deserves a day of celebration.

The Lord showed me today the importance of serving others. TraciLyn, my adored nurse navigator, has been the biggest blessing to me. She is truly one of a kind. She goes with me to my appointments, she takes notes, she puts up with my terrifying texts (like the cherries, or today I told her I got an "alarming" e-mail, and nearly gave the woman a heart attack). She has been a true example of selfless and unconditional love to me. It's really convicted me to serve others.

How many times have I had the chance to serve someone and let my laziness, or time, or distractions get in the way? A good friend of mine is from South Africa, he was telling me that in their culture people are so important that they don't even glance at the clock when they are spending time with someone. They're just there for people, all in, no distractions, and no agenda. It made me stop and think. I run so well off the schedule I like, and I constantly fill it to please me and go a million miles a minute. I want to be more intentional. The people God placed in my life are there for a purpose, and they are so special. I want to serve them and love them regardless of whether I feel like it, or whether I have time for it. Traci has shown me what it means to love your neighbor as yourself. I have been blessed more than I can say by her and I want to pass it on!

With that being said, you all have been so awesome in asking me what I need and how you can help. I want to turn the tables on ya, so please tell me what you need and how I can help you!

Crying, It's Okay

July 2, 2015

ᚠᚠᚠᚠᚠᚠᚠᚠ

Today I had the privilege of leading worship with my sister Chandler at camp. There is no one in the world I love singing with more than her. Sometimes when we sing together it's like we are just one voice. It's special and rare and makes my heart sing and my emotions soar. I love my sister for so many reasons and music is one of the things we love to do together. Worshiping God through music can feel magical, especially when you are going through trials. The lyrics just penetrate your soul and every emotion escalates.

I broke down after singing the song "The Stand" when it talks about standing with our arms raised high and hearts abandoned in awe of Jesus who gave His all for us. I was overcome with gratefulness to my savior and humbled by His great love for me. I went into the bathroom and just collapsed on the floor. The guttural cry was back. In anguish, I just cried.

I cried for the future. I cried for my family. I cried because it was Sis's birthday and I felt like cancer was ruining it. I cried for the unknown. I cried from being overwhelmed. I cried because I have cancer. Emotions flooded my heart and mind, and the entire time I cried, God was holding me. Heart abandoned, and soul surrendered I was reminded that all I have is His.

For the first time in a while, I just wanted comfort. I wanted to cry with someone I love, and I just wanted someone to hold me. I went into the chapel and saw JB sitting there. We made eye contact, and she just knew that I needed her. We went into the other room, and both collapsed together. As she held me, we both wept. It was a touching moment for me and one that the Lord sent me as an answer to my prayer. How blessed I have been to have a family that I am so close with and that loves me so much.

I felt so much love at that moment from my cousin. I have always looked up to JB as a big sister and a role model. When we were in high school, we decided to have a sleepover. We went to the store and bought every junk food that sounded good. Cap'n Crunch, caramel popcorn, rice cakes, M&M's, gummy worms, you name it. We shared a mutual love for Cap'n Crunch and made it a tradition to buy it every time we had a sleepover. Here we were, years later, and while I lay with my head on her lap, nearly drowning in tears, she says, "I could go for some Cap'n Crunch right now... but I can't have gluten, and you can't have sugar. The devil really planned this one out!" We just burst out in laughter, like genuine, joyous laughter. I love you so much JB! What a light and blessing you are in my life.

People keep telling me that they are trying to be strong for me. On the flip side, I've tried to be strong for people. You guys, God is our strength. I don't need to be strong for you, and I don't need you to be strong for me. We have to come together in an authentic and honest fellowship. The Lord tells us to mourn with those who are mourning; it doesn't say stay strong and hide your feelings from those who are grieving.

These vulnerable moments I shared with my cousin JB showed me that. She made an excellent point in saying that crying doesn't mean you're weak, or that you don't trust in God, or that you don't have peace. JESUS WEPT. He did! He cried out in anguish to God, and He didn't make mistakes. Emotion is a beautiful thing that the Lord blessed us with. We have feelings, so we aren't robots, please don't be afraid to show me that. I won't hide my true emotions from you, and I will always be honest about how I'm feeling. I encourage you to do the same with others. The Lord gave us people to help share burdens. Don't carry it on your own and don't rob people of the chance to be there for you.

Enough about crying! I do however want to say JESUS WEPT, and not just once. You remember Lazarus? You remember Jesus in the Garden? He wept because He felt the pain of going through trials, and finally, he went through the ultimate trial. He was 100% human and 100% God. He felt real emotion, and He didn't just expect us to go through it alone. How awesome is it that we serve a God that not only took our place but went through that trial as a human?

I cried because I have cancer. Emotions flooded my heart and mind, and the entire time I cried, God was holding me. Heart abandoned, and soul surrendered I was reminded that all I have is His.

I am so encouraged to know that the God I serve cares about me so much. He has such a beautiful plan. I mean Jesus went through the trial of being tortured and dying, but in the end, we were saved because of it. TRIAL = BEAUTY.

I had a rough day guys, I really did, and I am willing to be honest about that. But as the day ended, the Lord reminded me of His divine presence and faithfulness. 2,500 dollars has been raised on the GoFundMe page which is going to pay for a considerable chunk of my Stanford bill. My blog has received 5,000 views which blesses me because I know God is using my story in the lives of many. I have continued to receive encouraging messages from everyone which keeps me positive and motivated to fight, and three different people today told me that they are planning a walk-a-thon and making t-shirts to help support me. Wow. Just wow. I have no words to express my gratitude. I am humbled and in tears by God's goodness and that He has used you all to show me that I am loved and He is here fighting cancer alongside me. God is so faithful, I have ended my tough day on a good note. I am going to bed encouraged, refueled, blessed, humbled, and ready for whatever the day brings tomorrow. Thank you, thank you so much.

Replace your fear and doubt with the truth of God's word. Psalms helped me get through the day:

> *"In the day when I cried out, You answered me, And made me bold with strength in my soul. All the kings of the earth shall praise You, O Lord When they hear the words of Your mouth" (Psalm 138:3-4).*

Mt. Cancer

July 3, 2015

I had a strange thought yesterday that I've been entertaining today, and I feel like it makes sense. Maybe it doesn't but bear with me. You know how they say trials are like climbing a mountain (at least I think they do), and you have to focus on the goal, the goal being the top of the mountain peak. A mountain is a tough, uphill climb, but once you reach the top you have a stunning view, and it makes the whole climb worthwhile. Then you get to go downhill, and while it may be a little rocky at times, it's still way easier.

I started thinking about my "Cancer Mountain" and how the mountain peak, the goal, was to be healed. That was my mindset for a while, until yesterday upon leaving Stanford the reality hit me that I may never be healed. The mountain suddenly looked as if it were an eternity of uphill, as if there was no peak, and I felt a moment of hopelessness.

I asked God to change my perspective because a mountain with no peak is just a horrible place to be. Then I started thinking; maybe the goal isn't to be healed, perhaps the peak isn't a full recovery from cancer. My mountain peak is becoming more Christ-like. With each uphill step, whether it's a step in my cancer battle, or a step where someone was holding my hand, or a step in achieving a good grade in school, or a step when someone blessed me with their words, or a step in faith, or a step in not having road rage for the day, no matter what that step is, my goal is stepping closer to the cross. And wow, with that as the mountain peak I don't ever want to give up.

I've been feeling overwhelmed and humbled (in a good way) by everyone's kindness and support. I started to feel almost helpless like there was no way I could ever repay you all. I was talking to my beautiful cousin Jess and she said: "People believe in you Hade, that's why they do these things. The best way you can repay them is by proving them right and fighting this with all you have." Wow. That was so encouraging, and it has helped me.

I will fight this, not by my strength but with God on my side. I am continually motivated by everyone's inspiring words, and I lift up a prayer for those of us who have no family, friends, support, or who don't have Christ. Without Christ, I honestly wouldn't make it.

Nutrition has been a huge part of this whole cancer thing. Apparently, sugar doesn't help cancer so for those of you wanting to send me something, please refrain from tempting me with sugary treats! Even though it's a very kind gesture and I truly appreciate it.

Anyway, it's been a struggle for me. Everyone else gets to eat whatever they want, and while I still have the choice, I have to pick what's not going to feed the beast obviously. Instead, I have to starve it!

My Mom is a nutrition freak (I say that in a good way) she knows so much and has such a passion for health. She has been great in encouraging me and making me tons of different bone broths and smoothies. It's hard to have a good attitude about having a cup of bone broth

Trials don't happen to people because they did something terrible and God is punishing them. Trials happen because we are sinners and the Lord is bringing us closer to Him. Just food for thought!

for breakfast instead of Cap'n Crunch, so I've been praying that the Lord would help me change my perspective. She made me this smoothie yesterday that tasted like dirt the first time I sipped it and hay the second time. Unfortunately, it didn't get better. She knows that it was gross so I don't feel bad blogging about it!

If anyone has good smoothie recipes that use less fruit and more veggies, please do me a favor and pass them along! That being said my mom is a very caring, selfless person and has taken a lot of time to care for me and I really am grateful. Sorry, Mom, that I get grumpy sometimes over kale!

I got a letter today from one of the campers from last week. It was so sweet and said, "Roses are red, violets are blue, you're the most prettiest in the world." It came at the perfect time because I've been so tired and have low energy, so my motivation to be around the kids hasn't been the best. It doesn't help that every time I see a camper, they say "What's that on your face?" and my best response is "It's my battle scar." Then they look at me like, "yeah, okay…"

Receiving that letter though reminded me that these kids at camp need us. They need love, they need support, they need role models, and above all they need Christ. The girl that wrote me the letter told me that she wants me to be her big sister. What a privilege and an honor it is to be that in someone's life. Thank you, Ciara! You are a sweet blessing to me. That was just the push I needed and an answer to prayer (once again). I want to find the energy and the patience to allow the kids to enrich my life during this time.

While I was living in Spokane, I started volunteering with Union Gospel Mission to lead a bible study at the juvenile detention center. Going into it I was terrified. What if I didn't say the right thing? What if they think I'm judging them? What if I don't change their lives?

Ryan, the leader of UGM said something in a meeting that changed my perspective forever. He said "You are going to go in thinking that you're going to help these kids and change them. But instead, go in knowing that they are going to help you and change you." I had never thought that a kid, let alone a kid in juvie, could ever help or change me. I lived on my own Christian pedestal and I didn't even know it.

Jesus didn't separate himself from the woman at the well, or the kids that ran up to Him, instead He sat with them, ate with them, and loved them. The time I spent with the kids at juvie absolutely changed my life.

They taught me that we all go through trials, and quite frankly they all look the same when you strip it down. The 13-year-old girl sitting across from me who had a 2-year-old and was addicted to heroin had the same insecurities and fears as me, a 21-year-old girl who didn't have a boyfriend and had never done drugs.

We all sin. We all fall short of the glory of God. Praise God that I was raised in a home where I didn't have to turn to drugs to deal with the problems of this earth. Some would say, "Why did that girl get cancer? How is that fair?" You guys, I am no better than anyone else and cancer is not a punishment.

Trials don't happen to people because they did something terrible and God is punishing them. Trials happen because we are sinners and the Lord is bringing us closer to Him. Just food for thought! Love you all!

Worth Celebrating

July 4, 2015

4th of July! As I walk around camp seeing everyone sporting their American flag socks, shirts, headbands, and underwear, I wanted to stop and really think about the blessing it is to be an American. I have the resources and access to advanced medical technology that can help me in my recovery. I have an abundance of food and water to keep my nutrition at a good level so I can prepare for treatment. I have a computer where I can keep everyone updated via Facebook and various social media. I have the freedom to write a blog where I openly discuss my faith. I could go on for days, but the point is I am blessed to be an American.

My GoFundMe page has gone over my initial goal of $5,000! I am at a loss for words. When I first started the page, I typed $500 in the goal box. That's how much my first surgery was so I felt like if God wanted to bless me with the money to cover that, then I'd be super grateful. As I was creating the page Traci said, "Why not go for higher? You never know what might happen!" So, I asked her what she thought, and she threw out, "Let's try $5,000!" I stared at her in disbelief. $5,000? I've never even had 5,000 dollars in my bank account at once. It was unfathomable, but I realized that our God is bigger than a number. So, I went with it.

The first day the GoFundMe account was opened, $600 got donated. I was stunned at the Lord's faithfulness. As the days passed more and more generous and heart-wrenching donations were given. The goal of $5,000 started to look like it could happen! Nine days, it has been nine days. $5,636!!!!!! I have no words. I am just humbled by your kindness, support, encouragement, and generosity! I am also humbled by the power and care of our God, that He would use all of you in this way to help me through this trial. My family couldn't be more grateful, and I can tell you, you sure taught me not to doubt God or His people!

A lot of people that I've never met have donated and reached out to me. Initially, I was like, well why would a stranger give to someone they've never met? As I dug a little deeper (a.k.a Facebook stalked), I found out that so many of you have a connection to me somehow. For example, two girls donated to me because they said my friend Ty from

Moody so blessed them that they wanted to bless me, or a few of my Dad's students donated because they loved my Dad as a teacher or a coach. There was even a woman who knew my Mom from her Miss Klamath County beauty pageant days who donated.

It made me realize that no blessing goes unnoticed. You truly never know how your example and impact in someone's life may impact another's. I mean we've all had those days when we feel like we have done so much, or been such a good example, or we've done something so nice and we feel like it has gone unnoticed, or we didn't get something in return. I mean, that's what karma is; you help the old lady cross the road, and later you win the lottery, right? Well, first of all, you shouldn't be blessing people hoping to gain something from it. That's not Christ-like and not selfless!

That being said, I realized as all these strangers were donating to me, that no blessing is wasted. That girl that you helped move, that old man that you mowed the lawn for, or simply if you bless people just by the way you live, act, and treat others, whatever it is, you may have no idea how it impacted that person and how God will use that to impact others!

It reminds me of a poem that a girl in my elementary class wrote about a smile chain. The poem took you on a journey following a smile. It started with a little girl smiling at someone like the mailman, and then that mailman smiles at the grocery clerk and on and on it goes until it comes back to the little girl. That's how blessings work you guys! Except it doesn't always come directly back to you, but maybe it goes to someone you love.

Take my dad's students for example. My Dad was just a good coach who cared about his team. He probably didn't even realize he was blessing their lives and now because of his care for them, they have reached out and blessed me even though they don't know me. It just encourages you to take this lesson and bless someone. Whether you bless them in a tangible way, or you choose to live out Christ's example, or you choose to do your best at work or be the best teacher you can be, just remember that although you may not "reap the reward" of your blessing right then, you never know how far it will travel down the blessing chain.

> *It started with a little girl smiling at someone like the mailman, and then that mailman smiles at the grocery clerk and on and on it goes until it comes back to the little girl. That's how blessings work you guys!*

I got an endearing letter today from a girl that I knew in my home town of Klamath Falls. In the letter, she complimented me because after reading the blog about saying what you think she decided to take my advice! I was so humbled to see that the blog is making an impact on people. But I want to point out that all glory be to Christ. He is using my situation and story to further the Kingdom, and I take no credit! He has blessed me beyond belief to be able to see even a glimpse of what He has in store for this trial. My battle with cancer goes way beyond me, and I encourage you all to remember that next time you're going through a trial. The crazy thing is, it may never even be about you! You might go through something that is meant solely for another person watching how you deal. Doesn't that make you want to strive to be the best example you can be? It sheds new light on the tough things in our lives.

> "Do not repay evil with evil or insult with insult. On the contrary, repay evil with blessing, because to this you were called so that you may inherit a blessing" (1 Peter 3:9).

I love you all. I want you all to enjoy the 4th, and I am going to go enjoy it.

Warriors

July 5, 2015

"Be a warrior, not a worrier." I saw this while scrolling through my Pinterest today. I used to be the type who worried about things so much that I'd lose sleep. I can remember all the way back to second grade when I forged my Mom's signature on a reading slip, and I didn't sleep the entire night because I was so afraid to talk to the teacher. When I went in the next day, the teacher was totally chill about the whole thing. It's funny to think back over the years. Have you noticed that worrying doesn't change the outcome of the situation at all? Losing sleep over something doesn't make it all of the sudden any better or easier! I can't tell you how many times I've worried about things and got all worked up, and it ended up being okay. Worrying isn't trusting that God is sovereign and works all things together for our good. So choose trust, it will be a much easier route. I am so glad that the Lord gave us the truth of scripture to silence our worries.

> *"Do not be anxious about anything, but in every situation, by prayer and petition, with thanksgiving, present your requests to God. And the peace of God, which transcends all understanding, will guard your hearts and your minds in Christ Jesus." (Philippians 4:6-7).*

I don't want any of you to worry about me or anything else. I know it's so hard, but I'm choosing not to worry and I want you to do the same! Practice in the little things, like a reading slip, and take your worries to Christ. Memorize this verse and let it help you in those tough times.

I went to church today with Mom and Dad. The church here is awesome. There were these three guys that sat on the end of our aisle that looked like they weren't in their right mind. I don't know what the heck got into me, but I started to get serious anxiety that they were going to shoot up the place. Now I know that's a terrible thing to think and super judgmental, but I got so worked up about it that I even got my cell out and had the dialer ready to dial 9-1-1. It made me think, I have a lot of peace and as morbid as it may sound I have accepted the fact that cancer might kill me. So why at that moment was I scared out of my mind thinking that they might shoot me? I'm sorry this is such a dark subject it just really bothered me today!

I just started praying. Praying that God would replace my fear with the truth. I repeated Philippians 4:6-7 and slowly but surely God gave me peace again. I put my phone in my bag, and I started praying for the men sitting at the end of the row. I spent the rest of the service in worship and thanking God for His word. You guys, it's real, and it is powerful! Let's choose to be warriors, not worriers.

I haven't felt 100% today. I slept so much that on a scale of human to fat cat, I definitely was up there with the cat. It's so strange, I know I have cancer, but I don't feel sick. I mean, I had cancer for three months before I was diagnosed and I didn't even notice. I always thought cancer was like the girl in *The Fault in Our Stars* (and some are!), you know how she has an oxygen tank and is frail and weak. But mine is more visible than anything (so far). I mean I look in the mirror and see the tumor in my neck and the scar on my face. And I feel tired. But other than that, I am so blessed to say that I'm doing pretty dang good!

I know the fight is coming; surgery, radiation, and whatever the future holds. That's why I am trying to prepare myself for battle. Today I mourned though. No guttural cries or weeping. Just a silent mourning. The strange thing is that I didn't weep for myself. I didn't think "Why me?" or "This isn't fair" I didn't even think "cancer sucks" (even though it does), I just mourned for my past. I started the reel of memories in my mind pre-cancer diagnosis. I grieved for the life I had. I mourned for the life that is changing right in front of my eyes. I mourned for the lives of my family and friends. They will never be

Worrying isn't trusting that God is sovereign and works all things together for our good. So choose trust, it will be a much easier route.

the same. I know that a lot of the changes are good. I mean my life has changed so much. The support from you all, and my relationship with Christ is closer than ever, that is the most important thing. I love seeing this push people to the cross, and please continue blessing me by your stories and encouragements too. I think more than anything I sometimes try to fill the unknown with my own thoughts of how the future will be with cancer. The truth is, I have no idea what the Lord will choose to do, and this is a form of worry, and I just told you guys not to worry!

I know I am going to hit bumps in the road. I saw a diagram today on Facebook showing how people deal with grief. I had to laugh as I went through this at how different my diagram has looked!

Shock: Yes, I mean who expects that they're going to have cancer!?

Numbness: The only numbness I felt was the numbness I felt in my face after surgery.

Denial: Well there was no way to deny that the lumps on my body weren't normal.

Emotional outbursts: Okay yeah, I definitely consider my guttural cries as such.

Anger: I was only angry that they didn't put me out before cutting my face open!

Fear: Yeah definitely and lots of it until I replaced it with the truth of Christ.

Searching: For what? I have Christ I have no searching to do!

Disorganization: Please, why do you think I have a nurse navigator!?

Panic: Nope, I've learned from past panic attacks that I don't want to spend 3 hours in the hospital on oxygen.

Guilt: Why? Like I said before, trials are not a punishment people!

Loneliness: With the amazing support group and love I've received I could never imagine being lonely.

Isolation: My mom is always by my side forcing nutrition in me, even when I don't want her to be, I've never felt isolated (love ya Mom).

Depression: I refuse to go down this path, that's a lonely, dark spiral down.

"Re-Entry" Troubles: Huh? Do they have to "Re-Enter" my face, does that count?

New Relationships: Amen! So many people have reached out to me, not to mention having cancer opens up the entire cancer community to me. New friends going through similar struggles.

New Strengths: Of course, God makes me stronger every day. I am learning to be a fighter, a warrior not a worrier, a health freak, an encourager, and a lover of things I used to take for granted!

New Patterns: I drink nasty smoothies and juices every day.

Hope: In Christ, so much you guys. Without Him, I'd be absolutely hopeless!

Affirmation: I've received an abundance from you all, and I hope to give an abundance through my life and this blog!

Helping Others: I sure hope so! Others have helped me more than I could ever have imagined throughout all of this.

Now obviously, I was being a bit sarcastic on some of those, but overall you guys, I have been on the good end of grief! With Christ, I have no reason to grieve. I am truly celebrating this trial and allowing it to change my life for the better. I encourage you to go beyond a grief graph. Prove it wrong and look to God to show you how to grieve and help you through it. Love ya!

Trial Signs

July 6, 2015

I catch myself people watching more than ever. Not in a creepy way, I just gaze out the window when we're driving, or look around at the various people in church, or at the grocery clerk ringing me up. I try to picture what their lives look like, or what they could possibly be going through. I know that if anyone were to look at me, or see my family at church, the last thing they'd think is, "Wow, they look like they're dealing with cancer." At least I'd like to think that's not their initial thought. It's made me realize that you truly never know what people are dealing with.

Just this Sunday, the lead pastor at the church we've been attending had to confess to the congregation that last Tuesday he got a DUI. You really NEVER know. Coming to this conclusion has led me to believe that because we don't know what goes on in people's lives or what they're dealing with, we shouldn't let that affect how we treat others. This was a huge conviction of mine when working in customer service.

Wow, people can be so annoying, rude, hurtful, needy, you name it. It took an extra dose of grace to be able to serve others when I worked in retail for my job. The day I was diagnosed with cancer I went to a CVS pharmacy to pick up some pictures. The guy was so rude and snappy toward me I really just wanted to say to him, "Oh, by the way, I just found out that I have cancer. Yeah, hope you feel really good about the way you're treating me!" How many times did I get snappy with a customer, or roll my eyes at the man at the bank who is taking forever to write his deposit slip? If we all walked around with a sign on our head saying "Just lost my daughter," or "Just got evicted from my house," or "My dad just got arrested" or "I was just diagnosed with cancer," how different would we treat each other? Everyone has something going on.

If we all walked around with a sign on our head saying "Just lost my daughter." Or "Just got evicted from my house" or "My Dad just got arrested" or "I was just diagnosed with cancer." How different would we treat each other?

Everyone has something hard that they have to deal with or some kind of trial. Big or small. How much better would I have felt had the guy at CVS taken an extra dose of patience with his breakfast and treated me with warmth and kindness? I'm convicted guys; it's a commandment to "Love your neighbor as yourself." It's not easy to do! I want to think about my interactions with people, and I want to be the 1% girl (the small percentage of people) that will be the one that made that person forget about their trial, even for just one minute.

Today I got an MRI. Thank the heavens that it wasn't as long as the PET scan! This one is a lot more relaxed, fewer rules and restrictions. The machine is super tiny so if you're claustrophobic, you've been warned. I felt like I was in some kind of space movie where I get stuffed in a tube and launched off. The annoying thing was that you can only swallow when the noise stops. It's the worst when you are told you can't do something because all of a sudden, the need to do that one thing escalates. I would feel the spit collecting in my mouth, and I waited anxiously for the sound to stop. I've never been so relieved to swallow! The noise in the MRI is ridiculous. Think squeaky rocking chair, atomic bomb, machine gun, car alarm, and sometimes a rusty car engine. Something about the noise made me cringe at first, and later lulled me to sleep. Yes, that's right, I fell asleep again. The tech had horrible bedside manners and without warning took me out of the tube and shoved an IV in my arm then pushed me back in. ALL WHILE SAYING NOTHING. Overall, it took about 40 minutes. I don't know if I mentioned it last time, but in my head, I saw Taylor Swift during the PET scan, well she was back during the MRI!

Thank you for your prayers! I found out today that I get surgery next Tuesday the 14th! Praise God that they were able to squeeze me in. Until then it should be a relatively easy week, just filling myself with grass tasting liquid and taking lots of naps.

The Lord continues to be so faithful. Today we went to FedEx to mail the MRI's to Stanford and Seattle. It was going to cost $30 to send two CDs! While the lady was ringing us up, I just prayed that the Lord would bless us with a discount or something.

"Hmmm, that's weird the card didn't go through" she said. The woman had already printed a tracking slip thingy and put the one package in the bin, and then there was a glitch in the system that wouldn't let her re-scan that package. "Well, I guess this one's on us! Consider that your Cancer donation from FedEx." $9.00 was the grand total. I couldn't even believe it! God is so amazing, and here once again He has blessed us.

Celebrating Cancer?

July 7, 2015

I received a Facebook message today from a girl that I've never met. I am so humbled and honored that people would reach out to me to encourage me and admit to me that they read my blog. I love hearing that God is using my trial beyond even my friends and family and allowing me to meet new people and allow them to enrich my life!

This girl is 14 years old and very inquisitive for her age. She asked me "After everything you have been through and getting cancer, how do you stay so positive and not question God's plan?" Now, this is a very thoughtful question and caused me to pause and think. The first thing that came to mind was the verse, "For I know the plans I have for you, declares the LORD, plans to prosper you and not to harm you, plans to give you hope and a future" (Jeremiah 29:11).

But before I go any further in answering that question from my perspective, I want to be transparent in saying that I haven't always been positive and I have questioned His plan! This is human nature and it's okay to take your moment in that. It's important to make it just that - a *moment*. Not a constant mindset or state. That being said, I just wanted to assure you that I'm no superhuman and although I have faith in our mighty God, I have had my moments as well! I would say first of all I cling to the truth of God's word. That Jeremiah 29:11 rings true as well as, Philippians 1:6, "Being confident of this, that he who began a good work in you will carry it on to completion until the day of Christ Jesus." The whole Bible is God's living Word to give us peace, comfort, and faith in times of trials. Go to that before anything else. Knowing God's promises helps me to stay positive because although He doesn't say it will be easy, He does say He will never abandon us or make us walk alone.

Then I go to the Lord in prayer. Prayer has proven to be a powerful thing in my life and especially during this trial. I have cried out to God in prayer for help, for strength, for faith, for Providence, I have asked Him to remove any doubt or fear, I have been honest in my times of unrest, and He has been nothing but faithful to answer. Although it doesn't always come down on a silver platter in our time of need, life isn't like *The Hunger Games*! Sometimes you are called to be patient, sometimes you have a "FedEx" moment like yesterday when God answers prayer right away.

You have to rest knowing that He desires the best for you and He will use your life for His glory.

Sometimes reading the Bible and prayer doesn't feel like they're enough. I don't think this is a bad thing; God gave us fellowship and community for a reason. I have clung to every encouraging word or gesture made by those who love me. Jesus chose three men to be His BFF'S and then nine people to be His closest followers. They were a support group, and a family to one another. Surround yourself with people who love you and care about seeing you grow. Anytime I even think about being negative or depressed, the Lord uses people in my life to intervene. It's so important to have people in your life that speak truth to you, but it is also essential to be a person that speaks truth and encouragement in the lives of others. If you have a standard for the kinds of people you want in your life, you must first meet that standard yourself.

During trials, I encourage you to magnify the things worth celebrating. I have said this before, and I'll say it again, cancer has made me appreciate the little things I took for granted.

During trials, I encourage you to magnify the things worth celebrating. I have said this before and I'll say it again, cancer has made me appreciate the little things I took for granted. The intricacy of God's creation shown in a little sunflower, the overwhelming joy shown on a kid's face when they get candy, the way music can stir up a deep emotion inside people, whatever it is that you can find joy and life in, do it. In the times when I have felt sad or melancholy, I focus on one thing, for me, I usually focus on the lyrics of a song or a specific instrument that moves me.

As far as questioning God's plan, that's a good question because I feel like I haven't had to focus on *not* doing that. The saying, "If God brings you to it He will see you through it," rings a lot of truth. God didn't just pick me up and dump cancer on me without preparing me. He truly doesn't give you anything He can't help you handle. Not by my strength, let me clarify, the strength I have comes from God and is way beyond me! But as I look back on the smaller trials in my life, God has never failed me.

In those past trials, the struggle was real! I wasn't at all positive, and I asked God why all the time! Baby steps, it's not an overnight thing. It's kind of like a winding road. There are times when the path is straight, and you can see everything ahead, and there are times when there is a turn, and you have no idea what's coming. We can't see the bigger picture. But that's faith; trusting that God will not lead us off the cliff. Sometimes we might hit a bump, sometimes our car breaks down, and sometimes you may never know why. There have been trials in my life that I went through and I still don't know why! But the "why" doesn't matter, not if you believe that God is Sovereign and He is good. I almost ask myself, why not? The answer comes back with, "Because I'm scared," or "Because I don't want to." We aren't called to serve ourselves, and we aren't called to live comfortable lives. If we never went through trials, then we'd never grow, and we'd never be pushed toward the cross. God is good! There is peace in that, you guys. Peace doesn't mean comfort and it doesn't always come easy.

Beautiful People

July 8, 2015

I'm home! If any of you want to stop by the house Saturday from 6pm-9pm I'd love to have visitors! If you don't have my address and want it, just message me. It feels so good to have a few days to rest in my own bed and surround myself with more people that I love. I used to hate this town (Klamath Falls, OR), but now that I've lived elsewhere I have gained a new appreciation for the small town feel and beauty of my home.

My parents are amazing, and they have an entirely organic farm. Mom is in heaven being back home where she can pump me full of all the veggies she and my Dad have worked hard producing, and lots of organic eggs from our chickens. As much as I moan and groan about all the juices, smoothies, fermented carrots, and not getting to have carbs or gummy worms, I really have noticed a difference. I feel like eating a nutritious, organic diet has benefited me in that I don't have headaches, I don't get any bloating, I don't ever feel like I'm in a food coma, and I think my hair and skin feel better!

Many people have talked about how much your diet affects your everyday life and how it especially affects your cancer journey. Many people say that after changing their diet, they have either cured themselves of cancer or have made their situation a lot better. I also want to point out that I am really grateful that my Mom has put so much time and energy in feeding me a healthy diet. Although I am a total drama queen, it has been a good transition and I hope to continue this lifestyle, and I encourage you to look into it as well!

I got to see my Grammy and Aunt Sherise last night. I have been so blessed to grow up with strong women in my life who are not only role models to me but some of my best friends. They told me about this awesome moment they had when my Aunt Jen, Aunt Sherise, and Grammy just shared a good cry. That brings so much joy to my heart. I want you guys to know that I like hearing about those moments. Not that I'm thinking "Awe, they are crying for me because they love me that much." That's not why it brings me joy. It brings me joy because moments shared like that are beautiful moments of vulnerability.

Crying is the most vulnerable state a person can be in and sharing that with others, that moment when all your walls are down and you truly feel loved as the other person embraces and comforts you, those are the times that bring us together. Those are the times when we are transparent and authentic. It doesn't make me sad or give me the wrong idea when you share those moments with me, or when you take that moment *with* me.

Like I mentioned before, I don't need anyone "being strong" for me. I need people to be real with me. Tell me how you feel! Many people have told me that they appreciate that I'm raw and vulnerable in my blog. Well, just like people appreciate that, I appreciate that too. The worst-case scenario is that cancer is going to kill me. I know that, and I've accepted it. I have peace in God's plan and seeing the ones I love, or even seeing strangers allow this to bring them closer together gives me joy. And that is what I want to look back on, not the times when everyone held it together and kept their "cool" for me. This is part of the fruit guys! The Lord has blessed me enough to allow me to see the fruit of my trial. People are coming together in authentic fellowship, leaning on Christ, growing their faith, loving themselves and others with a Christ-like love. That's what this is about. And at the end of the day, I have a reason to smile in the midst of all this.

A beautiful journal was donated to me recently, and a quote was marked in it that read:

> *"The most beautiful people we have known are those who have known defeat, known suffering, known struggle, known loss, and have found their way out of the depths. These persons have an appreciation, a sensitivity, and an understanding of life that fills them with compassion, gentleness, and a deep loving concern. Beautiful people do not just happen."*
> —Dr. Elisabeth Kübler-Ross

This quote is something magnificent in all its truth. I started thinking of every example of someone I would consider a beautiful person. Esther for instance, in the Bible, I always admired her for her strength and what do you know, she found her way out of the depths of suffering and loss for sure. I would say that every person in the Bible including Christ himself knew loss, suffering, defeat, and rose from the depths of struggle. The key point here being "found their way out of the depths." Notice how beautiful people aren't a product of sitting in their loss, defeat, or suffering, or ignoring it, or running from it. FIND YOUR WAY OUT! Now, I really don't know how people hope to do this without faith. I think of it like

Jesus guides me out. Without Him, I'd be stuck. We all have the choice to be beautiful people. Choose to find your way out, choose to let your struggles define you in a good way. Seek help from Christ, you guys. He will never leave you stranded. He will always guide you out of the dark. Beautiful people don't just happen.

I mentioned before, I don't need anyone "being strong" for me. I need people to be real with me.

Quick update/praise! We are at a total of....of.... $8000!!!!! I am stunned as I type that many zeros, God is so faithful and I am just humbled and so grateful for your support. You are going to help save my life. I have my surgery at Stanford for sure this Monday. I'm not sure what time yet. I am so beyond blessed that they were able to squeeze me in. Also, Traci, my amazing nurse navigator angel got a room *donated* for my parents for three nights while I'm in the hospital! The blessings keep flowing, and it reminds us that our God is so good. The surgery is on my cheek where they have to clear the margins around the tumor, and they will be doing a neck dissection. It will take an estimated 4ish hours. Praise God for your support! Thank you, thank you a million times thank you!

Get Uncomfortable

July 9, 2015

I got to see my grandma that we call Mame, yesterday. I love that girl so, so much I can't even express it in words! Mame, consider this a note to you. Mame, you are the most selfless and generous person I have ever met in my life. You give without seeking anything in return. You never hesitate to help the ones you love even if it is a sacrifice to you. You have shown your love to your family daily in various ways, and your example has hugely impacted me. What a strong person you are and how dear to my heart you are. You have changed my life for the better. From Easter outfits, giant cartons of Goldfish, tea parties, my car, the chance to go to Europe, the opportunity to go to college, the most memorable Halloweens, and now as you help me fight for my life. You have radically changed my life, Mame, and I could never express enough gratitude. You are an amazing woman, and I will seek to be as humble and giving as you are. Even when you are helping me, you only express your gratitude for us. I love you a bushel and a peck!

To those of you who decided to read that, I hope you take something away from the kind of person you should strive to be! What a fantastic example of unconditional and sacrificial love. That is the love our God has for us, and that is the kind of love I will strive to show others. That is the love that changes and saves lives!

Today started off super stressful. I got reprimanded by one doctor, the next phone call told us that our insurance would not cover the cost of radiation if I get it in Seattle, and the third call was from Dr. Sunwoo letting me know that they found more cancer on the MRI! I started off discouraged like I was bombarded with bad news. I got myself worked up and worried, offended and scared, not trusting that I will get the care I need and not trusting that God will be faithful to provide finances. Then I just paused. WAIT.

You may say something, and someone will despise you for it. Later as they change and mature or their circumstances change they may look back on that moment where maybe you felt uncomfortable, and they may be significantly impacted.

First of all, God is in charge of my care. Not the doctors, not the secretaries, not the nurses. Sure, they have pulled strings to get me into surgery and save my life, but God made those appointments available. He is in control, and the only way I'm NOT going to get the proper care according to my standards and my human expectations is if God has a different and better plan.

He is in control, He is faithful, He is loving, and He has begun a good work in me and will see it through to the end. Then I was reminded that God has been more than faithful to provide finances - so if the insurance doesn't cover radiation at Seattle, then there are other options, and it will work out!

I honestly was happier that they caught the other cancer via the MRI because now they can take that out during surgery as well. It's in my salivary glands near my ear so it will add a few extra hours onto the already 4-hour operation. You better suggest some exciting reading material or movies to my family as they wait! Praise God for technology and doctors with a keen eye.

I want you guys to know that sometimes I make jokes about my situation not to be sick or hide from my true feelings. Sometimes it helps me to be positive and lighten the mood! After Dr. Sunwoo listed off the extra risk factors I now face, one of them was the small chance of permanent paralysis on one half of my face. I jokingly said to my parents, "Hopefully that doesn't happen because I'll be really sad if I never get married!" to that Dad responds, "At least part of you will be!" HAHA, bad joke. For those of you who didn't get it, if half of my face is paralyzed it will have a permanent, droopy, sad face look. Sometimes you gotta enjoy those jokes!

I want to thank everyone for not only reading my blog but giving me feedback, input, and showing me how it has changed you or your perspective on things. This makes my heart so happy! God is using the writing gift He gave me and the knowledge He gave me from my surroundings and His Word, and I am so happy to see it impact people. We are up to 9,000 views! My goodness, you all must have a lot of friends because I sure don't have that many! Thank you for sharing this with others. You truly never know what sentence, what story, what verse, or what quote may help a person in their situation. That is why it's so important not to let your insecurities hold you back.

If I let my insecurities get the best of me I would have never even started a blog in fear of rejection or judgment. Be authentic, and be transparent. It gets uncomfortable you guys! And that's okay! You never know what seed you will plant. You may say something, and someone will despise you for it. Later as they change and mature or their circumstances change they may look back on that moment where maybe you felt uncomfortable, and they may be significantly impacted. We have to trust that God will use our words for His glory. We may not like it, and we may be afraid, we may never even see the impact. But if you never take that chance, you'll never impact anyone, and you will sit alone in your comfort.

Excuse My Expectations

July 10, 2015

᚛ᚖᚖᚖᚖᚖᚖ

Today I was pondering the past two weeks as I retold the recent events to several friends of mine. I think one of the hardest things about trials is that we are forced to die to our expectations. If you think about it, if we had zero expectations about how our life is supposed to be there would be no disappointment or bitterness. We'd gladly accept things as they are and anything above that would be considered a blessing. That's been a tough lesson throughout this trial.

I expected to live until an old age. I expected to get married and have kids. I expected to go live in my cute new apartment in Spokane. I expected to be a healthy 21-year-old. I expected to wake up this morning. My world has been turned upside down because I was living life expecting all these things instead of being thankful for the blessing that each of these things is.

How many times have I stopped to thank God for the privileges of this life? How many times have I complained about my job, my family, waking up early, or being hungry because the chef is taking forever? How many times have I been bitter because a loved one was taken from me, or disappointed because I didn't get to move back to Spokane right away because I have cancer? Our very breath is a blessing. OUR VERY BREATH. Take a second while you are reading this to take a deep breath. That is not something you're promised. Our very life is not something to be taken for granted.

Instead, we can hope. Hope for the white picket fence life, hope for the career of our dreams, hope for enough money to feed our families, and thank God when our hopes and desires are fulfilled, not curse Him when they aren't.

Expectation: "a strong *belief* that something will happen or be the case in the future."

Hope: "a *desire* for a certain thing to happen."

Had I not set my expectations on living until I die peacefully at an old age, or moving to Spokane after the summer is over, or expecting that my savings would go toward buying a new camera and not cancer treatment, I wouldn't have faced disappointment. I hope that I live until an old age, I hope that I get to go back to Spokane eventually, and I hope that one day I can upgrade my camera for my photography. But guess what? If my hopes aren't fulfilled, God is still God and He is still good. He has a better plan for me and my life. A plan in which He knew when He placed me in my mother's womb.

I read a quote recently that was talking about expectations and it said something like "Expectation leads to disappointment, disappointment leads to anger, and anger leads to bitterness." It's a downward spiral to a really dark and hard place, and I can see the truth in this.

I encourage you all to think about what you *expect* for your life, and work on changing your perspective from *expecting*, to what do you *hope* for your life? Hold those plans loosely; better yet, don't hold them at all. Give them to God and let Him carry them for you!

It's been amazing to me how many people have reached out to me. I mean we're talking people I've never met, people I haven't seen in 12 years, young, old, all different countries and all different walks of life. So many people have said something along the lines of "I know we haven't talked." or "I'm sorry it took you getting cancer for me to reach out." I've even caught myself thinking, "I'm sorry it took you reaching out to me because of my cancer for me to reach out to you!"

At first, I felt guilty, like wow, I need to be more intentional. I don't want to only reach out to people because they are having a hard time, but then I started thinking about how unrealistic that is. I mean why is it a bad thing? I actually would venture to say it's not! God gives you different people in the different seasons of your life for a specific purpose. Some are meant to be your best friends for a long time, some are intended to be your lunch buddy in middle school, and some are meant to give you words of encouragement during your trial. I don't want you to feel guilty that it took me getting cancer for you to reach out! Being intentional doesn't always look like calling someone once a week, or getting coffee once a month, or sending them letters letting you know you're thinking about them. I want to suggest that you should be intentional in that you live a Christ-like life. Then the love that overflows from you will affect the people surrounding you even if you didn't write them a card. Your example and your life are what affects people.

I encourage you all to think about what you expect for your life and work on changing your perspective to what do you hope for your life? Hold those plans loosely; better yet don't hold them at all, give them to God and let Him carry them for you!

I guarantee you that people will remember your character and not if you called them every week. DO NOT get me wrong, being intentional, going to coffee, sending cards, etc. is such a blessing and a very rare characteristic. Those of you that I've lost contact with over the years, I remember you for your character, for the life I witnessed during the time that I knew you. That is what affected and impacted me for the time that the Lord had you in my life. Make your life an example, make your impact matter during the season they know you. That should be your intention!

Cuz I'm Free Fallin'

July 12, 2015

It was so hard for me not to write yesterday! I was tempted to stay up all night writing about the thoughts, convictions, and emotions stirring in my brain, but I didn't. I don't want to feel guilty for not writing. It's not my job to write. I love to write, and I want to write. I never want it to become a thing that I have to do.

That being said, I had an amazing day yesterday. I started the day going with my Aunt Jen and Uncle Darren on their new zipline. Cliché once again, I feel like cancer has made me want to try more, adventure more, and do more things that I love. In the past, I may have decided to sleep in more rather than wake up early to go on a zipline. What an incredible experience! Flying through the air, wind on my face, adrenaline pumping, and enjoying the stunning view of the mighty pine trees and beautifully crafted terrain of Klamath Falls. For a moment, I felt totally free. Free of the unknown, free of emotions, free of fear, free of cancer. I basked in the excitement of the adventure. It was incredible down to the very last jump.

I used to be fearless, a daredevil ready to take on any height. I was the kindergartener that loved the Drop Zone. But at one point I learned how to psych myself out, how to hesitate and peer over the edge. I learned how to freeze my body in fear and have a mental block that refused to move. For a while, I didn't even go rock jumping. There I was, standing on the zipline platform, 60 feet off the ground ready to jump, my mind was tempted to hesitate, to stop me. I realized that I paralyze myself with fear, and I do not want to be controlled by fear any longer. In my mind, it was confirmed that we only have a short life, all of us, not just the girl with cancer. I don't want to be dictated by fear in any way, and with that, I leaped. The first few feet were a free fall. I had a moment of panic before I realized that I did it. I conquered it, and I was no longer paralyzed by fear. I stood up and walked. How freeing it felt. How amazing it was to feel like I could do anything.

Ziplining is a great metaphor. How many times and in how many ways have we been paralyzed by fear in our lives? How many times have we let fear dictate and choose what we do? Fear of letting your child go to college because they might get hurt. Fear of pursuing that one guy because you're afraid you aren't good enough, fear of chasing your dream because you might not be successful, fear of being bold because you might be rejected. Fear of saying the wrong thing because you might offend someone. We paralyze ourselves all the time.

If you search and dig, fear is the root of so many weeds poisoning our beautiful garden in this thing called life. I encourage you to go gardening, dig through and don't only cut off the top of the weed, find the root, find the root and yank it out. Get rid of the dictator that rules over you. Take the 60-foot jump and find freedom. But also know you can't do it alone. I didn't just leap off the edge at 60 feet and land on two feet on my own. I was hooked up to a lead rope that helped me land softly and securely. It was scary knowing that my life depended on that little rope. It's scary to let go of your fear and place your trust in something outside yourself. God is our lead rope, you guys! You have to take a leap of faith, ditch your fears, and trust that God is going to guide you to the ground and help you land safe and sound.

If you search and dig, fear is the root of so many weeds poisoning our beautiful garden in this thing called life. I encourage you to go gardening, dig through and don't only cut off the top of the weed, find the root, find the root and yank it out.

After the excitement of ziplining, my day continued to get better upon the presence of my beautiful friend Kelsey. Kelsey is an amazing role model for me. Her willingness to drop anything and help those in need is a humbling characteristic. She is the girl who drives 2 hours to get a tank of gas for strangers stranded on the side of the road, the girl who is at your house with your favorite ice cream when you just got dumped, the girl who buys you pizza when you've been drinking vegetable juice for weeks (yes, she did), the girl who drives 2 hours to spend a day with you when you need a friend, and the girl who would shave her head for you if that time comes. I am in awe and humbled by her selflessness. Even when people don't return the favor or are not grateful she has shown perseverance and proof that she gives without seeking. We got manicures together so while I feel gross and not girly in the hospital, I can gaze upon the beautiful mint green polished nails, and feel like at least my nails look pretty. Then we both decided to continue my amazing day with a splurge pizza send off. That decision was quickly regretted as the grease and cheese made our stomachs hate us. But man, it was so good going down!

The last hurrah of the day was the open house my Mom set up for people to come to see me before surgery. I had no idea what to expect.

So many people came to see me and support me! It was incredibly humbling and enriching. Moms told me that their daughters read the blog and learn from my example, people gave me encouraging verses, and so many funny stories were shared! It was the exact sendoff I needed so thank you all for blessing me with your presence.

We are now back in California as a family spending some time together as I prepare for surgery. My parents are at the Creekside Inn, and Sis and I are staying at the Epiphany Hotel, and boy is it fancy! WHAT A BLESSING. I feel like a Cancer Kim Kardashian with the service and room we've received! It's so cool, and I have nothing but positive thoughts and feelings going into surgery. Surgery is tomorrow morning at 6:15 so my prayer warriors get ready for it! I have no idea how drugged up I'm going to be, but I will do my best to write whenever I have a lucid moment and a sound mind. If not, you may have some deciphering to do! Who knows, maybe I'll write some amazing John Lennon type thing in my drug-induced state. Love you all!

No Grey's Anatomy

July 14, 2015

Cancer battle part two is finished. Here I sit, I.V. in one hand, two drains in my neck, stitches covering my face, a flappy hospital gown on, a groaning roommate, and the sound of beepers indicating life functions. You know the funny thing is I used to want to spend the night at the hospital as a kid. I used to think about eating Jell-O and getting apple juice while everyone cared for me. I used to see the movies where you are in the spacious room covered in flowers and balloons and a giant window. Reality can be so harsh. Life isn't like *Grey's Anatomy*, unfortunately.

From the beginning, it was a hurry up and wait for the 6:00 AM check-in where we sat around anxiously awaiting surgery. Then I strip down and get to put on the most attractive gown and head wrap. I'm thinking a fashion trend? The anesthesiologist doctor was extremely attractive, so turns out my cousin Jess was right about that one, you know what I'm saying. I sat in the room wearing the gown, the head wrap, the wristband tagging my identity, the ugly purple hospital socks, and an I.V. sticking out of the top of my hand. No date for me LOL.

For the first time ever, I felt sick. I felt like a cancer patient, and I knew that I would be accepting this sickness as a part of my life. Before it was easier because I just had a few tests and they repeated to me that I had Merkel Cell Cancer, but I still felt like me. Sitting in that room as I awaited the surgery, knowing that I would come out never being the same, I felt the cancer label imprinted on my life. It made me cry. I cried knowing that the face I had at that moment would be changed forever. I cried knowing that I would be carved into and cut on for the next 7 hours. I cried for my family as they anxiously awaited while the hours ticked by, and I cried for being sick. I took my moment and composed myself as I was reminded of all the blessing that have taken place so far. The fact that I was even sitting in that room waiting for surgery at Stanford by the best doctor there just 16 days after my diagnosis was a blessing in itself. And I found peace knowing that you all were in constant prayer!

Turns out the surgery took much longer than expected, and 7 hours turned into a very long 11 hours. Dr. Sunwoo spent 11 hours separating nerves from tissues, removing 80 lymph nodes and trying to remove all the cancer.

I don't even remember where I woke up. There is a fuzzy recollection of being in the recovery room and seeing Dr. Sunwoo as he put a suture in my neck drain. I remember juice. Apple juice which is so good by the way. Then I remember talking to the man wheeling me to the hospital about his cool tribal tattoos.

The night spent in the hospital was horrendous. I think I got a total of one hour of sleep, if that. The drains in my neck weren't working, so I had to get them fixed every hour, and my roommate snored louder than a hibernating bear. Seriously, I think the MRI and it's creaking and clacking is just a form of preparation for the noise you experience in the hospital. At least I had an awesome (and as I recall super-hot) nurse, Dana, who was super friendly, caring, hospitable, and funny. He helped walk me around and kept me entertained all night. I have a new respect for nurses, what a job! You people are so selfless and patient, and I admire every single one of you! A good nurse can really make a huge difference in a crappy hospital stay.

I was so drugged up yesterday, I didn't get a good look at my face. Today I did. It was hard at first. So many stitches, bruising, swelling, and long lines. As I stared in the mirror, I noticed every difference in the face I knew so well. But then I gained an appreciation. These are my battle scars. They are proof of a fight for my life. They are beautiful because I know the story behind them. And you know what, I am getting used to this new face. I hope to help people feel beautiful in their own skin. Find meaning in your

Sitting in that room as I awaited the surgery, knowing that I would come out never being the same, I felt the cancer label imprinted on my life. It made me cry. I cried knowing that the face I had at that moment would be changed forever.

"flaws" and flaunt your scars, your imperfections. Find peace in knowing that you love them and find confidence in them and don't retreat to insecurity.

I had a good day. I got to eat some solid food, French toast was first on the list, yum. My Mom's beautiful friend Kathy came to see me and enriched me with her warmth and kindness. I got to spend some quality time with my Mom and Sis. I am so grateful for their willingness to hang out with an old sickie like me! And I got a lovely little "Warm Embrace" gift from camp director Ed and his wife, which explains how I feel around them and the people of Camp Redwood Glen. Also, a few of the nurses

I've encountered have said that they appreciate how positive I am, how it makes their day better to see someone just 21 going through this very hard thing and to see that I am taking it and making it into something good. That was so good to hear and just a reminder that your attitude can really have an impact on anyone. You can be a witness without even saying much!

I'm still groggy from the drugs, so I'm going to end it there and say goodnight. Pray that I get released tomorrow! Love you all.

Fighter

July 15, 2015

When I was a kid, I loved to play this video game called The Sims. It is a life simulation video game, and you control everything about the Sim people. I feel like I am a Sim. Not controlled by my own mind but controlled by nurses one minute, drugs the next minute, doctors another time, nutrition at one point, and then cancer takes a turn. They tell me when to pee, when to sleep, when to eat, what to do and when to do it all day long. My mind has been in such a blur from the pain meds that I just float along until I get my next instruction, like press (z) and leave me to finish the task (for those of you who played/play Sims you understand). It makes me feel sad for people who live like this, especially those who choose to have their mind blurred out and filled with a giant cloud of nothingness. To just exist day by day, I refuse.

Here I sit, typing away, and I finally have a change of scenery. I have escaped the hospital prison, and I now reside in a room back at camp. Hallelujah! I slept one full hour with no needles being shoved into my arm, no beeping, and most of all no Pam groaning "Ohhhh owwwww NURSE PAIN MEDS PLEASE, GOD!"

Pam: she was definitely my trial while recovering from my surgery. So many sleepless hours listening to her snore or complain made me tempted to absolutely lose it. Fortunately, or Unfortunately, when I write something in my blog, I try to follow my own advice, so I had to repeat in my mind "Trial Signs." There she sat, bitter and lonely, awaiting a surgery to help relieve her from pain. She didn't have one visitor come in while I was there and after a later discussion, she wasn't planning on having any. I knew that I needed to find an extra dose of patience and grace and show this woman love. That sure didn't mean that I didn't wake up when she turned on the light every hour and think "Really God, really? I can't just have a solid night of sleep?" When I was getting ready to leave the hospital today Pam said to me, "Haley (my name is Hayden), you're a brave girl and you are going to get this. You have a great atti-tude, and I want to wish you the best of luck my Libra." And we left off on a good note, and you know what, that feels good guys. Trial signs - treat people like they have a big blinking one above their heads.

The pain is pretty bad today. Up until this point I've been numb from surgery, but slowly there is a tingle in different parts of my face as I regain feeling. Then I'm reminded that my face and neck were cut up and my body isn't too happy about it. It was an 11-hour surgery as most of you know by now. I can't even imagine being a doctor and standing there cutting and moving things for 11 hours! Besides sleeping, I can't think of anything that I've done for 11 hours straight. Anyway, so he cut out several tumors in my lymph nodes near my jawline, he cleared the margins on my face around the previous tumor, he removed my salivary gland where more cancer was found, he also removed over 80 lymph nodes in my lower neck, and then he cut off a chunk of my neck muscle, turned it and attached it to fill in the gaps in my face where he took out so much tissue. Wow. Just wow, you guys. We have amazing technology but how about these bodies that God gave us! I had two drains in the back of my neck to remove fluid buildup. I know it's super gross, but today Dr. Sunwoo was able to take one out. It was a gnarly feeling having him pull out a tube that goes in through the back of my neck all the way down into my lymph nodes. Then he had to stitch me up which was painful but geez, the dang local anesthetic shot is worse! Actually, no, I've decided that Heparin is the worst by far. It's the blood clot shot they give you every 8 hours in the arms and stomach.

I'm on the road to recovery after my second cancer battle guys! This is exciting news and it feels good to be taking another step forward. I posted a picture on Facebook last night of all my new battle wounds and was overwhelmed by the response! 500 likes and so many messages later, my blog is up to 12,000 views. I have lost count, but the GoFundMe page is past the original goal, and I've received so many encouraging letters and care packages. Thanks, you guys! You know it was hard posting that picture at first. Everything about it goes against what society calls beauty. I have no makeup, my hair is matted with blood and goo from surgery, I am in a white hospital gown, and I have giant marks all over my face. So why did that picture get 500 likes? Because it's real life. Because we all can

Let's change that. Let's be the "Wow you can tell she's a fighter and she didn't go down with that trial." Because that's exactly right, Battle scars are beautiful.

relate to the ugly marks from trials in our lives. Because society tells us to cringe and hide them, to keep them covered up and keep people comfortable, I want to challenge society to rejoice in the beauty of overcoming trials, to be proud of the marks left by the trials in our lives that we've conquered.

The marks on my face are going to get stares, and they are going to get the "Mommy, what's wrong with her face?" They are going to get the "That girl would be so pretty if she didn't have those big scars." I've been that girl, you've been that kid, we've all done it. Let's change that. Let's be the "Wow you can tell she's a fighter and she didn't go down with that trial." Because that's exactly right, battle scars are beautiful.

I feel like hospital. I smell like hospital. I taste like hospital. Love you all, I'm going to go try to feel human again starting with some deodorant!

Help Wanted

July 16, 2015

ᕤᕤᕤᕤᕤᕤᕤ

Today hurts. I feel weary, exhausted, helpless, and in a lot of pain. The numbness from the drugs has completely worn off, so I can feel the throbbing of each stitch and the pull of the drain in my neck. The pain meds don't make the pain go away, they just make me forget about the pain momentarily because I'm so dazed and sleepy. Literally, right after I take the pill, I am sitting there completely alert and paying attention to my surroundings, then I will feel this dull buzz and poof, goner.

It's humbling being in a position where you rely on others to help you with everything. This is something I experienced in the hospital first. The nurses were in charge of giving me my meds, helping me get to the bathroom, cleaning my body, helping me get dressed, all the things you are used to doing on your own. You don't even have the strength to be stubborn and tell them you have it under control because you don't. I was at the mercy of their help and hospitality, and it truly makes the small victories, like walking by yourself that much better.

Now my care is in the hands of my family. Get yourself a good support system you guys, honestly, they have been utterly selfless in all this and willing to help me in every way. My sister and mom gave me a bath today. Now that's not the most comfortable situation, but sitting there while they worked together to help me was a touching moment for me. Like sharing a good cry, being dependent on others for help makes you vulnerable and makes all walls come down. I honestly knew and felt in that moment that these two girls in my life would do anything for me and they love me unconditionally.

In that same way, my dad took a Q-tip and meticulously cleaned every single stitch on my face with precision and gentleness even though it was a bloody mess. Why is it that we are always so hesitant to get help? We would much rather be stubborn and say "no, no I have it handled" than allow others to extend a helping hand. Why is seeking help or accepting help looked down on as a weakness?

I can't tell you how many times during my cancer journey so far that I have received help in some way and thought, "Oh no, I can't take this" or "How will I ever repay them?" But how humbling it has been to receive so much help. It has not only been so enriching and fulfilling to be helped, but it has taught me a lot about what it means to be a good helper to others. By not allowing others to help you, you rob them of the chance to pour into you and grow themselves. If for nothing else you have to let others help you for them. For example, it has been very hard for me to allow people to donate to me. My aunt told me, "We have to do what we feel called to do to help you in any way we can. If something were to happen to you, we want to have peace knowing we did our part." God calls us to love one another, we have to choose to be selfless by helping others, but we also have to decide to be selfless by letting others help us.

On that same track, people don't know you need help if you don't ask! We aren't like Edward Cullens, the mind reading vampire from the *Twilight* series. Humans can't go around reading minds. Don't be embarrassed or insecure about sharing your struggles, so you can let the people that God placed in your life come around you. If we all kept our struggles hidden from each other, then we'd never get help or be able to help others. Since I've decided to be completely open and honest throughout my fight with cancer, I have been blown away by the things people relate to, the help I've received, and the help I've been able to give.

Be transparent, allow others to help you carry your burdens, we were never meant to walk these things alone. Allow the Lord to carry the load and allow His people to help you in ways that will help them and help you.

One girl told me that she was afraid to wear capris because of a scar on her leg, and now after reading the blog she has the strength to wear capris. Now had I been ashamed and embarrassed about my scars and the struggle it is to have my face cut up, then we wouldn't have had that chance to help one another. Be transparent. Allow others to help you carry your burdens, because we were never meant to walk these things alone. Allow the Lord to carry the load, and allow His people to help you in ways that will help them and help you. I have been blessed by the support and I have been completely transformed by the things the Lord has allowed me to see since the beginning of this trial.

I'm weary, and I'm weak, I'm in pain, I'm not ashamed to admit that I'm struggling. I need help from the people around me to even shower. But you know what? There's absolutely nothing wrong with that. I am still a fighter, and I still have strength from the Lord to battle this and recover.

Like the Bill Withers song *Lean On Me* says "Just call on me brother, when you need a hand—we all need somebody to lean on."

Challenge yourself to pick one person today and ask them to help you with something you're struggling with. Start small if you have to, or take a leap of faith. Let people surprise you. Love ya!

Identity Crisis

July 17, 2015

Facebook is like a buried time capsule of every stage in your life. I am so entertained by going all the way back to 2009 and reliving who I was as a freshman in high school when it was cool to update your status every day and do "Truth Is" challenges, and continue scrolling up to 2015. That's six solid years of history!

Today, as I reread embarrassing statuses and looked at a trillion selfies, I tried to picture who I was and what made me who I am today. I looked into the eyes of that freshman with black hair, black eyeliner, and black braces. I remember the feeling of leaving middle school and entering high school feeling like I could be anyone I wanted, the athletic girl, the prep, the nerd, the goth, I had the freedom to choose a label.

As freshman year unfolded I struggled with identity, no matter who I tried to be, I wasn't content. Nothing was good enough, and nothing satisfied the standard of perfection I had for myself. Sophomore year rolled around, braces came off, and I was no longer at the bottom of the food chain. I started to do some soul-searching, looking through magazines, TV shows, and social media. I searched for a role model whom I thought had it all together. That was when I was introduced to the concept of comparison.

Comparison was addicting. From the girls in the magazines to the girls at school, from the length of our hair to the shade of our skin. I would pick things about myself that were better than the opposing figure, that would build me up. Then I would tear myself back down as I noticed everything about the opposing figure that was better than me. It was a losing game that no one could ever win.

Comparison is the thief of joy, and slowly but surely, he was robbing me. Junior year I was drowning in insecurities. I was at the lowest low of my self-esteem, identifying in nothing. I was so consumed with what other people thought of me I couldn't find joy. Then the thought came to me that perhaps if I could be thinner I could find some worth. That's when I started puking to try and fit the skinny body standard. That didn't help either, so I was striving to do anything, find anything that would make me feel like I was worth something. Sports, art, boys, fashion, popularity, grades. I searched for fulfillment and kept finding myself empty. I hated myself, and I wanted nothing to do with God because He was just another person for me to fail.

As I scrolled through the end of my Junior year on Facebook, my heart was heavy for the lost and hopeless girl I was. What a merciful God we have that He didn't allow me to have cancer during that time, I honestly would not have been able to handle it. The girl back then with these scars marring her face, she would weep, she would curse God, she would become depressed, and she wouldn't survive.

Being an "almost" Christian. Being so close to being a Christian—but you aren't! The Lord used that sermon to grip my heart and bring me to my knees. I couldn't believe it, I had been living a life claiming to know Christ, but I didn't actually KNOW Him.

Senior year I reached a breaking point. God does that you know, brings you to the end of yourself, so you have nowhere to run but to the cross. And it's a lovely experience.

One day I was doing a Bible study with my Mom and sister, up to this point, I had lived out a fake religion for 17 years and never had a personal relationship with Christ because of my fear. We listened to a sermon on being an "almost" Christian. Being so close to being a Christian—but you aren't! The Lord used that sermon to grip my heart and bring me to my knees. I couldn't believe it, I had been living a life claiming to know Christ, but I didn't actually KNOW Him. I didn't know Him enough to know that He loves us unconditionally, that He died for us, and we can't fail Him. That out of every relationship we could ever seek on earth, God is the only one who is unchanging and will never abandon us.

From that day on I wanted to know the God that I claimed to serve. I wanted to develop a personal relationship with Him and not just live out a religion where I had a holy checklist that I would never get perfect. I went from being a Christian robot.

Pray: check
Read your Bible: check
Go to church: check
Don't sin: check

To truly understanding what it means to have a relationship with Jesus Christ, and seeking to not only know God but become more like Him. I have an identity in Christ, and He silences all insecurities and fears of this earth. He alone gives me value and worth, and he is the place I find unconditional love.

It didn't happen overnight. Oh no, there were many more lessons learned, and I am still learning today. But I have joy, no matter the situation, I have a reason to rejoice because I have a Savior who cares about me. So, this girl today, marred with scars, infected with cancer, not sure what tomorrow will bring, she is happy. I am happy, and I am prepared for this battle with the Lord by my side. If God can take the timid, insecure, fearful high schooler who would photoshop her selfies and take them down if they didn't get a certain number of likes, and change her into the strong, confident woman who is not ashamed to post her struggles, then He can change you too. To God be the glory and the credit for molding me into the person I am today and preparing me for this trial.

Which Field Are You?

July 18, 2015

I listened to a sermon today upon the suggestion of Garret, a guy from my old school whom I look up to very much for his steadfast faith and love for others. It was entitled, "Trials/Temptations" by Matt Chandler. I would highly recommend it to anyone who is seeking some good, solid teaching and advice about trials. Matt talks about a quote by A.W. Tozer and I wanted to share it with you guys because it is such a stunning analogy of the purpose of trials in our lives.

Here are two kinds of ground: fallow ground and ground that has been broken up by the plow. The fallow field is smug, contented, protected from the shock of the plow and the agitation of the harrow. Such a field, as it lies year after year, becomes a familiar landmark to the crow and the blue jay. Had it intelligence, it might take a lot of satisfaction in its reputation: it has stability; nature has adopted it; it can be counted upon to remain always the same, while the fields around it change from brown to green and back to brown again. Safe and undisturbed, it sprawls lazily in the sunshine, the picture of sleepy contentment.

But it is paying a terrible price for its tranquility; never does it feel the motions of mounting life, nor see the wonders of bursting seed, nor the beauty of ripening grain. Fruit it can never know because it is afraid of the plow and the harrow.

In direct opposition to this, the cultivated field has yielded itself to the adventure of living. The protecting fence has opened to admit the plow, and the plow has come as plows always come, practical, cruel, business-like and in a hurry. Peace has been shattered by the shouting farmer and the rattle of machinery. The field has felt the travail of change; it has been upset, turned over, bruised and broken.

But its rewards come hard upon its labors. The seed shoots up into the daylight its miracle of life, curious, exploring the new world above it. All over the field, the hand of God is at work in the age-old and ever renewed service of creation. New things are born, to grow, mature, and consummate the grand prophecy latent in the seed when it entered the ground. Nature's wonders follow the plow.

Stunning huh? This picture so moved me. Now to put that in a real-life example, here we have Hayden 1 (the one without cancer) and Hayden 2 (the one with cancer). Hayden 1 had a seemingly good life, relatively easy, extremely comfortable, and prone to exist day to day as long as her expectations were fulfilled and things went her way. No real passion, no deep thought, no experience of love, just not much depth to her life. She is the first field, the one afraid of change, fearful of the hardship the plow brings, not willing to put in the effort to see fruit grow. Now, this Hayden looks like she has it made, like the field that lays comfortably in the sun, but at the end of her life what would she have to show? If the field has no fruit, if her life has no growth, what is the purpose?

Then you have Hayden 2. That field that is uncomfortable because the farmer is plowing, disturbing her peace and causing pain. Hayden 2 has cancer, a trial that she never expected. It hurts, it's uncomfortable, it's scary, it demands your attention. This field doesn't lay out and bask in the sun, and this field doesn't live out in comfort, unchanging. But Hayden 2 is experiencing life. She has passion. Deep thoughts are constantly stirring in her, and she has experienced a surreal, unconditional love, and there is so much depth and growth in her life. This field has beautiful fruit, beautiful life bursting forth from its soil. Hayden 2 is going to look back at her life and be amazed at all that God did and how much she was able to grow from the hard times. She is going to see the fruit of her trials and think, wow that was a great life. I see the purpose, and I would never choose the comfortable life.

Embrace the trials with joy! It seems so silly and so not of this world to do that. When life is going great we want to give ourselves the credit, but when it doesn't go our way, oh then that was God's fault.

Embrace the trials with joy! It seems so silly and so not of this world to do that. When life is going great we want to give ourselves the credit, but when it doesn't go our way, oh then that was God's fault. Don't choose to be the comfortable field that bears no fruit, that serves no purpose, decide to embrace the plow. Choose to work hard, persevere, and bear fruit. Beautiful people do not just happen. Everything good comes from hard work. A good body comes from hard work at the gym. A good marriage comes from the hard work of dying to yourself. A good career comes from the hard work of a disciplined work ethic. A good life comes from the hard work of trials. Cheers to the fields who do not fear the plow!

Today was much better for me. I had more energy, and I was in less pain. The swelling has gone down significantly, and the drain is draining less. I am counting down because on Monday I get the drain removed and hopefully the stitches! Right now, I kind of feel like a doll that has too much stuffing on one side of her head and keeps flopping to one side. My neck is very weak, and it hurts to stand for too long so please pray that with some physical therapy that I can regain some strength! Love you all, and I am continually stunned by your support and encouragement.

Finding Beauty

July 19, 2015

I went to church today. I just needed to get dressed up and feel like a normal, functioning human. We sang this song that I've sung a million times and any churchgoer, or anyone who listens to the Christian radio station has probably heard it a bunch and even sings along. It's called, "Hosanna in the Highest" and it's just a classic. Well, for the first time, a specific lyric stuck out to me, "Break my heart for what breaks yours, everything I am for your kingdom's cause." I started weeping.

How many times have I sung those powerful lyrics? Did I even understand what that means? Now I do. Everything I am for your kingdom's cause. It doesn't say only the stuff I want you to have. It doesn't say everything that I'm willing to part with right now or everything that I think you should have. It cries EVERYTHING I HAVE for your kingdom's cause. It's completely selfless, and it's completely following the example Jesus gave us when He gave His very life for the kingdom's cause. I have cancer. I have no idea what my future looks like, and for the first time, I understood what it means to give everything I have for the kingdom's cause. How humbling and beautiful that is.

I had a few moments of insecurity today about my scars, stitches, droopy mouth, slanted eye, and giant drain. I went to church where I felt really good, confident, like I wanted people to see that I'm choosing not to stay secluded in my room because of this.

Then I went out in public to Trader Joe's for the first time, and that's when I got the stares I expected. Little kids, eyes wide, adults, some with eyes of judgment, some with eyes of "Wow, badass", some with eyes of confusion. It doesn't matter what they thought because their eyes were glued to me. I tried to remind myself that it's not always a bad thing when people stare, I tried to remind myself that these are my battle scars and I know my story, they don't. But it was hard. It was hard feeling like I was an attraction at the zoo. I got overwhelmed and ended up leaving, feeling defeated. I sat in the car and prayed that the Lord would remind me that inner beauty is a treasure, and I prayed that He'd show me the beauty in my scars, the beauty of conquering this battle and that is something to be proud of.

Like always the Lord answered my prayer. My cousin JB, and friends Clare and Anna came over and wanted to do a photo shoot of me. Now those of you who know me well know that I am the photographer and it is a real struggle for me to be the model! Insecurity creeps in when you have all the attention on you, and it has been a massive struggle in my life. Slowly I have eased into feeling more comfortable in front of the camera, but after the day I had when I was feeling self-conscious, I thought that this might be a bad idea. Then the Lord reminded me that faith grows outside of your comfort zone and He wants you to be excited to overcome your fears.

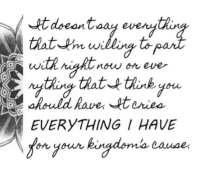

It doesn't say everything that I'm willing to part with right now or everything that I think you should have. It cries EVERYTHING I HAVE for your kingdom's cause.

I also was reminded that because I was unashamed to post a picture of my scars, Brittney was inspired to wear capris for the first time, bearing her scars. So, I agreed to the photoshoot, I decided to find beauty and confidence in the marks on my face.

What a stunning experience. Not only were the girls so amazing in their encouragement with an "Ow ow! Lookin' Good" here and there, but during that moment I realized, everyone is staring at me, just like at the store, but they are staring out of admiration and respect. They know the struggles behind these marks, it made me convicted. Anytime I see someone now who might have something wrong with their body, or might be marred by scars, and I am going to think about their story and find a way to respect them, not judge them. I felt more beautiful than I ever have in my life. Not because I was all of a sudden, the skinniest I've ever been, not because I magically grew a big booty, not because I grew gorgeous hair, not because I turned into Angelina Jolie. No, if anything my outward appearance is the least attractive it's ever been.

For the first time I felt radiant, I felt like I saw my heart, I was seeing myself in God's perspective. It was beautiful, and I felt joy. It didn't matter that my mouth is droopy because I can't feel it, or that my face was throbbing because I have hundreds of stitches, or that my tube was pulling on the inside of my neck. All that mattered was the woman that I know God is molding me into. I hope you all get a chance to peer into your inner beauty and feel all other vanity fade away. I hope that every person who thinks that they have flaws can rejoice in their story, that they can celebrate in showing that they conquered something and there is no shame in that.

Love you all! For those of you who want to share my blog, please don't feel the need to ask for permission! I am humbled and honored to have my blog reach out to others. Please pray that I can get my drain AND stitches out tomorrow at 4!

The Big Picture

July 20, 2015

Today was a perfect day. I started the day with french toast, which is just happy food that brings me warm feelings of childhood and all good things. Then we drove to Stanford where my favorite surgeon Dr. Sunwoo took out my drain and all my stitches! It was so freeing you guys, like how I imagine a person who gets a cast off for the first time, or when you get braces off, it's just freeing. Surprisingly it was reasonably painless which is an answer to prayer because I had a little anxiety earlier about there being so many stitches to remove.

Dr. Sunwoo stated not once but twice that he is so pleased with how well I'm healing. Mom gives nutrition all the credit and wants everyone to understand that it's the juice, LOL! If I'm honest, I'm genuinely noticing a difference from being so healthy. I have more of a glow (no not a green alien glow from all the salad), I lost weight, I am recovering faster, my skin is a lot better, I have had zero bloating or stomach pains, no headaches, I've needed less sleep, I have more energy, and I'm sure there are more benefits that I'm forgetting but I'm embracing the lifestyle of healthy eating.

So just when I felt the day was at its peak greatness with the stitches and drain gone for good, I got a much better surprise. As I've mentioned before I was saving all my money to buy a camera because I love photography. Well, the Lord had a different plan when I had the first surgery (a minor in-office procedure) costing a whopping $600. Like I mentioned before about dying to my expectations, I had to wrestle with this one. Here I was working hard, and I had a plan to buy a camera so I could advance in what I thought could be a photography career. I was disappointed, sad, mad, and it felt unfair. I didn't do anything to make the lump appear on my face so why should I have to pay to get it removed!? It felt different; you pay for a cavity because you didn't brush your teeth, you pay for a broken leg because you jumped off the swing, etc. The injustice of cancer was a hard pill to swallow. However, I saw only one pixel in the grand scheme of God's bigger picture.

I remember crying in frustration to a good friend of mine and she, in her wisdom, said, "Just remember how many times God has come through for you. You don't see the bigger picture now, but if you are faithful in prayer and if you serve and trust God He will provide in His timing and what He knows is best for you." That brought me a lot of comfort, and from then on, I haven't mourned the loss of my potential camera.

After my stitches were removed, we had to drive to Best Buy to get a camera charger for a camera that my mom's friend Kathy gave me. I was so wiped out by then that I was going to stay in the car and take a rest. My Mom comes in the back of the car and says, "Come on you have to come in." I said, "No Mom, I'm really tired and I don't feel 100%. I'm going to stay in the car." She insisted, "No, no I don't know what to get, so you have to come in and help me, plus walking around is good for you." Seriously Mom? At this, my blood starts boiling. I said in a short tone, "Mom they aren't going to have the charger you need, this whole thing is pointless, and I just got my face pulled at—leave me in here!" to that she said a stern, "Now come on." AS SHE HOLDS BACK LAUGHTER. At this point, I was so annoyed. How could she be laughing right now? Why the heck is this funny? "Mom you're treating me like I'm a five-year-old, why do I have to go in!?" She said, "You're acting like a five-year-old. Just come on, I need your help!" At this point, I was so frustrated that I didn't even have the energy to argue with her. I stomped out of the car, in dramatic rage city style and I exclaim in frustration "You don't respect me!" Finally, we get into Best Buy, and I'm replaying the whole situation in my mind and just fuming. We get to the camera

I remember crying in frustration to a good friend of mine and she, in her wisdom said, "Just remember how many times God has come through for you. You don't see the bigger picture now, but if you are faithful in prayer and if you serve and trust God He will provide in His timing and what He knows is best for you.

section to look for a charger I know isn't going to be there and we are standing in front of a display case of gorgeous, high-end Canon cameras. "The chargers are located over there," I said pointing, and at that moment a little *Lightbulb* came on in my head. "I know," she said.

We weren't there for a charger. Emotions clouded my mind with excitement, hope, joy, guilt, and shame for the 5-year-old tantrum I just threw. I started crying as I looked to my parents in disbelief. "An anonymous donor wants to buy you this camera so you can fulfill your passion," my dad said, and I could feel my heart swell up and then almost crumble at the thought that someone would be so kind and generous. You know that saying that we use flippantly, "You made my day?" I could confidently say to you at that moment, "You made my life."

God is incredible you guys. What a beautiful reminder that we honestly don't see the big picture. He gives us pixels, sometimes snapshots, but I encourage you to take a look at your life, think back on times where you struggled with something and try to see if you can find where God took that struggle and worked it into His divine plan for you. Use these examples in your own life so that next time you see a pixel, maybe it's bigger like cancer, you will find peace in saying, "God's got this. It will be okay."

Livin' On a Prayer

July 21, 2015

It's been interesting to receive so many messages, texts, and calls. So many people's lives have been touched by cancer in some way. Some have never dealt with it before, and some are dealing with it currently. There have been some messages that say," Hey Hade, I have no idea what you're going through." Or "Hey Hade, I know my trial is small compared to yours." I want to encourage you not to let a label make you insecure or uncomfortable.

My trial right now is cancer. It's a big and scary title, but the truth is that God could be using cancer to grow me in the same way He is using your dog dying, or your parent's getting divorced, or school presenting itself as a challenge or getting laid off of from work. Don't compare your trial to others; it will make you insecure. Some people have thought, "Maybe I shouldn't ask her for advice because she might think that I'm dumb for having a hard time with the fact that I can't pay rent, while she has cancer." Or "I would love to offer her some support, but I've never been through anything like she has. I would love to give her some encouragement or advice but I can't even get through my summer with these rowdy kids, and she's dealing with cancer."

Do you see how this could make you fearful?

The truth is, God gives us wisdom and grows us through experiences and trials in different ways. I want to help support you as a sister in Christ whether your trial seems big or small. I want you to help support me as a sister or brother in Christ whether you feel like you can relate or not. I have been changed by those who have reached out to me to offer support, prayer, help, relating, or words of encouragement. Don't let your comparison hinder you from reaching out to your brothers and sisters. We all have trials, none of them look the same, but we have the same God whose ultimate goal is for us to be more like Him.

God is faithful. You know I used to struggle with prayer, even as I learned more and more about developing a relationship with God and not just living a religion. Prayer is the easiest thing yet the hardest thing. Here we can sit with our best friend and talk for five hours straight. Here we text our friends, Snapchat, Facebook, FaceTime, and are always flapping our gums. Yet prayer is something that we have to "set aside", or "find time" to do? I used to have tons of insecurity about praying. "What if I say the wrong thing or what if I don't sound passionate or holy enough?"

You know those people who are "good" at praying? The ones who use big, biblical words or the ones who say Jesus but also, Daddy, Holy One, God, Lord, Father, King of Kings, Alpha and Omega, and they seem to know everything. Or the people who crescendo and decrescendo, or the ones who can go on for 10 minutes. Good for them, but that's not me. I used to HATE circle prayers because I would sit there and rehearse what I was going to say in my mind. Praying was so hard for me because I would find myself getting distracted, then I'd get mad that I was distracted. I've learned over the past few years that there is no "right" or "good" way to pray. Just PRAY. You can pray about anything. Here I was the other day, praying that

> My trial right now is cancer. Its a big and scary title, but the truth is that God could be using cancer to grow me in the same way He is using your dog dying, or your parents getting divorced, or school presenting itself as a challenge or getting laid off of from work. Don't compare your trial to others; it will make you insecure.

my FedEx package would be cheaper. There is nothing that God doesn't know or can't handle. Nothing is small or dumb to God. He is even faithful when it comes to mail, something I would have never prayed about! I've started praying at the moment.

My Mom is an excellent example of this because she prays at the moment out loud. I used to kind of think it was weird, but wow it has genuinely changed my prayer life. Instead of saying I should pray about that later, even just in my head, I say a quick prayer for the situation. There is no designated time that you have to pray. If you need to set some time aside, then do it! I've noticed that my drive to work is a great time to pray. I turn the radio off and spend some time in prayer.

Another thing I've been learning, is to pray without expectations. At times I pray expecting a particular answer, and then I get disappointed if it looks different than what I had hoped for, and think that prayer doesn't work. Hey, guess what? God is not a magic genie in the sky people! Praying with expectation is selfish and not praying with the right motives. For example, I don't pray that God will cure me of cancer, thinking that because I pray to Him every day that He'll do it. I pray that God will use cancer in my life to grow me to become more like Him and point others to Him. He may heal me, and I do ask Him for that, but the truth is He may not. I hope that He does, but I pray that His will be done and that He gives me the strength needed. Don't pray with your expectations. You will be disappointed. Believe in the power of prayer people! It's amazing. It may not turn out exactly like you planned or in the timing you thought was best, but God will answer your prayers in His way. The very best way. Commit yourself and dedicate yourself to prayer, and see how it will change your life. It has sure changed my life, and it has changed my cancer journey for the better!

For those praying for me, I still need a flight for Traci and me to Seattle to see the specialist there. Also, we don't have a place to stay there so prayers for both of those things would be great! Also, I have temporary paralysis in my lower left lip that Dr. Sunwoo is confident will heal over time, the quicker, the less annoying! Thank you!

Giving Up

July 22, 2015

My Mom said to me this morning that she had been crying a lot, which is understandable when your kid has cancer, but that wasn't it. She said, "I was crying all morning. But I wasn't crying because you have cancer. I was crying because I have been humbled to my knees by the kindness and support people have shown. It was a good cry. The kind of crying that brings praise and tears of joy!" I smiled because I could relate to her and had cried that very morning for that same reason!

People have stunned me. During this hard time in my life, I would have never guessed I'd have half the support that I've received. It's been so humbling and such a tremendous blessing! And you know what? So many of you have said, "No thanks needed, the best thanks you can give us is to fight."

It's challenged me. I genuinely wish I could bottle up this feeling and sell it. The feeling I get every time someone messages me and says they are impacted and strengthened by my trial, that they decided to change their perspective that day, or that they see God in this when they haven't seen God in a long time. I wish I could sell a cup of how my heart bursts with joy when I ask you to pray for me, and then God answers - like when I receive a hotel room for the time I need it, or when I receive a donation and have peace knowing it allows me to see the doctors that might save my life. Or when I meet a stranger that was brave enough to reach out to me with encouraging words. I have made a promise to bless others the way you all have blessed me. Instead of selling them the feeling, make them feel it! I want to live like I can't take it with me. You have challenged me to be quick to serve others, to respond to the call for help, to give what the Lord has given me, to give without expecting anything in return.

I remember as a kid I was pretty stingy. To this day it's so hard to give with no strings attached. I mean giving with expectations isn't truly being generous. Like "Oh, I'm going to give her the best birthday present this year, so she feels like she has to get me something good in return." Or "Oh, I am going to give them the biggest donation because then they'll see that I am just the kindest, more generous person and they'll like me." Want to challenge yourself? Give something anonymously. I promise you it will reveal to you your true motives! It's tough for me to do that. I'll be the first to admit that I love taking the credit, and makes me feel like a good person.

There have been a handful of times where I have given anonymously, and it KILLED ME. I was always thinking about who they thought it was, if they had a clue it was me, or if they liked it. I would eventually start to break down and "drop hints". Well clearly my motives had "strings attached." As I learn from those of you who either don't know me or have done kind things for me anonymously, I am convicted! I want to start practicing by doing something nice for someone every day and never reveal that it was me. It forces you to give for the other person, not for yourself. You do something kind for them, and if they don't know it's you, then you truly made their day better, in that your day should be better.

Want to challenge yourself? Give something anonymously. I promise you it will reveal to you your true motives! It's tough for me to do that, I'll be the first to admit that I love taking the credit, and makes you feel like a good person.

I'm not saying that I am less grateful to those of you who have done something for me or that you shouldn't have put your name on it! Please don't hear me wrong! And not all of you struggle with that. Some of you genuinely want to bless others, and therefore you are blessed. But it is good to challenge yourself in your giving. In the end guess what, it all belongs to God. He gave it to us, and He allowed us to have it. We need to be good stewards and show Christ in giving back to His people. We are called to help others, imagine a world full of stingy people who never helped each other out! Ew.

Update: Thanks to Lori Burns and Rebecca Ezell, Traci and I have a place to stay, so thank you! My lip is still on the struggle bus to struggle town, and I'm trying to have patience. My face is healing quite nicely, and I am slowly getting off the pain meds, so my mind is much clearer. I love you all so much. Please never stop letting me know how you're doing, how you could use prayer, and how the Lord is using my trial to impact you. You have enriched my life and helped my fight!

Don't Count Your Blessings

July 23, 2015

I got this cute little devotional from the Claybaugh Family, and I was reading in it today about "Counting Your Blessings." This is a classic Hallmark phrase we've heard all the time, and I can only speak for myself, but I've never really given it much thought. Anyway, the devotional kind of surprised me in that it doesn't go the classic Hallmark route about the importance of counting all your blessings, instead it goes, "Uhm hello, even if I counted for a week I couldn't list all my blessings!" I was pleasantly surprised by this approach, and it's so true! It would be overwhelming to list off every single blessing starting with the fact that I'm CURRENTLY DRAWING BREATH. It goes on to say it's okay to take your time to rejoice in the big blessings and not spend all your time trying to thank God for every single blessing, instead take time to bask in His love. David didn't even attempt to thank God for every single thing in one of His hymns. It was the fact that He focused on adoring and loving God. Real gratitude comes from God's nature and so, in us loving Him more, we are more grateful. Are you tracking with me here?

So, I've been a little overwhelmed with all the blessings that have surrounded me the last few weeks, not to mention just the blessing of my entire life. I started to get a little stressed, like "Oh geez, how am I ever going to show enough gratitude?" and "Oh geez, a Facebook message to people isn't enough, they won't think I'm truly grateful." So, I started writing all these cards, and then I just stopped. I could spend days writing hundreds of thank you cards to everyone, DAYS. After reading this devotional, I realized that there is no way I can, in my human strength, human terms, and human understanding show my gratitude. So instead I am choosing to relax, and bask in the love you have all shown me. I am grateful, so grateful and you know that, so with that, I am going to rejoice in the blessing of life, rejoice in the blessing that with all your combined efforts you are saving my life. So, thank you.

On the gratitude note, let's act like every day is Thanksgiving, shall we! I don't know if it's the era, the generation, or the country we live in, (probably a mix of them all) but man are we an ungrateful people. It's baffled me being here at camp how many kids are being raised to take, take, take and expect things handed to them on a silver platter.

Not just here and not just kids though, it just seems to be the norm in the majority of the population. I want you to pause for a second, hold up ten fingers, and think of ten things you can be thankful for right at this moment. For example, reading a blog written by a girl you may or may not know, on a computer, tablet, or laptop, in the comfort of your home

On the gratitude note, let's act like every day is Thanksgiving, shall we! I don't know if it's the era, the generation, or the country we live in, probably a mix of them all, but man are we an ungrateful people.

or maybe a coffee shop, using WIFI. Now be honest with yourself, how many times have you stopped to thank God for these simple ten things? How many times have you thought, wow how grateful I am and what a privilege and blessing it is to have these things!

It's humbling to see the things you take for granted sometimes. That's one thing cancer has forced me to see, how many things I indeed take for granted. I'm holding up my ten fingers right now. 1. I'm thankful for my beautiful friend Kelsey who took me to get this Shellac on these ten fingers I'm holding up. 2. I'm grateful for the scenic forest I see when I peer over my laptop and out the window. 3. I'm thankful for my Aunt Tonyia because she got me a massage today which made my day begin on a wonderful and relaxing note. 4. I'm thankful for the yawn I just yawned because I was able to take a long and enriching nap. 5. I'm thankful that I get to write a blog where I share my feelings and thoughts and people read it. 6. I'm thankful for the parent's I have who bought me the vegetables to make the juice that I just drank. 7. I'm thankful for the fuzzy socks my feet are cuddled up in and for Nicole who sent them to me. 8. I'm thankful for the joyful noise of kids outside, laughing, and playing. 9. I'm grateful for the country we live in where I can write and not fear for my life. 10. I'm thankful that I woke up today and was able to put on a shirt without needing anyone to help me. That was easy, and I could have gone into the thousands. I encourage you to look around you, everything surrounding you came from something, somewhere or someone. Don't pick the ten easiest, "Thanksgiving" answers, challenge your perspective and find new things to be thankful for. Love ya!

Staring at Doors

July 24, 2015

I have to start this off with a mind-blowing praise. Traci and I were awaiting the Angel Wings airline to get a flight set up for us. Unfortunately, they have to get volunteers for each "leg" of the flight, so you end up with several different pilots. Well, it wasn't coming through and time is drawing near, and everyone working on the flight situation was getting stressed, but Traci and I, while feeling the pressure of the importance of getting a flight, still had a strange sense of peace. We both just kind of said, "God's got this." Not in an "I'm going to sit back and enjoy a margarita way" we just knew that He is faithful to provide and doesn't call us to be anxious about anything. Sure enough, Tanaya, a woman that my Dad used to teach, messages me and tells me that she has the flights to Seattle covered for Traci and I. It gets better! As exciting and praiseworthy as that was, she also has a friend who has a voucher that will get me back to Medford, and Traci is covered by the hospitals points to get home! The flights are all taken care of. PRAISE GOD, He is so good and the power of prayer is stunning, you guys.

I want to run with that idea of the balance between sitting back and letting God work but still doing our part by not doing nothing. So many times I hear people say, "Let go and let God" and then sit. They just sit and say that God is going to open a door for them, they are just waiting for a sign, then they will go forward. I remember falling into this trap myself. I was in high school, that awkward senior year when you have to make what seems like the life-altering decision to attend college or not to attend college. I remember getting so stressed out feeling the pressure to figure out how to begin of the "rest of my life." I read that little quote on Facebook. "Let go, let God" It seemed so much easier, to sit back and watch as God did His thing. So I sat. And sat. And sat some more, wasting time, waiting for God because I had "let go." To put it in analogy form I was standing in front of 3 doors, all of them seemed to be closed. Go to college, not Go to College and go to Europe to be a nanny. Instead of trying the handle, I just assumed that if I sat there and stared at the doors then God would magically open one for me and I'd get up and walk through.

When has a door ever opened by you just staring at it? It doesn't unless you're Matilda, the girl with magic powers and can move things with your mind. It wasn't until I understood that "letting go" doesn't mean giving up. It doesn't sit back and sip a Mojito, and it doesn't mean be lazy and blame God for not opening doors. It means to let go of our expectations. It means you can't be prying open, tugging, and banging on the door, you expect to open, but you still have to do some work people! God is not a magic genie that grants wishes. Your job is to work hard, step outside of your comfort zone in faith, and do all things unto the glory of God. If you do this, He will make a way. Stand up and let God take your hand to the door and open the door with you; you can trust that He will choose what is best for you and won't lead you astray.

It wasn't until I understood that "letting go" doesn't mean giving up. It doesn't mean sit back and sip a Mojito, and it doesn't mean be lazy and blame God for not opening doors. It means to let go of our expectations.

Even if you open the door to a giant lion's den waiting to kill you. The door might seem scary, I get that. Had I stepped back and seen a door titled "cancer" do you think I would have picked it on my own? No, but God led me to it, and He will lead me through it. That's what it means to "Let go and let God."

It's easy to say, "Well I don't know what my purpose is. I don't know what God wants me to do in this life." That's normal, and that's human nature! What isn't okay is to allow that statement to let you sit. The Bible is clear that your purpose in life is to glorify God. He placed passions, desires, and interests in our heart! That's so cool to think that He made us all unique and placed different gifts within all of us. Now, He didn't do that so that you could sit around and not put them to good use. There is no magic formula, and there is no magic pill to reveal your purpose in life. But if you're glorifying God, there is no wrong way to go! Either God is sovereign, or He isn't. So many times I've heard (and done it myself) "Well, what if I'm not meant to be with this husband?" Or "What if I made a wrong choice by choosing this career?" Guys, if your motives are not of selfish ambition and you are glorifying God in it, then He allowed you to be with your husband or choose that career. Great news! Even if you did choose a career because of money and it is not glorifying to God, or you married that man because he's hot and your marriage does not glorify God He can make it good! God is still Sovereign, and He is always good and He allowed that situation to happen so He can use it for your good and His glory. He uses sin sinlessly. Amen.

Wonderful Wonder

July 26, 2015

I had a rough day yesterday. It was the last day of camp and the first time the reality of the summer ending hit me. Fear crept through my thoughts as I started to worry, "How will I handle cancer outside of camp?" If you think about it, I've only known how to deal with cancer while being here at camp. Surrounded by the majestic forest, my sister and four cousins, my parents, and my special nurse, Traci. Camp Redwood Glen has provided me a tight-knit community of believers who love me and care about me, kids around having the most joyful time of their lives, having enough sleep and enough food, and people praying for me 24/7.

What happens when I am surrounded by buildings and the pollution of the city? Or when I am in a place where no one knows or cares about me. Or how will it be when I no longer hear the joyous songs of kids and receive their love in hugs, or when I have the stress of a job and don't get enough sleep? These fears began to cripple me. They surprised me and hurt me all at once. Once the negative entered my mind, it poisoned everything in my day. My cousin Micaela from out of town came over and all of us girls got pedicures. Instead of looking around at the lovely faces that I call my sisters, I looked around, heard them laughing and talking about their lives and future plans and all I could think was, "Will I be there to see them get married?" "Will I ever be able to have a reunion with them like this again?" I let the thoughts ruin my time instead of celebrating the reunion and joy I have when I am with them.

We then went to downtown Santa Cruz to walk around. As I was sitting there, I watched as couple after couple walked by, hand in hand with love in their eyes. I became angry at their happiness. "Will I ever fall in love?" "Will I get to be married?" The pressure of time started to weigh on me, the thought that maybe I have less time than every other human on Earth. I was sad. It's sad to me to think about the day I wasted being anxious and letting the bitterness win. It's sad to me to think about all the people out there who live every day like the day I had yesterday. They just exist. They are mad at life, angry with God, bitter toward people, and sad. My heart breaks for those who have no hope, who find no joy in the hard times. If every day of my cancer walk looked like yesterday, I wouldn't even fight.

Today is a new day! God blessed me with another day, and He helped me out of the fearful rut I got myself into. I have hope. There may be pain in the night, but JOY comes in the morning. How true that is for me today, you guys. I woke up, thankful for the time the Lord gave me at this beautiful camp. I spent the day with people that I love, and I savored the moments we got to share.

"May we never lose our wonder
Wide eyed and mystified
May we be just like a child
Staring at the beauty of our King"

The pastor at church talked about wonder today and how sad life would be without it. He said to renew your sense of wonder is to do three things.

1. *Remember* God's wonders: I sat there and replayed in my mind all Gods wonders from the creation of a single and complex cell to the beauty of the worship team singing.

2. *Celebrate* God's wonders: I felt joy creep in as I started to praise God for the miracle of life itself. For the beautiful things, cancer has brought into my life. I even began to celebrate cancer itself.

3. *Request* God's wonders: I asked God to continue to reveal His wonders to me. So that I may not just merely exist as a body sick with cancer, but as a joyous soul living for Christ. My sense of wonder was rejuvenated by the joy and peace that came with it. The sadness and worry from yesterday dissipated and Satan did not win.

Hey Seattle!

July 27, 2015

We are in Seattle! We made it safe and sound thanks to Tanaya and Rebecca. The flight went very smoothly, even though I left my I.D. with Mom who has it in Oregon, Oops. I made it through without too many problems, I just had to get frisked, and they had to check all my stuff. Good news, I'm not a terrorist! The hotel is PERFECT with a view of the space needle and within walking distance of Pikes Place. Nurse Traci and I walked around the city a bit, and since she has been stuck in the woods (a.k.a camp) for the last two weeks, she loved the city life. I am so beyond blessed by the help I've received. Thank you all for helping make this Seattle trip possible! I meet with the specialist, Dr. Nghiem tomorrow, the radiology oncologist, and Dr. Bhatia. I'm hoping that they will be able to give me a lot of answers as far as what my treatment plan is and what stage I have. Please be praying for wisdom and a clear plan!

I've been waiting for these appointments ever since I had surgery. I've had mixed feelings about it. It's been hard not to feel kind of like cancer is a dictator. It decides when I eat, when I sleep, where I live, where I go, when I go, etc. One minute I am a 21-year-old who had been living on my own for three years and was in control of my own life, and overnight I am handing everything over to cancer. It's so easy to feel that way, but as I was praying about it, I realized that I was never in control of my life. God is in control. Cancer does not dictate my life, and the doctors, nurses, or my parents, aren't trying to take control, they are trying to help me fight. So, I don't get to pick where I live necessarily? I have to change my lifestyle, and I might not get to do some of the things I used to do, oh well! My life doesn't stop while

> *I am handing everything over to Cancer. It's so easy to feel that way, but as I was praying about it, I realized that I was never in control of my life. God is in control.*

I deal with cancer, it doesn't begin again if I get healed. Cancer is just one part of my life now, and I am choosing to let it make my life better, not worse. Whatever the doctors tell me tomorrow, I am prepared. I am going in with no expectations. I am just going to trust that God is good and He will do what is best for me! A short blog post today because I am exhausted from traveling! I will let you know ASAP when I get some answers tomorrow, love ya!

Walk the Walk

July 30, 2015

Hey strangers! I am just kidding because I've been a stranger, so I apologize. I have had a crazy few days, but as most of you know, I am now visiting my cute little apartment in Spokane. Seattle was really fun, and we were able to do touristy type things like Pikes Place and Beecher's. On Tuesday we had appointments from 10 in the morning to 6 at night. It was SUCH a long day. Unfortunately, we left with more questions than answers, so I don't have any news for you. Without getting into medical jargon that I have a hard time understanding, I am waiting on the doctors to decide the abdomen nodules. They are suspicious enough to look into it but not alarmed enough to say that they are cancerous. Please pray for wisdom as they try to decide how to determine whether they are bad news or good. Once they figure that out, then they will be able to tell me that I am Stage 3b, which in that case I will be doing radiation, or Stage 4 which in this case I would be put on a clinical trial.

It's so good to be in Spokane. I adore my little apartment, and it's been hard not to envision my life here and hope to come back. I am trying to focus on enjoying the time the Lord has given me to be here and see some of the people that I love. Cancer has been revealing a lot to me lately, as those of you who have been reading my blog have noticed. One thing I've noticed recently, as I go from place to place is who makes the time to see me.

It's been so cool and encouraging to see strangers or people that I don't know very well, or even people I'm close with come around me and support me. I have been so blessed by those of you who have taken the time to talk the talk but also walk the walk. You have shown me what it means to invest in people's lives, and you have shown me the importance of selfless love.

At the same time, I have been shocked by the people who don't walk the walk. The people who claim to be invested, or the people who I considered close to me who haven't come through with even an encouraging word. I have tried my hardest not to be offended or hurt by this, and I have tried to remember that people get busy, they get scared, they get nervous, or feel like there are so many people reaching out to me and they don't want to bother me. But if anything, it has shown me what I don't want to be. I understand this better now, but we are supposed to be there for each other, to be the body of Christ and mourn with those who mourn and rejoice with those who rejoice. We should be investing in each other's lives and pouring in regardless of how tired we are, how busy we get, or how consumed with our own lives we get.

I am totally guilty of this! I have talked the talk plenty of times without so much as sending a Facebook message to my friend in need. I know now how that feels, and it sucks. It isn't how God called us to be. Especially as Christians, we should be practicing selfless love. Please know that it means the world to me for you

I have been shocked by the people who don't walk the walk. The people who claim to be invested, or the people who I considered close to me who haven't come through with even an encouraging word. I have tried my hardest not to be offended or hurt by this, . . . it has shown me what I don't want to be.

to take the time to reach out to me even if it's just a Facebook message. I hope you walk away from reading this with the same conviction that I've had. Be there. Don't say you're a friend and don't say you're a brother or sister in Christ unless you are going to be there. You make time for your brother or sister if they are in need, and it's no different in the community of believers. I have an obligation as a sister in Christ to be there for those of you in need regardless of my time, my needs, or the status of our relationship. I want you to hold me accountable, and I also want you to challenge yourself. If you are one of those people who has been absent in the time of need, whether it be your friend, me, your mom, or your brother or sister in Christ, take the time right now to walk the walk.

Never Alone

July 31, 2015

It's boiling like "hot lava" hot here. I never thought I'd come to Washington to say, "Send me back to California where it's 80 degrees!" I don't even know how people function in this weather, and I think that the swollen parts of my face are rebelling against the heat by doubling in size. It's not fun you guys, and there is a reason I didn't move to Africa! But that's enough complaining because I am happy to be here and in my (once again) adorable little apartment.

It's evening, and I'm sitting here gazing over the computer screen at my friend Garrett and my roommate Reagan as they are talking about life. What a beautiful scene. We each come from different parts of the country, we have different backgrounds, we have different career goals, we are different ages, yet we have this bond and unity in our mutual belief in Christ. I have spent the afternoon in authentic fellowship with these guys, being transparent about our summer and lives. The good things, the hard to understand things, the lovely things and everything in between. This is what being intentional looks like. These lovely people came over to spend quality time with me, and we have spent the afternoon just talking, laughing and being in community. We weren't all on our phones texting, checking social media, we aren't looking at our watch continually wondering what we are missing or where we should be.

If you're with people right now, close your computer, get off your phone, pause reading this blog, look up, ask them a question, anything at all. Engage in a conversation with them and take the time to appreciate that you have them and you aren't alone.

I feel so sad hearing about people that are alone. I am continually hearing at the doctor's office, "Oh, you are so lucky that you have so much support. People come in here all the time by themselves." How sad is that!? I guarantee you every person that walks this alone has at least one person that could have been by their side. Don't ever let someone go through their trial alone. Like I said yesterday, be there. Don't let insecurities hold you back! Take a chance outside of your comfort zone.

That being said, I was convicted yesterday. I realized that I have been shifting my dependence from God to a community. Don't get me wrong; I stand by the message in the blog yesterday! I think community is vital, BUT people will fail you. People aren't perfect, and if you put them on a pedestal they will fall off. God has been showing me that I expected too much from people instead of

If you're with people right now, close your computer, get off your phone, pause reading this blog, look up, ask them a question, anything at all, engage in a conversation with them and take the time to appreciate that you have them and you aren't alone.

depending on Him for comfort and peace. God gave us community for sure, and we should be seeking that and helping each other, but God is the perfect one. He will never fail us. He will be with us wherever we go and in whatever season we are in. He is the one we need to seek and depend on for comfort and help. As long as we have Him we should never feel alone.

No huge update. The doctors think they can do a fine needle biopsy on the node in my stomach which means another needle shoved into my stomach. Not exactly excited, but hey, at least they'll have answers!

Dreams

August 1, 2015

Do you ever wake up after having a ridiculously realistic dream and feel like it really happened? Like you wake up after dreaming you were late to work, and you feel panicked and stressed, or you wake up after having a dream that you started dating that cute boy and you smile to yourself feeling like it was true? That happened to me this morning. I had a very realistic dream that I had a beautiful baby boy. My family joined me at the hospital as we all admired my son and we were crying in celebration. I woke up this morning excited, ready to see my son, so when I opened my eyes to an empty apartment a pit formed in my stomach — just a dream. But I felt defeated, I felt crushed, and I felt really sad. I kept telling myself not to go there, but the realness of the dream made me think, "Will I ever get to experience the feeling of holding my own child?" I went there in my mind, and I was sad.

The day continued, and I tried to keep my composure as it felt like one thing after another went wrong. The doctors called to tell me that they need me to come back to Seattle on Monday to get a radiation plan set up just in case I end up with Stage 3b. Then they couldn't tell me if I would be able to get my biopsy done at the same time. Anyway, I was stressed because everything was so vague and I couldn't plan. I felt Traci's absence in those moments, and it made me even more grateful that I had her by my side as long as I did. As I was stressing out and starting to get anxious, my friend Micaiah came alongside me and supported, encouraged, and prayed for me. She, with her selfless spirit, immediately began making calls to see what she could do to help. I was terrified of going to my appointments alone. I don't know if I'm overreacting or not but the thought of being in a big city, trying to gather all the new info, and possibly getting a needle shoved in my stomach, all while being alone really didn't sit well with me. In my stressed state, I started to understand how poisonous anxiety is. It tried to affect every aspect of my day, and I kept repeating God's blessing to myself, and I tried to remind myself that He is faithful, but I felt weary. Micaiah and her family came through for me and showed me what it means to be generous and show Christ. Her family has never met me, yet they said that because I am a sister in Christ, they would do everything they could

Micaiah and her family came through for me and showed me what it means to be generous and show Christ.

to help me. Turns out they are going to take me to Seattle, and THAT is what it means to treat each other like brothers and sisters! What a blessing.

As the day continued on, we went to a house warming party at Garret's place. We all sat in fellowship and shared stories of the summer and blessed each other with the warmth and support of community. As we prepared to leave, everyone gathered around me and prayed for me. I was stunned. I can't explain the love of this group of people and how God is using them to encourage my anxious heart. This was the community I was seeking. God knew what I needed to mend my heart. To have the people that I call my brothers and sisters in Christ physically surround me and support me was amazing and calmed my spirit. I was so happy that God answered my prayers and sent me the authentic, loving community during this time of need. I ended today feeling refreshed and ready to face these appointments with new friends by my side and God walking with us. Love you all!

Enemies

August 3, 2015

I'm in Seattle...AGAIN. Someone, please help me out because I know that so many people love this city... so clearly I'm missing something! I came here with a good friend of mine Micaiah and her awesome Grandma. What a blessing it has been to have them by my side! They are both very selfless, and generous people and their caring examples challenge me.

Good news, my appointments didn't go nearly as long this time, thank the Lord! I had to do more labs this morning, and then I started a radiation plan. The plan consisted of a CT scan, in which, of course, I fell asleep! This one was a little more involved because they had to make a cast for my head to rest in, they had to stretch out my arms so my shoulders would stay flat, and then they made this funky custom mesh mask that squished my eyelashes and matted my hair.

For those of you who have been praying that I would get a biopsy tomorrow, THANK YOU! They scheduled me for 2:30. An update, they started a radiation plan but there are still nodes in my stomach that are abnormal, and I found out today that there is a spot in my groin that also showed up. They are doing another fine needle biopsy, to my dismay, but that will determine whether cancer has spread or not. If it has spread, I will be doing a clinical trial for treatment, if it hasn't then I will be doing radiation. I am at peace, either way because God has been so good to me and He will continue to be faithful!

I am continuously blown away by all the posts on the Defeat Cancer Walkathon (go like them on Facebook to receive all the fantastic updates!) everyone from individuals to businesses have come together to help my family and I. There was a post recently talking about how the staff at the Mazatlan Grill gathered up their tips and filled an entire jar for me, and then someone stole it. When I first read this, I was outraged at the injustice of it all. I was hurt, and I was ticked off that someone would look at my picture as they empty the jar onto their bed. I was thinking to myself "Justice will be served!" as I secretly wished Karma was real and would make them pay. Then I stopped.

First of all, that money doesn't belong to me. It belongs to God, and it is a privilege that I have people who care enough to help me, it's not my right. Secondly, I had to remind myself that God has been beyond faithful in providing for me. Maybe the person who took that money has two little kids currently starving? Perhaps they are homeless and haven't had an actual meal in months? Or you know, maybe they have

So as hard as it is, I am going to pray for them and love them in my heart. I encourage you to think about someone in your life that you've resented, hated, been bitter towards, or angry at because you felt that they wronged you, and stop. Stop and pray for them, stop and forgive them, stop and love them.

a drug addiction, and at that moment they saw an opportunity and took it. None of these reasons make it right, sinning is sinning and stealing is wrong. But it does me NO good to be bitter, angry, and condemn them to hell in my mind because now I am sinning and that's not what we are called to do. So as hard as it is, I am going to pray for them and love them in my heart. I encourage you to think about someone in your life that you've resented, hated, been bitter towards, or angry at because you felt that they wronged you, and stop. Stop and pray for them, stop and forgive them, stop and love them.

"You have heard that it was said, 'YOU SHALL LOVE YOUR NEIGHBOR and hate your enemy.' "But I say to you, love your enemies and pray for those who persecute you, so that you may be sons of your Father who is in heaven; for He causes His sun to rise on the evil and the good, and sends rain on the righteous and the unrighteous. "For if you love those who love you, what reward do you have? Do not even the tax collectors do the same? "If you greet only your brothers, what more are you doing than others? Do not even the Gentiles do the same? "Therefore you are to be perfect, as your heavenly Father is perfect" (Matthew 5:43-48).

Needles

August 5, 2015

Hey friends! I'm back in Spokane and as much as I'd like to say I'm here for a good chunk of time, the reality is I have no clue. Seattle was a good trip even though I had seven needles stick in me during the duration of this visit. The needle biopsy actually went better than the one in my neck. This one was in my groin, which makes me feel slightly awkward but whatever, it had to be done. It was pretty gnarly because I was watching the needle move around and then jab the lymph node on the ultrasound. It was uncomfortable at best but thankfully not painful. There was this weird thing where they twisted the needle into the lymph node like a corkscrew then clicked a trigger, and clipped a chunk of tissue - that part was really funky. Anyway, basically they will run tests on the tissue and if it's positive for cancer then I have Stage 4 and if it's negative then they will probably have me come back in to do a more invasive procedure looking at the lymph nodes in my stomach. Please pray that the results come in soon so I can know whether I can finally go back to Klamath Falls or not!

I'm exhausted from this last Seattle trip, and while it was good to get to know Micaiah and her Grandma better, I am glad to get a chance to rest! I am so thankful for their company and that I didn't have to go alone.

It's been cool to see who God brings into my life when I'm bold about my faith. It's still hard sometimes, insecurity creeps in, and I hesitate to mention God to strangers. But lately, I've been challenging myself, even if I may hesitate at first, I stop and ask myself, "What's more important, you feeling comfortable for one second or furthering God's Kingdom?" Ouch. So the last two times I've given up my initial comfort, God has allowed some cool people into my life! One woman was working at the Macy's in Seattle, and as she was helping me pick out my perfect foundation, we started chatting. Anyway, she ended up being an awesome Christian woman with a beautiful heart, and I would have never had the privilege of seeing that had I been insecure about sharing my faith!

Another example was today when I was getting my hair done, which by the way was an extremely fun and impulsive decision made by my good friend Caiah and me. I started talking about my "cancer story,"

I stop and ask myself, "What's more important, you feeling comfortable for one second or furthering God's kingdom?" Ouch.

and for a moment I hesitated to talk about God but then once again I had to remind myself that God is the POINT and the most significant and best part of the story! So my hairdresser also turned out to be a Christian, and she had also dealt with cancer when she was seven years old. God performed a miracle by saving her life and what an excellent experience to be able to celebrate that with her! God is so awesome and even though I write a blog that thousands of you see, I am still working on my insecurities! God is faithful to present opportunities for you to practice if you are struggling in an area ask God to challenge you. Love you all!

Conflict Bomb (Part 1)

August 7, 2015

I decided to write the blog after I heard back from the doctor's, hence the reason I didn't post this morning! The node in my groin came back negative! While this is obviously great news, it still doesn't mean I am not Stage 4, because there are still stomach nodes in question. But God is good, and I am trying to see the amazing good news that my groin is cancer free! Praise God!

Yesterday was a great day. I spent the day with two of my great friends, Minnie and Molly, and then we went to the college group at church. At the college group, the pastor talked about conflict and tips to resolve it. It was super interesting and convicting to me, so I wanted to do my best to summarize his sermon in my words so you all can learn a thing or two as well! As he was speaking I sat there and tried to think honestly if there was any unresolved conflict that I had with anyone. I encourage you to do the same as you read on! If you're feeling good about your relationships, then take these steps to heart so you may be prepared when conflict comes. Because it will, we're human and flawed!

#1. Assume the worst about your own heart. Now, this is not something you hear every day in today's society! Society tells us that we are the best, most beautiful, always right, and most amazing people on the planet. Why do you think it's so hard in conflict? We want to be right, we want our pound of flesh, we want justice, and no one wants to admit that they're wrong. It feels better to make the other person pay, and it feels better to feel like we "win." How radically different would it be if we remembered instead that we are the biggest sinner in the room? How humbling would it be if we assumed the worst of our own heart and motives? I think you would be quick to pipe down in an argument when you turn your eyes to your own heart. Has that girl been gossiping about you? How many people have you gossiped about this week? Your husband lied to you? How many times have you lied today? The point being none of us are perfect and when you remind yourself of that fact, you can allow others some more grace.

#2. Act on wisdom, not emotion. This one is hard, especially for me! We humans thrive on emotion. Why do you think drama T.V. is so addicting? How many times do we react and get defensive right away? I can tell you there are a handful of times out of hundreds where I've taken the time to reason before I react in a conflict. Anger, sadness, all the emotions that fuel the fire within are so easily misguiding and they can make you have some severe regrets, so let's try acting out of wisdom instead of emotion.

#3. Avoid the plague of slander and gossip. Why is this SO HARD!? Seriously, I remember back in Jr. High when I decided to give up gossiping, I didn't even last a week. I felt like I had nothing to talk about and that was extremely revealing to me. But how many times have we seen the poison of gossip and slander? Do you guys remember that veggie tales movie called "The Rumor Weed"? A big ugly weed grows and eventually takes over the city. It's so true though! Think about school, your work, camp, your church, and think about how much conflict could have been avoided had we all decided to stop gossip?

Assume the worst about your own heart. Now, this is not something you hear in today's society! Society tells us that we are the best, most beautiful, always right, and most amazing people on the planet.

#4. Apply gentle words in the moment. How about this one to detonate the atomic bomb of conflict! Imagine yourself arguing with the one person you pictured in your mind. Imagine them heating up in anger and you just whip out, "You know what, you are such a generous person, and I'm very grateful for you." Imagine their reaction to that!

To be continued... Love ya!

Weary

August 8, 2015

Today I am weary. I am stressed. I am tired. I am discouraged. I woke up in a bed that's not mine, in a house that's not mine, in a town that no longer feels like mine. I have to go to Seattle again tomorrow, and I just cried. I actually bawled. I cried out of a longing to rest, longing to have answers, longing to stay in one place, and a longing for family. I've been going nonstop since I've been diagnosed and I feel like today it really got to me. I went from Santa Cruz to Stanford to Klamath to Stanford to Santa Cruz to Seattle to Spokane to Seattle to Spokane and now to Seattle again. I think I am craving stability, answers, and familiarity. I don't exactly know, I just feel exhausted.

I just cried. I actually bawled. I cried out of a longing to rest, longing to have answers, longing to stay in one place, and a longing for family.

I took today to be by myself, and I just prayed that the Lord would help me change my attitude and give me supernatural energy to continue on. One more week, I am praying only one more week, and then I will actually have answers and start treatment. Thank you all for being supportive during this. I know that this is necessary to fight for my life and I don't want to let the weariness get me down. Please pray that I can keep a positive attitude. Also, if you have any advice on how to make my trips to Seattle more enjoyable please tell me! I have seen and done everything downtown and I would love to see the more laid back, less touristy part of Seattle.

That being said, I am leaving in the early a.m. and I am driving my sister's car to Seattle where I will meet up with her. I have a meeting with the specialists on Tuesday, and we will discuss the stomach biopsy.

I will finish the blog about conflict I promise! I'm just stressed today and needing to take some me time, and I'm sure you all understand!

> *"Come to me, all you who are weary and burdened, and I will give you rest. Take my yoke upon you and learn from me, for I am gentle and humble in heart, and you will find rest for your souls." (Matthew 11:28-29).*

Conflict Continued (Part 2)

August 9, 2015

Thank you all for the support yesterday! Today was a much better day. I hit the road at 4 am this morning and made it to Seattle with no traffic, no GPS, and no bathroom breaks in 4 hours! My sister Chandler and I took some time to sleep before we spent the evening on the "hipster" side of Seattle and ate at Linda's Tavern. Apparently, it was the last place Kurt Cobain from Nirvana, was seen alive. Then we found our way to Bill and Syd Sliker's home. They have been friends of our dad's since he was a kid and they have graciously allowed us to stay with them for the duration of our visit. Seriously, once again I'm blown away by the kindness of people, and I have to proclaim, "There may be pain in the night but joy comes in the morning!"

Now on to the promised continued blog post about conflict...

#5. Access the invincible power of Christ. How many times is your first instinct to pray in the heat of conflict? How many times are you firing up your weapon and decide to take a few seconds to ask the Lord for help? I wonder how that would change the conflict. I mean I really think we take for granted how amazing prayer is. That our God would give us the freedom to at any time talk to Him. Excuse me, what!? So cool!

The pastor continued preaching an awesome sermon, but there were a few more things that jumped out to me.

A. "Remember that Christ was fully human and he experienced the deepest insults and injustice." He didn't have to endure that. He's God, and He could have just poofed into oblivion and then expected us to deal with the hardships on Earth. He was KILLED, He was TORTURED, and He was INNOCENT. And you know what He said? "Forgive them, Father, for they know not what they have done." Forgive them, He prayed as the crown of thorns pierced His skull and as His hands throbbed at the sharpness of the nails. Mind blown! I don't even want to say that I'm sorry when my sister Chandler and I are arguing over something as stupid as who should drive! Wow, talk about a humbling example and one that would make any person think twice about their anger in a fight.

B. "All of the injustices you experience are a loving gift of God's hand to transform you to the image of Christ. They are not an accident, and God doesn't change the situation so you can be happy." Oh, wait, it's not about us? It's not about what we want, what we think is best, or about what makes us happy? Huh, shocker! That entirely goes against our human nature and our society! But wow, talk about a perspective change, the injustices against you are to transform you into the image of Christ. He gives us the opportunity to act in love and become more Christ-like during a conflict. No, it's not easy, but these things take time and hard work.

"All of the injustices you experience are a loving gift of God's hand to transform you to the image of Christ. They are not an accident, and God doesn't change the situation so you can be happy."

C. "Difficult people and circumstances are God's reminder that they can't satisfy your soul." Imagine a world where no one let you down, where your circumstances were perfect, and there was no disappointment or conflict. You just cruise through life nice and comfortable. Your soul would be satisfied and why would you need God? You'd do perfectly fine on your own so why ask for help, or cry out in frustration, or step out of your comfort zone, or lean on Him in faith, or worship Him, or look to the Bible for answers, or pray? We would be self-sufficient robots. God uses these things in our lives to remind us that only He can satisfy. Love ya!

The Dying Girl

August 10, 2015

We just got back from a 4-dollar movie. Why can't more movies be 4 dollars? It's just a perfect price because it's not enough to be upset over if the movie sucks. Anyway, the film was called, *Me and Earl and the Dying Girl.* I was delighted that Sis suggested that we go and watch it because she didn't hesitate or get weird about the fact that it was about a girl (SPOILER ALERT), who dies of cancer. It made me feel like a normal person, and she didn't give it a second thought when she asked if I wanted to see it.

The movie was good, kind of your typical off-beat indie film, but it was funny, interesting, and it felt like real life. There were problems, ugly people, ordinary families, and it was just refreshing to watch something that was real life. Of course, it ends up being a sad story about cancer; I get it. They have to draw you in and make you emotionally attached and then end with a dramatic, heart-wrenching finale. I got nervous for a while, worried about seeing a girl my age fight the same fight, nervous about seeing her lose, worried about seeing myself in her as she had her ups and downs, nervous about watching a girl I relate to die. I wasn't sure how I'd react. But honestly, I didn't look at the weak, sad girl and say, "that's me." Instead, I looked at her and said, "Never let yourself go there." I watched as she went from a healthy, joyful girl, and as she slowly let the cancer monster devour her. I watched as she became depressed, sad, and eventually gave up. I watched her die. I've had days where I caught a glimpse of that girl, the dying girl. When you look, you may not see a difference. She's a young girl, and she has cancer. I am a young girl, and I have cancer.

Why isn't my story a sad story? Sure, I'm not dead, but that doesn't mean I might not die. But even if I did mine wouldn't be a tragic story about a girl with cancer who gave up. Why? The difference is I have HOPE. I have hope because Christ has given me a living hope.

What's the difference? Why isn't my story a sad story? Sure, I'm not dead, but that doesn't mean I might not die. But even if I did, mine wouldn't be a tragic story about a girl with cancer who gave up. Why? The difference is I have HOPE. I have hope because Christ has given me a living hope. I will never give up no matter how dark and weary the days get, no matter how weak or ugly I feel because He gives me strength! I have God on my side, and He is bigger and better than any Cancer Monster I will face. So, I left not feeling discouraged by seeing a young girl with cancer die, I left feeling sad that she didn't have the hope that I have because even if my body dies here on Earth, I have a hope that I will live eternally. This is not a sad story.

Tunnel Vision

August 13, 2015

I spent a good two hours crying today and a good two hours at the dentist. No, they did not occur at the same time.

First, let me backtrack to my last day in Seattle. I had an appointment with my medical militia, is that the right term? I don't know army terms but I like to think of them as the leaders of my battle against the cancer monster. It's a stronger image than a team. Anyway, they felt that it was essential to explore the nodes in my stomach, so I go back to Seattle on Monday to get a more invasive biopsy surgery done. This one is more complicated because the stomach nodes move around. Kind of like when you let that cute little kid help you bake, and all they ever want to do is crack the eggs and eat the batter, but when you let them crack the eggs they always get pieces of the shell in the egg whites and every time you think you've grabbed the shell it moves? Well, that's how the lymph nodes in my stomach act, so they have to put me to sleep and cut me open so they can grab one. AFTER this surgery they should have answers as to whether I have Stage 4 cancer or Stage 3B.

I know I have said it many times, but If I have Stage 3B I will start radiation on Wednesday in Seattle. If I have Stage 4, I will wait to discuss the different clinical trials that are opening soon. I just want to know.

After my CT scan on Tuesday in Seattle, we drove 8 hours, and rolled into my driveway in Klamath Falls, Oregon at 4 a.m.—in one piece thank the Lord. At 8 a.m. the next morning I had a dentist appointment, then an hour break, then another dentist appointment, then an hour break, then a chiropractor appointment, then the day was done. Today I woke up and had another dentist appointment and I came home, spilled water, dropped my phone, then went into my bedroom, sat down, and cried.

This is the part where I guttural cry for two hours. You know how people say there is a light at the end of the tunnel? It feels as if I am digging my way through the tunnel and one day I see a speck of light, and the next day I get dirt in my eyes and the light is gone. I feel like I have no map and I am wandering aimlessly through, just hoping that I'm going the right way. Typically, when you get through a massive clump of dirt you see the light, it may be far away but at least you see it, and you can move towards it. I don't feel that way. When you have a major surgery you plan for it, you get it done, you recover. Then you say congratulations and thank God you got through it, and it becomes a thing of the past. When I get through digging through a massive clump of dirt, there is just more dirt. When I get done with labs, scans, biopsies, and surgeries, I don't have that feeling of relief like now I can move on with my life. After surgery comes the next lab or biopsy or scan or treatment. This is my life now. It will never be the same. I remember when I went to college group, the guy doing announcements said, "What are you doing with life? School? Work?" The only response I could think of was, "I'm fighting cancer."

God didn't call us to live comfortable or predictable lives. If we did, we wouldn't change, and we would never long for heaven. It's about perspective.

Now don't worry, I'm not going to leave you there feeling sad for the crying cancer girl stuck in a tunnel. I'm not defeated, I'm human. Two hours passed by while I sat in the dirt, not digging, not moving toward the light, just sitting. In these moments I can understand why people give up, why they say screw it and let cancer win. It's exhausting, it's stressful, it's hard, scary and it can feel hopeless. My Mom mentioned something to me earlier; she said, "It's kind of like people in the military, they get comfortable with where they are at and then all of a sudden they are sent to a new place. Or someone who is paralyzed in a car wreck. They are driving their car like normal and all of a sudden, they can't walk. Even a teenager who moves out for the first time; they are living with their parent's, and then all of a sudden, they have bills to pay. It's life-changing."

The point being, we go through life changes all the time. Just because this is one that isn't always fun or easy, this isn't the first time my life has been changed. When I learned to talk, when I got saved, when I learned how to do my hair, when I moved out, when I had my first boyfriend, you name it, our lives change every day. My life will never be the same. It just won't. There is nothing I can do to take that back. But even if I didn't have cancer, something else would happen that would change my life forever, and do you know why? God didn't call us to live comfortable or predictable lives. If we did, we wouldn't change, and we would never long for heaven. It's about perspective. I'm human, and I get sad, and I feel hopeless, and I feel defeated sometimes. I'm learning how to live a life WITH cancer, not to live a life OF cancer, if that makes sense. I take my moment to sit in the dirt, then I pick up my shovel with God as my guide, and I keep digging.

Five Second Challenge

August 14, 2015

~~~~~~~~~~

I went to the chiropractor again today. He said that he could feel the weight of all the stress in my muscles. That's so strange to me, the connection between mind and body. I would have never thought that my stress would affect the muscles in my body, now that I think about it I understand what being tense means. But I got to sleep today, so that was pleasant and things are coming into perspective again. Like I've said, take your moment to be human but don't let that be a constant mindset. Get up, dust off, and fight.

I have SUPER exciting news! I've mentioned it on Facebook but I'd like to elaborate. Someone suggested to my Mom, who suggested to me that I should start a YouTube channel. The idea seemed brilliant, but daunting at the same time. How the heck was I going to handle making videos on top of everything else!? Then during my last Seattle trip, my phenomenally talented sister Chandler brought up the idea and expressed interest in making the videos! She is gifted in videography, so together we have started a YouTube channel and boy, you guys, it's STELLAR! I can only say that because my sister is extremely talented and the first video was so perfect that it made me cry. I can't wait to share it with you all so stay tuned and expect it on SUNDAY!

I am currently sitting in my spacious living room, the sunlight peeking through the curtains, my mom and sister cuddled up in their rocking chairs, my pops eating apple pie next to me, and *"The Scent of a Woman"* playing on the big screen. I wanted to take a moment to cherish this scene. You know I decided that I need to relish the moments that I take for granted, and I need to take a moment to notice sweet scenes like a family movie. This is peace, and this is how I find rest. I used to think that peace and rest only came in the form of sleeping, sitting, reading, or anything quiet and serene. I'm understanding more now that peace can really be found in any situation if you take the time to see it. I want to challenge you and myself to take five seconds in each situation to look around and cherish the moment. Whether it be a family movie or your morning cup of coffee, maybe it's your work meeting, or a lengthy doctor's appointment, even that moment when your twin boys are fighting and screaming. I think that if I can take five seconds to be grateful and find peace in these moments, then I think I can relieve a lot of the stress and tension in my life! Let me take one more look at this moment. I have peace knowing that the people on my left and right are my family, my best friends, my biggest fans, my supporters, and my team. I have peace in knowing that we all have a moment to watch a movie and sit in the calm. I have peace knowing that we have this wonderful house that I have spent many days, and have had many memories in. I

I am currently sitting in my spacious living room, the sunlight peeking through the curtains, my mom and sister cuddled up in their rocking chairs, my pops eating apple pie next to me,...I decided that I need to relish the moments that I take for granted, and I need to take a moment to notice sweet scenes like a family movie.

could go on and on, but I challenged us to five seconds. But wow, I already appreciate this time, and I already have a rest that I have been seeking. Perspective my friends. It is all about perspective. Take five seconds right now to find peace in the moment!

I head to Seattle on Sunday, Monday at 5:30 a.m. I go in for surgery so prayers for safe travels and wisdom for the doctors would be much appreciated! Love you all!

Super Glue

August 17, 2015

~~~~~~~~

Okay folks, I am in Seattle again! Boy let me tell ya, that was NOT an easy trip. Yesterday we left at 9 a.m., and we didn't get here to the Collegiana until 9:30 p.m. We had bumper to bumper traffic nearly the entire time. As some of you know, I have road rage and traffic tries my patience more than almost anything, so it was an excellent opportunity to practice reminding myself that I cannot change the situation by getting mad, and I'm not going to get there faster by being impatient.

Anyway, we finally got into downtown Seattle, and we had to get the key to our room for the Collegiana from the University of Washington Tower. Everyone kept pointing us to the UW tower which was not helpful to directionally challenged people like my mom and me. Where this UW Tower was located was a complete mystery to us. We got lost multiple times because there was construction, of course, because it's Washington and they don't have summer, they have construction. LOL (Their joke not mine)

So we pulled into a sketchy parking lot and without a word, my mother hops out of the car with her map in hand and NO PHONE and just waltzes down some dark alley alone! I was left sitting in the car replaying every Law and Order scenario in my head. "What if a homeless guy finds her and hurts her?" "What if a group of drunk guys tries to mess with her?" Every creepy creep that walked in her direction made my anxiety sky rocket. Just as I am beginning to speak truth to myself and get out of that terrible mindset, this man, about 26 years old, apparently high, staggers up to the car and tries to open the door! WHILE I AM SITTING IN THERE! Oh my gosh, my heart started racing, and I slammed my hand onto the horn. He jolted out of his zombie high, and I yelled at him to leave. He ran off in the direction of my Mom and left me there wanting to cry! It was so scary to me, you guys! Talk about a way to welcome us into our potential new neighborhood! Of course, Mom came back fine and got quite a kick out of my little story.

So, I woke up bright and early and headed to UW Medical Center at 5 a.m. and got prepped for surgery. This one was an easy hour-long surgery, and I was able to leave around 11 a.m. to head back to the Collegiana. Unfortunately, we did not get the answers we were seeking, so prayers that the results will come in tomorrow would be much appreciated! I have three incision marks, and my pain is mild compared to my other surgery. And get this, they super glued me shut! I almost feel like a college bro that cut his foot and couldn't afford band-aids, so he just dabbed some glue on it. It's kind of funny to me. The doctor was able to get a good sample using the laparoscopic technique, so that was a blessing!

Our home for the next seven or eight weeks is the Collegiana, and it is for patients of UW and Seattle Cancer Care Alliance. It is close to UW, so that is convenient. I was kind of nervous because I had no idea what to expect, I mean, it's kind of like a dorm-style housing. It is an older three-story building in the U district not far from the college. It's offered at a cheaper rate than any apartments or hotels. I am pleasantly surprised! The room is nearly the size of my apartment in Spokane with three beds, a little sitting area, and a good-sized bathroom, and an eating nook. We are right next to the shared kitchen, and we are on the top floor, so we don't have any noise from any upper floors. We had the opportunity to meet our neighbors, a woman named Rose and her daughter. They are from Kansas and guess what, Rose has Merkel Cell cancer! Now while this is not an exciting thing, I mean I wouldn't wish that on anybody, but of all the cancers for my neighbor to have the Lord blessed me by giving me Rose! It was so cool to be able to meet someone in person who is going through the same thing as me. To be able to relate to how she is feeling and having her going through the same treatments and dealing with the same fears and questions. It was just refreshing. She has a very positive outlook on the situation, but please add her to your prayer list!

...but of all the cancers for my neighbor to have the Lord blessed me by giving me Rose! It was so cool to be able to meet someone in person who is going through the same thing as me.

I'm still on drugs, so I'm not going to try to say anything more than a factual update, but I'm recovering well, and I appreciate all the prayers! Oh, and as some of you saw, we released our first YouTube video yesterday! The channel is called "themerkelmiracle" if you want to look it up. I am so excited to allow you to see my journey on a virtual level and I hope you all enjoy the channel. We created it as another way for you all to follow my journey, but we are also praying that it can provide another form of financial aid for my medical bills. The more subscribers, views, and likes to the channel the more opportunities we have to raise money. Yet another blessing! Thank you all and love you all.

The Outsider

August 19, 2015

Hello, my beautiful friends and family! It's been a few days since I posted, and I'm totally aware, so I apologize. I'm still trying to recover a bit from that last surgery. The incision marks and inside my stomach feel kind of like one big bruise. It's not unbearable, but it is something that bothers me a bit.

Mom and I have been busy here in Seattle! I am determined to change my perspective and find the aspect of Seattle that makes people adore the city. I think we are onto something! We explored downtown a little bit, and we even took the trolley like true locals. Then we went and had dinner with the Sliker family. Such a friendly, warm, and welcoming family and the food was so good! Today we went to this adorable little park called Green Lake Park. Mom and I have a mutual love for people watching so we enjoyed that for a solid hour. We were looking for a church to go to on Sunday and Mom thought about attending a Wednesday night service. Well, I found a college group instead and that looked promising, so yeah, I was that girl who brought her mom to college group. Hey, she has no shame, and she liked it, and they loved the fact I brought my mom! We sang, ate, learned from God's Word and had a fantastic time of prayer together.

On that note, I'm back to community. From elementary to high school, to college, to churches, to camps, to Europe, to Spokane, the Lord has been faithful to provide me with a robust community everywhere I go. As I walked into this unknown situation with a group of kids I'd never met, I had a little anxiety. I mean a new place, a new city, and you know you're an outsider. One thing I feel like the Lord is always trying to remind me is that I'm not an outsider. That's a label we put on ourselves. ESPECIALLY if you are joining a Christian community that has been united by the belief in the same God. We are brothers and sisters, so I am trying to challenge my perspective and get involved. As I sat there listening to them talk to one another, watching them worship, watching them pray for each other, it was beautiful, but I got a sinking gut feeling that I recognized this community. I looked around and felt like I saw my friends the Nickels from Klamath, and the twins from Texas, I saw the Fusion group from Germany, I saw Garett and Collin from Moody. I could go on

and on. At first, the re-
alization brought me
down, here I was feel-
ing sad that those
people from my old
communities were no
longer with me, and
these people before
me don't know me.
Not to mention, I'm
not 100% myself. I start-

My challenge to you is to check your perspective. Are you an outsider? Is that keeping you from seeking community, following Christ, volunteering, or making new friends? How does God see you? And do you need to work on not making others feel like an outsider? Just some food for thought.

ed to pray that the Lord would help me trust in His faithfulness. Many new situations start out uncomfortable.

The Lord then gave me this notion, "What if this community isn't here for me? Instead, what if I'm here for this community?" Wow. This has rocked my perspective guys. It has moved the spotlight from me and my needs to them. How can I contribute? How can I serve? How can I help make this community tight-knit and Christ-centered? How can I be a resource of the Lord and use my gifts and talents, or even my current trial to help this community? And in that selflessness, what can I learn from them? It's not about my comfort or insecurity because we may not be best friends. I am a Sister in Christ to them, and wherever the Lord sends me, I can go confidently knowing that His people will always be there. So after reading today's post, my challenge to you is to check your perspective. Are you an outsider? Is that keeping you from seeking community, following Christ, volunteering, or making new friends? How does God see you? And do you need to work on not making others feel like an outsider? Just some food for thought, love ya!

Quick update: There is no update! I was supposed to have the test results on Monday after surgery. It is now Wednesday, and I have noth-ing. So, the Stage 4 vs. Stage 3B feud continues, and I will let you know, when I know!

She-Wolverine

August 20, 2015

Finally, an answer! As most of you have heard by now, my stomach is cancer free! My stomach nodes are cancer free! Praise God! You guys, I don't have Stage 4 cancer. The power of prayer is so evident, and God is so faithful. Instead of starting a clinical trial, I started my first day of radiation today at the Proton Therapy Center in Seattle. This is one of 25 treatments, so let the countdown begin! It was relatively quick and easy, they snap this alien mesh mask on my face, and I sit under a laser machine while it zaps all my cells. I felt like a she-wolverine or an alien or an x-man or something. You know how they get experimented on, and all of a sudden, they turn into this superhuman? Yeah, maybe that will happen to me!

I just wanted to point something out to you all. I mean, I am so thrilled and relieved to know that cancer hasn't spread in my body, and that is a huge blessing! God is faithful, and God is good. BUT what if I would have received different news? What if the cancer had spread? What if you were all praying for the cancer not to spread and for me to have Stage 3B and the results ended up being stage 4? Would the attributes of God change? Would He be less faithful and less good? Isn't it so easy to treat God as our own personal genie? When things go well we all sing His praises and jump for joy and thank Him for answered prayers, but when things go what we see as wrong we stop praying. We resent and curse Him, and we turn away. We prayed for healing, and in His mercy and wisdom, He has made my stomach cancer-free. That's grace you guys. I didn't deserve this, I am not entitled to this, it is not my right, and if we would have had different results God would still be God. He would still hear our prayers, and He would still have a perfect plan. That being said and keeping that in mind, I challenge you to check your heart while you pray. Whatever you are praying for, stop and ask, "If this prayer isn't answered in the way I want it to be, is God still good and will He still be in control?" Sometimes it goes the way we are hoping for, like the fact that my cancer has not spread! But sometimes it doesn't. That's okay too.

Seattle is our new home! I feel so relieved to have a plan, I mean I still hold plans VERY loosely because I've learned my lesson, but it feels good knowing that every time I put the green alien mask on, I am fighting for my life. This is the next step in kicking cancers butt, and I can consider the green mask my armor. The first week I'm not supposed to have many side effects, so that's good news. This radiation is called Proton Therapy. It's a different form of radiation that is more specialized, and it is less damaging. The doctor had to pull some serious strings to get me in this program because there is only one machine on the west coast. Praise God!

Also, next weekend is the walkathon! I don't know if you guys understand how amazing Lori and Nicole are? This is not merely a time of walking; there are going to be events and bouncing things, and eating contests and cars, and sheesh, you name it! I am so excited to see the community come together on August 30th. Not to support me (that's a bonus), but to be united during a trial and show the meaning of helping one another.

Mom or Enemy?

August 24, 2015

Hello friends! I know it's been a few days but I was sick Friday, and Saturdays I have decided to take the day off since you all have fun things to do on Saturday nights. Sundays I thought about devoting to YouTube. Like instead of having a new blog, you all go and watch the new YouTube video; how does that sound?

This weekend Chandler, my sister, flew into Seattle which makes me very happy. She is my best friend and I have needed her with me. I love having the three of us together. Mom and I have done an outstanding job having all this together time though. We haven't been fighting or annoyed with each other, so I'm proud of us. The three of us went to the EMP museum, I'm not sure what that stands for but basically, it's a giant music museum, and it's really cool. Then Sunday, we tried out a rad new church called "Cross and Crown" and their worship band is called "Ghost Ship" which is absolutely amazing, so go check out their stuff!

Anyway, I promised you all that I would be transparent, so here it goes. This weekend my conscience dealt my attitude some painful conviction, and it was not fun! Not that a guilty conscience is ever fun; in fact, it usually weighs on your heart and makes you focus on the log in your eye. I was convicted because Sunday morning while we were meeting new people at the wonderful new church we attended, I found myself embarrassed by my mom and her outgoing self. I started making excuses to the new people we were meeting for her behavior because my insecurity flared up. I found myself saying, "Oh don't mind her, she has no filter" and focusing on how embarrassed I was that she was bragging about my blog and passing out my blog cards to everyone she came in contact with. As the day progressed, I found myself grumbling as she handed me a juice to chug, or filled up another glass of water for me to drink, or when she encouraged us to bypass eating out so we could eat healthy food at home. As my attitude toward her got worse and worse, I started treating her like she was my enemy. Sunday a big conviction SEIZED my heart and the Holy Spirit said, "ENOUGH IS ENOUGH."

I had a radical perspective change my friends, also known as repentance. Since when did my mom, my biggest fan, and my biggest supporter become my enemy? In what ways was she doing anything that was hurting me? I sat and pondered the things I was growing in resentment toward her and found a giant log was sticking in my eye. She shares my blog because she is proud of me and because she is my biggest supporter. She takes the time to make my juice because she cares about my body being in the best fighting condition. She makes me drink water and eat healthy because it's good for me AND radiation is frying my good cells, and my body needs everything it can get to replenish the cells that are dying.

Conviction SEIZED my heart and the Holy Spirit said, "ENOUGH IS ENOUGH." I had a radical perspective change my friends, also known as repentance.

I thought about what it would look like if she just stopped doing all of these things, if my grumbling and snide comments and bad attitude finally put her down enough for her to just say "You win, bye." Wow, I could NEVER do this alone, I need her, I am grateful for her, and I have found a new appreciation for the sacrifice and hard work that she has put in not only during this time but my WHOLE life. So, this message is for kids, teens, adults, and those of you who need an attitude check. Who is it and what is it that you are growing bitter toward? Your husband for not allowing you to spend all your money on shoes? Your wife for making you go on a run? Your mom for making you go to bed early? Your dad for not allowing you to date that one boy? Think about whether they are doing that because they love you or because they hate you. Then check your attitude next time your biggest fan wants to help you out.

I'm sorry Mom for not appreciating the time and hard work you've put in to make sure I live a long and healthy life. I'm sorry for not realizing that you want what's best for me and you've never once done anything to try and hurt me. I love you, and I am going to do my best to have a better attitude and be more grateful for all you do! Now it is your turn to reflect. Who do you need to thank and apologize to? Kids, you all have grumbled about your parents when they say "In five years you'll understand and appreciate us." THEY AREN'T LYING.

Missed you all! The second YouTube video is up so if you enjoyed it, please like it and if you want to see more, please subscribe! Also, the walkathon is coming up on the 30th at 1 p.m. I am going to come home to Klamath for it. Please, please come see me and let me thank you personally and please share your stories with me. Love you all!

Your Last Day

August 25, 2015

My cold/flu thing is finally going away! Mom claims it's the juice, I don't know about that, I think maybe it's the fact that I took a 2-hour bath while I watched *Lord of the Rings*, that seems like a cure. Radiation hasn't made me sick yet!

Our neighbor here at the cancer house has Merkel Cell cancer like me. Isn't it cool that God did that? I mean, of all the different cancers and people, she is right next to us. Anyway, last night she came home from nearly the end of her radiation and found out that cancer has spread and she now has to come back to Seattle for a clinical trial. It hit me hard; the realization that just because we are doing radiation doesn't mean we will be done battling cancer or cured. I had a moment there where I had to think about the fact that I could get done with these six weeks of radiation only to find out that I have cancer somewhere else. She handled it well, and I am so proud of her, but please keep her in your prayers. I'm going to choose to move forward in my treatment knowing that I have no control over what happens and being scared and worried won't change what happens!

Rose mentioned something that I relate to. She said she isn't afraid of dying; she's afraid of leaving her family behind. That's been one of my biggest fears throughout this, what will it do to the ones I love if I died? The reality is, we never know when our time will come. Who will you leave behind? We may not be able to control when we leave this Earth, but we can control who we leave and what we leave behind. If you were to leave today would your loved ones be okay? Would they know that you love them? I want to leave knowing that I left nothing unsaid, that I resolved things and didn't leave anger or hate. I want to leave knowing that I made a difference and made an impact. I want to leave knowing that I glorified God, and as much as I hate the saying "Live like you're dying" how radically does that change the way you spend your day to day life? Would you waste your time being angry, or waste time getting involved in petty drama? Would you spend your last days sleeping or sitting in front of the T.V.? Would you spend your time complaining or being depressed? Would you waste your time being afraid or insecure? What would you do on your last day? Who would you spend it with? What things would you say? What relationships would you fix? These things can be revealing to you. It can show who is most important to you, what you might need to get rid of in your life, what you need to stop doing, etc.

We may not be able to control when we leave this Earth, but we can control what we leave behind. If you were to leave today would your loved ones be okay? Would they know that you love them?

Challenge yourself tomorrow; wake up and pretend that it is your last day on earth. See what happens! See what people you spend time with, what things you do, what things you say, and also pay attention to the people you DON'T see and the things you DON'T say, maybe those people and things shouldn't be a part of your life. I love you all!

Oops, Wasted

August 27, 2015

So, I woke up yesterday all set to take myself up in my own challenge. Yes, I actually try to practice what I preach, and well, it didn't exactly go as planned. (Read the previous post to understand what challenge I'm referring to). The morning started off well enough as I gulped down my slimy green juice without complaining. I enjoyed a conversation with my Mom and Sister, and then I go to do one of my favorite things - I went thrifting with Sis. All good things, and I did my absolute best to enjoy every moment. Then time for radiation treatment came along and even though it's not the one thing I imagined myself doing if this were my last day on earth, I still tried to enjoy it and be grateful for it! Up to this point, I felt pretty good about my challenge, and then complete failure as we decided to go to Sprint to get new phones set up... four long hours later...Yep, I failed at my challenge. And I didn't blog. Now you know why. But now we all have spiffy new phones and we got rid of our slider dinosaurs from junior high! What a huge blessing! I want to know how you all did? If you didn't accept the challenge guess what? If you wake up tomorrow, the Lord gave you another day, so no excuses!

It made me realize, we can sit there and hope and dream and try to picture what our perfect day, our perfect life, our perfect plan would look like but how often does it actually happen that way!? I didn't plan for my pretend last day to be spent in the phone store. I didn't plan for 21 years old me to get cancer. So, what then? Do we just say "Well that didn't work out so I may as well give up!" Or "Well crap now that was a waste, one more day in the trash." I did this you guys! I sat at the phone store and said "What a waste." But it wasn't if I look at it a different way. My Mom and sister and I had many frustrating moments but we had so belly laughs too, and we were together and now we have a good story. Do we really want to live life thinking that ordinary or

It made me realize, we can sit there and hope and dream and try to picture what our perfect day, our perfect life, our perfect plan would look like but how often does it actually happen that way!?

frustrating moments that don't go our way are just wasted? That would leave me believing that this entire cancer journey was a big waste. Or that you working at that minimum wage job after college is just a waste. Or you thinking that your teenage son who got arrested was just a waste. Or the fight you had with your friend didn't have any purpose. I don't ever remember the people in the bible saying, "Well God, I ended up in quite the mess, guess the rest of my life is just a waste!" Does God ever throw us away? Does He say, For YOU know the plans the plans, no, no, no... He says for I KNOW the plans I have for you. God wastes nothing, not even the four hours you spend in a phone store.

Love you all! In case you didn't get the memo, Sis and I will be singing at the walkathon which means we'll be there! So please be there too so I can meet you.

Greener Grass?

August 28, 2015

We are currently in the car driving to Klamath! I'm so grateful that I can come home to be at the walkathon! Please pray for safe travels. It's always quite an exhausting trip. I am starting to feel and see the effects of radiation. Today was my ninth treatment so I have dry mouth and I'm beginning to see my radiation burn. Other than that, everything treatment-wise is going great!

I've been catching myself being discontent with things. Discontent with my hair, discontent with being in Seattle, discontent with being single. It just becomes a funk that I get in sometimes when I catch myself always looking for the greener grass. Then I get online and see a world full of discontent people! Lip injections, a faster car, a younger wife, a better butt, better behaved kids. You long for a white picket fence then when you get it you need the new modern steel fence.

Our world tells us to be discontent, "Oh you need whiter teeth." "Actually, you NEED a bigger phone." We are bombarded with these messages, and it is nearly impossible to be content! I had to laugh while we were at the phone store as my mom pulled out my iPod from Jr. High complete with the touch circle thing that I spent many hours spinning. She has always been content with that because it works. It meets her needs, and it isn't broken, so she's content. Here I am, blessed beyond belief to even be alive, and I find myself being discontent. Here in the life that I almost lost, and I am discontent because of my hair color.

Then I realized, in this world full of material things that promise us happiness, in a world that entices us to get the "next best thing" or the "the bigger, cooler thing," we are left with a bunch of discontent people. I mean look at that celebrity that seems to have it all, the looks, the hot husband, the dream job, and all the money they could ever need, and they commit suicide.

I mean look at that celebrity that seems to have it all, the looks, the hot husband, the dream job, and all the money they could ever need, and they commit suicide.

So what then? You find contentment in the things you already have, like the ultimate contentment in Jesus! I mean, He doesn't change, we will always NEED Him, and He is already the best there is. He isn't selling you anything better. He doesn't promise you happiness in the "next best anything" because He is already the best! What more could we ever want or need? Everything else, I mean EVERYTHING else is a bonus.

Come on, Community!

August 31, 2015

I'm back in Seattle! This time Mom stayed home back in Klamath Falls, and my sister and cousin Jess came with me to stay this week. I went to Klamath over the weekend for the walkathon. Oh. My. Gosh. What a HUGE blessing that was to me. The turnout was baffling, and the support and encouragement you all offered me were incredibly humbling. Thank you to all who attended and made it possible!

It's so interesting to me to see how trials can bring people together. I mean it breaks down walls, heals wounds, and it makes people realize that life is too short to be anything but joyful. The day spent at the walkathon was a day of joy. I looked around and saw kids playing, moms and daughters walking together, grandparents taking pictures, and the community doing what they can to help. It was one of those moments when I saw family. I hope everyone gets the opportunity to see that kind of a community. It refueled and rejuvenated me to hear in person from you that this trial has impacted you! What an honor for me to be in this position, thank you.

Pour into a community, you guys. Don't let excuses keep you from doing so! Tonight, Jess and I went to a community life group at a church nearby and initially I felt like maybe we shouldn't go because I'm only going to be here for six weeks. Life is one continuous transition period. We are always going to be changing, leaving, moving, staying, whatever the case may be. We went, and we learned from the group, and we were poured into. People will come and go in your life, but God will use them for you, or use you for them! I am so glad I didn't let time keep me from meeting some new, awesome people. It is incredible to see

> *It's so interesting to me to see how trials can bring people together. I mean it breaks down walls, heals wounds, and it makes people realize that life is too short to be anything but joyful. It was one of those moments when I saw family. I hope everyone gets the opportunity to see that kind of a community. It refueled and rejuvenated me.*

how God uses people to bless you and uses you to bless other people! So I challenge you to pour into a community, no matter where you are or how long you are there.

Monkey Connection

September 1, 2015

We went to the zoo today, and it was Jess's first time! You could say she shared a special connection with a monkey, so her day was made. Radiation side effects are worsening, and I can barely swallow solid food now because my throat is so dry, so prayers for that would be helpful!

We went to a rad college group tonight! The speaker was authentic and transparent, and the community was genuine. Jess and I walked out and didn't introduce ourselves to anyone. As we walked down the street, I thought about my recent blog and how I challenged you all to pour into a community and allow the community to pour into you. I stopped dead in my tracks and knew that I needed to go back in there and develop a community. If not for them to pour into me, for me to allow the Lord to use me to pour into them. So, we went back in. It's so easy to let fear and insecurity hold you back from meeting people, but how rewarding is it when you go forward with the confidence in Christ! The fantastic thing about the Christian community is that you are walking into a room of your brother and sisters. You should walk in feeling like you could rely on any one of them and you should walk in excitedly anticipating how God is going to use you.

We did! We walked in and right away I was able to share the incredible testimony of the Lord and His work through me during my battle with cancer. Now if we would have continued walking away, I would have never been able to invest in a community!

God truly brings people into your life during different seasons. You will meet people, and sometimes they are long term and sometimes they are short term.

I want to reiterate the fact that God truly brings people into your life during different seasons. I struggle with this a lot. I used to think it was a bad thing that people would come and go in my life. I thought it was a character flaw in me and that I wasn't trying hard enough to stay in contact with people. While sometimes that's the case, you do have to put in the effort to be intentional, but that's not always how it goes. You will always meet people, and sometimes they are long term and sometimes they are short term. Either way, you can trust that they are there for a reason. Don't ruin the season by trying to guess if they're here to stay, or just temporary. Just enjoy the moments. Life happens in moments.

The Superpower of Impatience

September 2, 2015

So now I absolutely can't eat solid food. I tried eating a banana today, and it felt like I was swallowing razor blades! So, if anyone knows of a place in Seattle with a killer soup selection, I'm all ears!

Today was a day of learning about patience. Why is patience such a hard concept for some of us? And why is it effortless in some areas and on some days but not others? My patience was tested today, and boy was it tested. I arrived at my appointment at 3:15 like usual, and they took me back to put on my mask and get me ready. Well, the first time, my neck didn't curve right, so all the tape and snaps had to come off and they had to redo it. Two times, three times, six times, and two hours later. At first, I have an easy time being patient, it has to be done, and I understand that they are doing their best. Then I can feel them getting impatient, gosh I would too! I mean I would have given up and probably said some choice words. The entire time I was laying on the table I played it over and over in my mind, how does getting impatient and mad help anything?

This is an honest struggle for me! It doesn't speed up time, it doesn't change the order of things. In fact, it makes the whole situation worse. I tried to keep a smile on my face and pray that the Lord would give me extra patience as the mask was pushed on and off my face over and over again. Then I finally get done, all I want to do is leave, and my Sister was supposed to pick us up. Traffic. Five minutes, ten minutes, an hour goes by. This time I didn't pray, there were no deep breaths or smiles, I lost my patience. I got mad and frustrated, and I spent the hour watching the clock as if it would speed up time. Frustration turned to anger, anger turned to hate, hate to bitterness. You choose the order but a lot of sinning went down and for what? Did it help? Did it make the traffic magically disappear? No. So now as I sit and wait I write this in conviction. I am choosing to use this time for something good. I am taking advantage of the time I have to sit, and I can tell you what, it feels a lot better than being impatient! Cancer had given me a lot of perspectives; one being life is short. We need to spend more time enjoying the moments and less time being rushed, mad, frustrated, and impatient. We are a go, go, go culture, and we get annoyed when things don't go our way! I should be feeling blessed that the doctors would take the time to get my mask right, I should feel grateful even to own a car, and I should cherish this time I have to sit in a nice doctor's office and be with my beautiful cousin! Perspective, it's a wonderful thing.

...find something good to do during that time instead of letting your impatience turn into bitterness and anger because impatience isn't a superpower!

So, my challenge for you today is to find a moment that you can easily become impatient, during a traffic jam, a long office meeting, as you wait for your child to get out of soccer practice, whatever your situation is, and find something good to do during that time instead of letting your impatience turn into bitterness and anger because impatience isn't a superpower! You aren't going to make things change magically, you aren't helping or changing anything, so why do it?

The picture shows my current radiation burn. Not the best-looking thing but it's working!

Sugar and Spice

September 4, 2015

I had to get a CT scan yesterday with the hope that the radiologist can get the mask positioned correctly. This time was worse though because my patience had reached its max after the day before, and this time I was actually in the mask for an hour rather than them taking it on and off. As I sat there stuck in my green costume, I started to realize how tight it was and how I really couldn't move at all. I began to feel claustrophobic, and I had a panic attack! Then I was so frustrated, and I had such a headache from the mask being too tight that I teared up.

I got some stuff called Magic Mouth Wash to help my throat so I can eat solid food. The downside is that I will lose my taste, THE UPSIDE is that I won't be able to taste the juice! HAHA YES!

I have been thinking a lot about kindness lately. It's like the Lord knows that I am noticing genuine kindness and He was like "Oh you like that? Oh, here you go, you can see an example of that every single day!" Like I'm not sure if He is just telling me to take a hint and be nicer or if I need to take notes. Anyway, I want to tell you about a few incidences.

For starters, our neighbors at the cancer house, Rose and Jim, come over every single day and check on us to make sure we are doing okay. They were at the farmer's market and thought about how I drank a lot of vegetable juice and got me stuff to make more juice. They were doing a load of laundry and came over to see if there was anything we needed washed. I could sit here and list kind things they do all day. They are genuine and absolutely sweet people. They are the type of people that after you close the door, all you can say is, "Oh my gosh, they are just so awesome."

Then there's the Sliker's. They are family friends that live here in Seattle. They have hosted us at their house and had us over for dinner. They give us vegetables to juice every single week, and yesterday, as they were on their way to drop the veggies off, they called to see if there was anything they could pick up for us on their way. After they drove across town to deliver the fresh produce, they insisted on driving us to this little hipster town we wanted to visit - completely out of the way. Once again, I could go on!

Even today as we were trying clothes on at the store, the lady working there was super sweet and bubbly. It was so refreshing. Also, we went to coffee and lunch today with Yarik (a friend from Moody) and his cousin. They offered to buy our coffee and food without hesitation, and when I was about to get an Uber to go to my appointment they said, "Don't be silly we would love to drive you!"

What sets these people apart?

Selflessness: concerned more with the needs and wishes of others than with one's own; unselfish.

It truly goes beyond kindness when it comes to

I have been thinking a lot about kindness lately. It's like the Lord knows that I am noticing genuine kindness and He was like "Oh you like that? Oh, here you go, you can see an example of that every single day!" Just look around, God's kindness is everywhere.

what sets these people apart. They are selfless. You can do plenty of kind things with the "karma" mindset without even realizing, being kind with strings attached and being kind without your heart being in the right place. Boy, I am SO guilty of this. Giving people a ride but thinking about how much gas you're using. Buying someone coffee but hoping that they will pick up the lunch tab. Cooking someone dinner but yelling in a fight, "BUT I COOKED YOU DINNER!" Calling to check on someone but scrolling through Pinterest while they talk.

I'm humbled and encouraged by these loving examples in my life, and they have thought of my needs FIRST. If I were to do my laundry, I would get it done, and wondering if my neighbor had laundry that needed to be done would have NEVER crossed my mind.

Being selfless is against our nature you guys, so if you have the same conviction as me right now don't worry! It's something you have to work toward. You first need to find examples of your life. Take the time to notice when people do something for you that is selfless. Then when you are doing the average, mundane things in life (like laundry), stop and see if there is a way that you can be selfless in it. Go beyond kindness and be SELFLESS.

Losing my Hair

September 8, 2015

Hope you all had a fantastic Labor Day! If I'm honest, I had a pretty terrible weekend. Okay, actually just a terrible Sunday and Monday... continue reading to find out why.

Sunday morning started off really well. The church we go to is amazing, and the preacher is so on point and relate-able. Previous to church I had been kind of convicted about how I've been living the past two weeks. I've been too comfortable guys. I started to get into a routine with radiation and I began to kind of relax knowing that I'm doing all that I can to fight cancer right now. With that relaxation came comfort, but not the peaceful comfort, more of a lazy comfort. I began to take a vacation from life, from my walk with God, and from cancer. I wasn't making time for juicing, praying, blogging, etc.

Then I noticed that in this vacation mode my sin tendencies were magnified. I was getting impatient, defensive, annoyed, and angry. I was gossiping more, and my insecurities and vanity were slowly creeping back in, I just started to fall back into the person that I don't want to be. I had a little conviction in my heart previous to the sermon. Then the sermon did what any good sermon is supposed to do, it brought on the real deal conviction.

The pastor talked about how God uses sinners, he talked a lot about Peter and Paul as examples, but he said something that really stuck with me. He said, "It's not that we walk away from God, it's that we aren't walking in the gospel." I don't know what it was, but the Lord used that sentence to seriously convict me for being in vacation mode, sippin' margaritas in my comfort zone.

I remember when I was a kid I heard a pastor preach about praying that God would push you out of your comfort zone to grow your faith and serve Him. He mentioned that your heart has to be right, and my little kid faith heard "because you might end up in Iran being killed for God, or something like that." In my little kid brain, I was like, "No way am I praying that prayer, I don't think I could die for being a Christian!" Now as I look back on it, the pastor wasn't saying that, he was actually saying that if you pray for your faith to grow and if you want to be pushed out of your comfort zone, expect the Lord to bring you through hard things.

So, I sat there in conviction and prayed for the Lord to push me outside of my comfort zone, to shake me out of vacation mode and allow my faith to continue to grow (I already have cancer, what's the worst that could happen?!) (that's a total joke by the way). I walked out of church feeling refreshed and ready to get back to business. Little did I know that the business would begin right as I left the building.

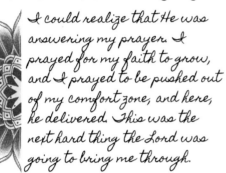

I could realize that He was answering my prayer. I prayed for my faith to grow, and I prayed to be pushed out of my comfort zone, and here, he delivered. This was the next hard thing the Lord was going to bring me through.

I ran my finger through my hair, like always. I don't know if I think it will help the style or if I just like the feeling of it, but this time was different, this time instead of my hand going through with ease, it came out with a giant chunk of hair. It was abnormal for sure, but sometimes you just lose some hair, so I continued on—all day. Chunk after chunk of my hair fell onto my clothes, into my hand, onto the floor, everywhere. I was losing my hair. It gave me a flashback to the times I as a kid I would lose a small pile of hair in the shower and sometimes worry that I had cancer. I mean, hair loss is probably the biggest symbol of cancer in our culture. When you google cancer all that comes up is bald people. I wasn't prepared to lose any of my hair, no one warned me. Remember how I prayed for the Lord to jolt me out of vacation mode? Yeah, well I sat there and stared at the bald spot emerging on my head, and I was reminded all so suddenly that I was indeed still sick.

I cried. The idea of a large bald spot on the side of my head wasn't the reason that I cried though. I cried because I could now empathize with the thousands of cancer patients that lose their hair. I cried because society makes me and them feel ugly for losing hair. I was faced with a choice right here, I could curse God for not only letting me go through cancer but now letting my hair fall out too, or I could realize that He was answering my prayer. I prayed for my faith to grow, and I prayed to be pushed out of my comfort zone, and here, he delivered. This was my Iran. This was the next hard thing the Lord was going to bring me through.

With that, I decided to move forward and embrace my new bald spot. I found what I thought was a cool hairstyle to work it...

Part 2 of the story will be in the next blog, stay tuned for the second terrible day.

Lost Some Hair, Gained Some More

September 9, 2015

ᶠᶠᶠᶠᶠᶠᶠᶠ

I decided I was going to rock the shaved side thing like Demi or Skrillex, I got my photos all ready and I was moving forward with a positive outlook on my new bald spot. It's just another battle scar, right? I wanted to show society that I wasn't about to be ashamed of fighting for my life. So, I entered the only barber shop opened on that Monday, a barbershop seemed legit anyway, after all, they shave heads all the time! A real pretty gal with flamin' red hair and tons of tattoos brought me to the chair. I told her right away about my situation and showed her the pictures. She was all for it, and she even proceeded to tell me that she was Macklemore's stylist! What!? How does that even happen? I guess she grew up with him and she cuts hair part-time more for fun.

Anyway, automatically I trusted her even more, I mean, Macklemore guys. She shaves a third of my head. I was expecting that, I mean it's better than it falling out all over the place. Then she tells me that it would be a good idea to blend my hair, so I don't have a giant bald patch, she suggested a little A-line, not taking off too much length. I was all for it. I've had an A-line a million times, and I like the look of it. So, she starts doing her trimming and cutting; meanwhile I took a deep breath, and my attention shifted to the wall covered in magazine photos. I looked up just in time to see her cut a massive chunk off the back of my hair…

I watched in SHOCK as the hair that had just grown out from my pixie quickly turned back into a pixie… It was too late, and there was no going back, my hair was ruined. I'm not confrontational you guys, in fact, I'd rather sit there while she hacked away my hair than say a word. At this point it was too late, but I still could have saved some of my hair! When she finally finished, to my dismay, she had used the wrong terminology. When she said A-line she meant asymmetrical. One side of my hair was pixie short, and the other side was longer. Super trendy if I were lady gaga or something, but I have never hated something more in my life! I felt like one of those characters that's half girl and half boy. Like I needed to walk around in half a tux and half a wedding gown.

The moment I stepped out of the salon I burst into tears. I cried the entire walk home, and I was more hysterical than when I found out I was losing a third of my hair. Quickly the girls offered advice, and we decided to get extensions at Sally's. Thank the Lord for Jess; she spent hours sewing them into my multi-length hair. I also had to part ways with the fun silver color, but it would have been a hit or miss as to whether the extensions would be the right color or not. I couldn't handle another miss. This time HAD to be a hit! And it was. I like having long hair again, and it's a nice change.

The funniest thing about this whole thing is that I don't have hair extensions because I have cancer and I'm losing my hair. I'm not trying to cover up the bald patch, and I'm not ashamed of my hair loss. I have extensions because by me trying to embrace the bald I ended up with the worst haircut of my life!

The funniest thing about this whole process is that I don't have extensions because I have cancer and I'm losing my hair. I'm not trying to cover up the bald patch, and I'm not ashamed of my hair loss. I have extensions because by me trying to embrace the bald I ended up with the worst haircut of my life!

Now, the hard part is trying to understand what the Lord is having me learn from this. I mean, the balding thing made sense and clicked with me, but a bad haircut? I mean, come on! I know it will probably be revealed to me later, or maybe the haircut wasn't even about me. Who knows? At the end of the day, it's just hair and it grows back. For those of you who have been or are going through hair loss, embrace it! I know society tries to make us feel ugly and I know there are going to be stares. But how beautiful is it that you have an outward appearance of your fight? You can walk around in confidence knowing that you are fighting, you are surviving. Don't let the hair loss keep you from remembering this time in your life, take pictures, go in public. There is so much beauty in this battle!

Stop Working

September 10, 2015

I'm alone. The apartment is so quiet and my only company outside of treatment has been a bunch of foreign Uber drivers. It's been so strange because I haven't been alone since before I was diagnosed! I almost don't know how to be alone, which is so odd because I am a very independent person and a bit of an introverted extrovert. But the last three months have been visitors, doctors, family, hotels, and hospitals, just go, go, go. At first, I woke up and wanted to cry as I stared at the empty beds by me. But later I welcomed the quiet. I relaxed, and it was much needed. To be alone with God, to be alone with my thoughts and just take some time in peace.

I had a great conversation with a friend of mine earlier. She was transparent with me in that she was having a tough time accepting grace. I could relate to that on SO many levels. Our whole human existence is based on us working for things. I mean, we work out to get a good body, we work hard at school to get a degree, we work hard at our career to have success, we work for things, and it feels good when we have a slice of glory knowing that we earned all that we worked for. It's so rewarding to work hard for something and to reap the reward, we want to show it off right? We want people to see all that we've accomplished.

What if our relationship with God was like that? I mean, isn't it so tempting and so part of our human nature to make it that way? Oh, if

That's why grace is so radical, because God says, "Hey there is nothing you could do to make me love you more OR love you less."

we work hard enough on our spiritual checklist, then I will reap the reward of God's love. Or oh, if we are just kind enough to people, or if I convert enough people, then I will receive the reward. But the problem with that mindset is it's all meant to glorify yourself. Your motives are off because you have the order: obey/work, love, believe. If you obey and do enough, then you will win God's love, and therefore you will believe in Him. It's rewarding, it's self-gratifying. It feeds our pride to think that we worked hard. That's why grace is so radical, because God says, "Hey there is nothing you could do to make me love you more OR love you less. I sent my son to save you, and it is finished." He says to Believe, Love, Obey/Work. Because you believe and love God, that in itself will motivate you to obey Him and work hard to become more Christ-like. That motivation is God-centered and focused on glorifying Him. So instead of focusing on what you are doing wrong and how you aren't doing enough for God, focus your heart on the gospel. Allow it to transform you and out of that you will obey! It's just cool to me to think that it's that easy. I challenge you to know the gospel, walk in it and when your life is God-centered He will help you.

I am nearing the end of radiation! YAYYYY! Love you all.

Pink Hair, So What!?

September 11, 2015

Mom is back in town! It's nice to have company again and we've become even better friends, so it's like being reunited with my friend.

We had dinner with an amazing girl named Shongi. We met her at a college group we went to at the beginning of our Seattle journey. She beams with love and joy, and it is inspiring, and it challenges me. She is a real example of what it looks like to live for God. She doesn't hesitate to live out faith, and she is not ashamed of her love for God. Her presence is convicting to me because even though I write a blog where I am not afraid to talk about my faith, I still find it hard to do so in person!

Today I took an Uber with a super hip granny. She had a strip of pink hair, and she had a lime green car decorated with furbies. Something in me just assumed that she was an eccentric, hippy type that worshiped mother earth. Judgmental? Heck yeah it was, and I'm not proud of it! But as I told her my story of cancer, I found it extremely hard for me to say anything about God. My fear of man crept in and paralyzed me. I knew that I would probably never see her again, I knew that my fear stemmed from a preconceived judgment based on her appearance, yet I let it control me anyway. At the end of the car ride, she stepped out, hugged me, and told me that she would keep me in her prayers. UGHHH. Conviction already set in. I have tattoos, I have had tons of different hair colors and cuts, I wear makeup, and how many times have I been angry feeling like people have judged me and judged my walk with God? How many times have I "caught people off guard" because I actually know something about the Bible? I had a cool opportunity to share with this woman what God has been doing in my life, and I didn't. Shongi's example convicts me because she loves everybody, she doesn't judge them or let fear get in the way. Her love for Jesus overflows into love for people, and that's how I want to be. I want to have boldness for Christ outside of my writing.

This whole concept was brought up again in my day because I was watching that show "Wife Swap" and a wife from a Christian family swapped with a wife that was from a family that had a husband, a wife, and a shared girlfriend. I watched as each side tried to shove their views down each other's throats. Both were at fault because their goal was to win an argument. Their goal was to be the right. Their goal wasn't to love, it didn't want what's best for one another. Jesus set an example for us. Look at how He treated the woman at the well. He didn't damn her to hell. He didn't sit there and argue with her to make her change, He didn't judge her by her appear-

...what is your goal in talking about Jesus? Is it to win an argument? Is it to condemn? To put yourself on a pedestal? Or is it because you love Jesus?

ance and say, "Well she's beyond helping now, she can't be saved so why even go there". He approached her in truth and love. I want my love for Jesus to be the reason that I talk about Him, and for that to be the reason that I'm not afraid! I challenge you to learn what the gospel is. What is your goal in talking about Jesus? Is it to win an argument? Is it to condemn? To put yourself on a pedestal? Or is it because you love Jesus? Is it because you desire to follow Him and in that, you desire to love others to as well? Because you want to follow His example?

Bottom line, check your motivation guys, and I am sure checking mine. By the way, I received my invitation to graduation today! They throw a little graduation party for us when we finish radiation, so that's cool. Mine is coming up because I'M ALMOST DONE WITH TREATMENT! Yay! Then I will be heading back to Klamath, and the rest is unknown. I almost cried today at the thought of leaving Seattle, as it's grown on me for sure.

More Merkel Miracles (Part 1)

September 15, 2015

Today was one of the first days that I felt the total symptoms of radiation. I feel like an iPhone with a battery at 1%. I was so tired and drained that I even fell asleep in the mask during radiation! I was able to push through the fatigue, and Mom and I went on a beautiful cruise tour of Seattle this morning. Loved it even though I could hardly stay awake!

Exhaustion is indeed a side-effect, but I figured that because I'm only 21, it wouldn't affect me that much, not like it does the older patients. Well, I was wrong! I also was told that the fluid in my cheek (that I thought was swollen) would be something that I deal with for the next several years because I have no lymph nodes to drain the extra fluid. Bummer. I also was told that my hair loss would be permanent, so basically yesterday was another day to wrap my head around the fact that cancer really does affect the rest of my life, not just this season.

Mom and I went to a dinner last night held for Merkel Cell patients. As I was standing in the elevator, I pretty much expected the doors to open, revealing 10-20 extra old people sitting around a table, and I was planning on leaving early to go to Bible study. As the elevator doors parted, I gazed out into a beautiful hall and to my surprise there stood more than 200 people dressed up in fancy clothes, a band playing music, a fantastic spread of food, wine, and lovely flowers, and waiters running around serving people. What?? It was a party. We walked in and prayed that the Lord would put us at a table that would bless us with some new relationships. We wandered around until we sat at a table with a husband, wife, and their daughter who was the only other person in attendance that knew who Justin Bieber is. LOL!

The husband, Steve, was a fellow Merkel Cell patient. It was so strange to peer across the table at someone who could relate to me. Outside of Rose, most people don't even know what Merkel Cell Carcinoma is. Then a man named Paul joined our table, he too was an MCC patient. It was an unexplainable feeling, the feeling I had sitting in a room full of people who can relate to me. It honestly felt like a family to me. I felt like I could walk up to anyone and they would support me, cheer me on, understand and love me. I connected instantly with Steve's family, and Paul and I were blessed by their stories of struggle and success.

After licking our plates clean, we went into another room to watch a presentation on the new technologies and advances in Merkel Cell. What a blessing to see the faces of the "behind the scenes doctors and researchers" making it possible for me to live.

It was an unexplainable feeling, the feeling I had sitting in a room full of people who can relate to me. It honestly felt like a family to me.

They dumbed down the medical terminology and made analogies for us to follow, and I was shocked at how amazing and intricate our bodies are and all that medicine and research are doing to help us survive. I gazed around the room and saw all the different shapes and sizes of scars, bald patches, and burns. Usually, my reaction would have been to gawk, or wonder, but instead, I felt a sense of pride. These are my people, fellow warriors - we are all fighters, and we all have battle scars. I also saw hope and love as families cried together, cheered together, and celebrated another year together. I knew that I had to say something, I had to let them know how this night was making me feel.

Pt 2 tomorrow!

More Merkel Miracles (Part 2)

September 16, 2015

I raised my hand to speak, and I said a prayer before the mic reached my hand. I didn't know exactly what to say, I just knew the Lord wanted me to say something. I stood up in front of everyone. They dismissed me at first, probably thinking that I was one of the patients' daughter. The moment I announced that I was a 21-year-old patient, all eyes were quickly on me and welling up. They looked at me with a hint of sadness, probably thinking that I was too young, that it wasn't fair, and feeling bad that I have to go through what they've been through at my age. These were the words that came out.

"Hello, my name is Hayden Crebbin, I am 21 years old, and I had been diagnosed with Merkel Cell Carcinoma cancer on June 26th. I didn't know what to expect from this dinner, but I wanted to thank all the doctors and researchers for their hard work in trying to find a cure. I would also like to thank the patients. Obviously, I'm one of the younger ones here, but I see hope in this room. That's why you're all here today; you have hope. And for that, I want to thank you because you have paved the way for me to have hope that I will live a long and healthy life. I am leaving this night encouraged we can fight this."

Or something pretty close to that! I teared up looking at the faces around me, knowing that they have been fighting cancer for quite some time now. Afterward, I was overwhelmed with love as patient after patient approached me to tell me about their success, to say to me that I too can fight this, to tell me that I'm going to make it. Then a man named Richard approached me. I gazed upon his face and noticed a swirly scar near his eye. I didn't want to jump to any conclusions, but it was too familiar. He began explaining his story, and it quickly matched my own. He was my scar twin! I can't tell you how that made me feel. Here a man not only knew what it was like to go through cancer, not only knew what it was like to go through Merkel, but he could relate to the fine details of my sickness. It was a blessing directly from the Lord to give me comfort.

The night was filled with such hope you guys, meeting survivors and fighters, and seeing the advances in the research to kill Merkel cell. The dinner left me feeling encouraged, and I am anticipating the next one because I believe that I'm going to be there! I am going to fight, I am going to continue fighting, and I know the battle will be lifelong but if a room full of people can do it, I can too! Love you all!

Dirty Dishes

September 18, 2015

Alaina is here you guys! The twins, Alaina and Paige are my friends from Texas that I met three years ago in Germany. They were au pairs the same time I was and man, they were an absolute Godsend to me during that time abroad. The remarkable thing is, they have remained faithful and amazing friends. They challenge me every day and show me what it means to invest in and genuinely care about the people in my life. It's funny though, we all met in Germany, then we traveled to Ireland four months later. Then Alaina flew to Sunriver, Oregon to see me a year-ish later, then Paige flew to Spokane to see me two years later, and now here I sit with Alaina in Seattle three years later. How amazing is that!? And how funny is it that all this traveling around and they've still never been to my hometown. Reminiscing with Alaina has made me see the value in having long-term friends. I mean, we've seen each other through so many life stages, and we've watched each other grow. That's a unique thing. Find a lifelong friend you guys, or friends. Make the time for them, invest in them, treasure them.

Meanwhile back at my apartment in the Collegiana, there have been a lot of dirty dishes left in the sink in our shared kitchen. Everywhere. There is a certain someone on our floor that dirties up all the dishes and leaves them for the maid or us to clean up! Ugh, it makes me so mad and frustrated. I want to do what we used to do at my house at Moody and just set all the dishes in front of their bedroom door. And the maid doesn't even say anything! I'm the worst you guys because in my mind I am super confrontational, but in

> *I don't have an ounce of love, generosity, humbleness, selflessness, or even self-control when it comes to the dishes. I feel it, and I know that I am not walking in the gospel while I am huffing and puffing under my breath because there is a dirty pan on the stove.*

person, I don't say a word. Even my haircut, for example, I DESPISED it, and I still grinned, paid, and left. I've had some serious conviction about the dirty dishes, and I'm growing bitter over the injustice of it all. The fact that they don't respect us, the maid, the fact that they are so blessed to be in a wonderful housing unit for so cheap! So I grumble and become a bitter, passive-aggressive person. It's not God-honoring. I don't have an ounce of love, generosity, humbleness, selflessness, or even self-control when it comes to the dishes. I feel it, and I know that I am not walking in the gospel while I am huffing and puffing under my breath because there is a dirty pan on the stove.

Then I realized that God is probably allowing this to happen on purpose for me to practice loving through the injustice. When I'm honest, I sit there and think, "They don't deserve it." or "I clean my dishes." Wow. HOLD UP. They don't deserve it, Hayden? Come on girl, what do we all deserve? For the wages of sin is…death. That's what we all deserve because we are all sinners. And yet, God loves me, and He wants what's best for me, He saved me, He has mercy on me, He has GRACE. And if I want to be more Christ-like I need to show that same love, compassion, and grace on the "dish leavers."

Where do you need to show love and grace this week? Your co-worker for taking an extra smoking break? Your wife for leaving the car on empty? Whatever it looks like, seek it out and change your heart to be more like Jesus. Love ya!

Burned

September 21, 2015

I'm burned. Burned by radiation, burned out mentally, emotionally, and physically. My radiation symptoms hit me hard this weekend with the promise from the doctor that this isn't the worst it will be, that comes next week. Yikes! I have sores in my mouth, a swollen throat, my neck, and face are swollen, the burns on my neck and face are raw and peeling, I feel flu-like, just all around ick.

I have one more radiation treatment left, and while you'd think that brings me comfort, I find it unsettling. I am afraid to leave Seattle, to leave treatment, to leave the doctors. What do I do when I leave? This is what I've known for the last four months, and now I feel like I'm leaving and I'm back to square one. It's like senior year when you are trying to figure out if a college or the military or a job is right for you. The thing is, God has never failed me. He has always provided a place and a job; He has always opened an exciting opportunity for another year to grow me. So why am I anxious and worried? I want to leave Seattle excited, excited for the time I got to spend here and the people I got to meet, excited for what's to come. I do not want to head into the unknown with a spirit of fear because I have a God who has a plan for me.

Life is truly a series of moments. I look back on life as I close the chapter on Seattle and realize that I have tons of other chapters that have closed in my life. One thing I noticed is that I get really attached to the comfort of the "moment" because it's known, it grows familiar, and in that it can become easy not to have faith or trust God in the unknown. When the chapter is coming to a close or closes involuntarily, I have a tough time dying to my comforts and allowing God to take the reins, and it's hard for me to give up control. Toward the end, I start to freak out, and my anxiety heightens until of course, the Lord shows once again that He is faithful, then I move forward, trusting Him again.

I want to leave Seattle learning from the past, the Lord is in control, and He even tells me that He has a plan for me, a plan to prosper and not to harm. I am choosing to leave in trust and believe that God will continue to take care of me. Take a look at your moments, the chapters in your life. How do you close them? Do you trust that God has bigger plans or do you struggle to let go of the control? Whether it is leaving high school, watching your daughter get married, or moving to a new city, be excited about what the Lord has for you next!

I am struggling you guys, and I am having a hard time staying positive. I haven't felt this bad

Take a look at your moments, the chapters in your life. How do you close them? Do you trust that God has bigger plans or do you struggle to let go of the control? Whether it is leaving high school, watching your daughter get married, or moving to a new city, be excited about what the Lord has for you next!

since my surgery, I feel weary, and on top of that, the Lord has been stretching my faith. I know that this will pass and the Lord uses these times of feeling at my worst to grow and change me!

I have to get my antibody test tomorrow at SCCA, and I will get a scan in three months. These tests will give me answers as to whether I am cancer free at this point or if there are new spots. Please pray for my symptoms to subside sooner than later and that we have a safe trip home!

Radia-DONE

September 22, 2015

I don't have a lot to say today except, I'M DONE! I feel ready for recovery and ready to start a life again. Well, a different kind of life. Cancer doesn't put your life on pause unless you make it so. I head back to Klamath tomorrow and play the waiting game until my scan in December. I am hoping to see a lot of you at the KU vs. DUTCH BROS football game at KU this Saturday at 6 pm! It's such a fun idea, and I am so blessed and honored to be a part of it.

I saw the lymphoedema specialist today about the fluid in my face, and she said that it flared up from radiation, so I will be getting more information when I heal up in a few weeks. My symptoms are worse today, that is to be expected, but it doesn't make it fun! Please pray for safe travels for Mom and me tomorrow and please, PLEASE always let me know how I can pray for you!

"You, Lord, hear the desire of the afflicted;
*you **encourage** them, and you listen to their cry"*
(Psalm 10:17).

Stranger in the Mirror

September 23, 2015

I wasn't going to write a blog today because Mom and I spent all day in the car driving home and I am exhausted. But as I lay in my bed, in my own home, with my own fully functional internet, I feel like I have more motivation to write.

I just cried a few moments ago. I stared at myself in the mirror and felt as if I were staring at another human. This is the first time I've been home in four months. I mean actually home where I can unpack and take a deep breath. The last time I stood in my bathroom, gazing in the same mirror, I was a different person. In my exhausted, emotional state I can't

I saw defeat. I didn't seek the beauty, and I wasn't grateful, I was discouraged. And at that I cried, I felt pity for the stranger in the mirror and longed for the girl who used to live in this house.

see a girl who is a fighter, a warrior, who had just celebrated four months of trials, who had made it through an 11-hour surgery and six weeks of radiation. A girl who has been radically changed by God, and who is ecstatic to be alive.

Instead, I saw a stranger. A girl with a haircut she would never get, with a swollen cheek, with a lopsided smile. I saw a girl with a bald patch, with yellow flesh oozing out of a horrible chemical burn. I saw scars that marked her otherwise pale face. I saw defeat. I didn't seek the beauty, and I wasn't grateful, I was discouraged. And at that, I cried. I felt pity for the stranger in the mirror and longed for the girl who used to live in this house.

I knew it would be hard to go back to what seems to be a normal life after four months of living the life that the doctors give me. I expected it to be different. But it's almost as if I was in a dream during all the craziness of treatment as I moved from place to place. I lived out of a suitcase, as I met new people and saw new places, and my life revolved around fighting cancer. Now as I come back to the familiarity, it feels like I should snap out of the dream. Like I should be coming home, and everything should go back to normal. But the mirror and my body tell a different story. They tell me that it's not over, that it wasn't a dream, and as I stare at the girl with raw flesh marring her face and neck, I know that my life indeed has been forever changed. I have cancer, and things will never be the same.

I'm a Mess

September 25, 2015

It's okay to be down, and it's okay to cry, it's okay to be upset, it's even okay to be broken. I'm a mess, I am flawed, and I am broken. But so is every human on earth! Guess what, does God leave? Does God say "Eh, you are a mess, I'm going to leave for a while." No, He allows situations to bring us to the end of ourselves, to allow us to be broken and humbled, but that doesn't mean He has abandoned us. That's beautiful guys! I am a flawed human who is a mess YET He still loves me. So, I am transparent about my moments of brokenness. That doesn't mean I have given up, or that I don't believe God is here. He is so present, and He draws me closer to the cross in my moments of brokenness.

I posted a photo yesterday of my burn on Instagram. It was so strange to think back on the pictures I used to post. I used to be so concerned and consumed with what people think, and I used only to post doctored up selfies, staring as I gauged my beauty by the number of likes a photo got. As I looked at the unedited, raw, and oozing flesh, a picture of a girl with wounds and flaws, I realized that my worth and my beauty is in Christ, and I lived out some depressing days when I relied on the number of likes on an edited photo to feel beauty and find worth. Anyway, I posted that photo and a guy commented on it asking if I was a burn victim too. I clicked on his name and was led to a profile of a young kid, about 16 years old, with eyes, a nose, and a mouth, and everything else was marred and scarred. He was a burn victim. Guilt welled up inside me as I looked at this kid. His attitude toward life was so positive, and here we are obsessed with editing and photoshopping our already normal face.

He had posted a photo of his full body scars, and the caption talked about how he would never take the burns back, he'd never go back and change the moment of the fire, and he'd never wish it away. At first, I didn't understand as I imagined all the stares he got daily. Why wouldn't you take that back!? Then I looked in the mirror and said the same thing to myself. I would never take cancer back.

That seems like a crazy notion that amidst the worst symptoms of my radiation I would say I wouldn't take it back. But I honestly wouldn't. Why you ask? Because it has changed my life. It has brought me closer to God than ever. I have met the most amazing people and have had the best support. I have gained a new perspective on life, and if nothing else, and if not for me, God has used cancer to impact others. The boy with the burns said a similar thing, and now I can understand. When I stop and think about all the blessings that cancer has brought into my life, I could never ever wish it away. I mean here I am at a low point in my cancer journey and Kris brings over a book full of inspiring messages from all the people at the walkathon, then to top it off, a group of fifth graders had a bake sale today and made not $10, not $100, but $412!!! I mean, God is so present and so good and every time I am down, He is so faithful to bless me. Thanks to you all for your support and love. I challenge you to be transparent. You're a mess, and that's okay!

Then I looked in the mirror and said the same thing to myself. I would never take cancer back.

My Funeral

September 28, 2015

I know many of you watched the most recent video, the one about the effects of cancer on my family. I cry every time I watch it. I know I already told you guys, but I feel like I want to elaborate on the reason behind the tears. To be honest, I cry because I feel like I am watching my funeral from the outside. The sweet words, the emotions, the pictures and memories that make me reminiscence on the amazing life I've had, and the way cancer has affected my family more than I even knew. I sat there and could envision their lives if I wasn't here. I could picture myself like in a cheesy movie where I am walking around at the funeral as a spirit, watching everything and everyone. But I didn't cry because I got a glimpse of being dead, I cried because I was so grateful to God that I was sitting there, in the flesh, watching this lovely video with my family and that I wasn't a spirit hovering above in a white haze.

A lot of people don't get that, and I imagined how heart-broken I would be if I didn't get the chance to hear what my family had to say or reminisce on old stories with them. So, with that, I was challenged. No one should pass away without knowing these things. Just because I am the one with cancer doesn't mean my day is coming any sooner or later than the next person. We don't know how *TELL THEM. That's my challenge to you, tomorrow spend the extra minutes, step outside of the comfort zone of your own brain and tell three loved ones something that you want them to know before they die.* much time we have or how much time our loved ones have. What makes us wait until that day? What makes us hold in the emotion, the stories, and the love until we are wearing black, standing over a grave? Why don't we tell each other what we admire about them, or what our favorite trait of theirs is? Don't rob each other of the chance to hear these things before your time comes. If that means you have to shoot them a text every day or say something the moment you think it, then do it!

Instead of looking at your daughter and thinking to yourself, "Wow, her hair looks extra beautiful today." or hanging out with your grandpa and thinking, "I appreciate how generous he is, I mean, he never hesitates to help us financially." TELL THEM! That's my challenge to you; tomorrow spend the extra minutes. Step outside of the comfort zone of your own brain and tell three loved ones something that you want them to know before they die.

Oh, and I started college classes today! I'm not fully recovered, but life doesn't pause and wait for you while you have cancer, it keeps going, and I'm not going to let it pass me by!

Maryanne

September 30, 2015

Healing. I am healing you guys. Emotionally, mentally, physically. I am starting to see the difference! I started classes as I mentioned before. I'm taking Social Media Marketing and Drawing with Adobe Illustrator. It feels terrific having a change of pace. Before, I was working toward the goal of saving my life. It was obviously my main focus and with good reason, and I don't feel as if those months were wasted, or that they were purposeless. I feel good being normal. I don't like that term, but I don't know how else to word it. I feel more like I'm doing normal 21-year-old things when I'm in school. Anyway, my burn is beginning to heal too which means radiation is exiting my body!

Something AMAZING happened to me today. Nate and I (Nate is one of my best friends and he is in town visiting from Redding) went to the store to get a treat. Now contrary to popular belief, I do still splurge on sugary goodness once in a while! So, we are in the store, walking up and down every single aisle because I am a very indecisive person and I like to see all my options. So we are walking down the cookie aisle, and I was telling Nate that I have been eating healthy so I'm allowed to splurge. I said all this while passing a woman in the same aisle. After a few good debates with myself and setting back one or two things, I finally settled on gummy worms, and Nate grabbed an Almond Joy. We made our way to the checkout and were just about to pay when the same woman from the cookie aisle made her way in front of us. Initially, I figured she forgot something and was going to ask the cashier for it, but then she takes out her money, looks at me and says, "I read your blog," as she hands the clerk her money to pay for our treat!!! WHAT, YOU GUYS!? I was stunned, I mean people do nice things for me all the time don't get me wrong, but to have a woman who I've never met pay for my groceries in person be-

...to have a woman who I've never met pay for my groceries in person because she reads the blog, that was just awesome.

cause she reads the blog, that was just awesome. I made a little bit of a scene in the grocery store as I attempted to show my gratitude in some "Awww's" and You're too sweet!" I found out her name was Maryanne.

She then proceeded to hug me, then hands me a $20 bill and says, "Use this to enjoy the rest of your splurge day." Wow, you guys, I am still just blown away by this act of kindness. It was so unexpected, yet it made my entire day. I was so inspired that I wanted to pass along the kindness and I did an act of kindness for a kid in my class today. Maryanne, thank you for being so kind and for showing me how much an act of kindness can affect a person's day or even life.

I am so thrilled by the blessings I continue to receive. God is present, and I hope you can see that by now. He is SO present, and you know what, the kindness of Maryanne, or the little girls who put on the bake sale, or Jordan buying me lunch today, or Lori and Nicole putting on a walkathon. God's hand is in it. It's not just them!

God answers prayers and He uses us to fulfill them! He has shown me that so much during this trial, so I hope you first, pray: pray for everything and believe that it can transform your life because it will, and second, allow God to use you to bless others! You never know what little act of kindness could be an answer to someone's prayers.

UCC, Blessings in Tragedy

October 1, 2015

My heart is heavy for Roseburg today. You can feel it all over, you can see it on the news, on Facebook, everywhere. I heard about it as I was walking into Triad getting ready to speak at the pep assembly. It sparked fear in me, a fear for the college I go to, a fear because it's so close to home, a fear because the shooter targeted Christians. Initially, all I could feel was fear, then I felt sadness, and then I felt hatred toward the shooter. Hatred for the evil that stirred inside him. In my heart of hearts, I condemned him to hell along with so many people exclaiming their hate on Facebook. I wanted to stay home and never go to school or church again.

Out of my hatred and sadness, I was tempted to ask God why? Why did those people have to die? Why did the shooter have to be so evil? But then I remembered something, and God is not to blame, God is not to question. We choose to sin. We choose to sin, and God uses sin sinlessly. Was this any different?

Sis and I decided to go to one of our old college groups called 120. The pastor talked about how nothing is as it seems. That we don't see what God sees. Some would be confused, and think, "What am I missing? Innocent people died! How is that not exactly as it seems?" I understand that. I would have had a similar mindset too. But how many people said, "She's only 21 and has cancer? How is that not as it seems? Seems unfair, seems unjust, seems unloving to me. Why God, why?" I want to remind you all that bad things happen. Terrible things happen because we have a sin nature and we are flawed humans. God doesn't promise that this life is easier with Him, He doesn't even promise that in earthly terms it's "better" with Him. But He promises that He is good, and He began good work in us and will see it through until the end. He does promise that we will have trials and that yes, He will give us more than we can handle, but *He* won't give us more than *He* can handle.

> He does promise that we will have trials but that yes, He will give us more than we can handle, but He won't give us more than He can handle.

God is still good. There was a shooting today and God is still good. There was an abortion today and God is still good. There was a rape today and God is still good. I have cancer and God is still good. It isn't easy, none of it is. But I can tell you right now that I sit here, a girl with cancer, and I see how God used one of the worst diseases and has turned it into something beautiful. He will do the same with this shooting. He will do the same with that aborted baby, He will do the same with that rape victim. So, mourn with our brothers and sisters who lost loved ones today, but do not live in fear, or anger, or hate because of this. Keep watch for the blessings that God has in store for the people of Roseburg. Be excited for the Lord who makes beautiful things out of the dust. And pray for Roseburg.

Pound of Flesh

October 5, 2015

For the first time in the last four months I feel like I have a future to plan for. You know what I mean though? Before, I was just going from place to place praying that I would be getting treatment and answers. Now for a solid three months, I feel like a 21-year-old. So, school has been fulfilling, and I have a new appreciation for it. Actually, I'd say I have a new appreciation for working hard to achieve your goals and dreams. Anyway, I'm excited to tell you guys that tomorrow I am starting an internship with Impressions (a photography, web design, graphic design company)! I couldn't be more stoked and grateful for the opportunity to learn, grow, and work hard at something I love!

I've been learning a lot about grace lately, guys. If you stop at the moment you are getting mad or frustrated and think through a situation; it can reveal a lot to you. I've been pausing a lot lately instead of just reacting right away. I take 10 seconds to take a breath and actually think through my actions. For example, I hope she doesn't mind me using this example but last week it was my first day of school, and I had told my sister that she could borrow my car AS LONG as she returns in time for me to get to school. I woke up that Monday, got my breakfast and my green juice, got all ready and glanced at the clock. Class was at 12, and it was about 11:00 so I was doing great on time. I had a lot of things to do before I left for class, and the next time I glanced at the clock it's 11:40. Hmmm, school is about 5 min-

> *Next time you are faced with a situation where you could be mad or frustrated, stop, pause, and instead of just reacting, take the time to make the choice to act differently. Pay attention to how hard it can be to go against your sin nature! But also pay attention to how awesome grace is.*

utes away so I was starting to get a little concerned. Finally, it's 11:55 and I am stressed out and frustrated. I jump in Dad's GIANT truck and chug along to school barely making it for my first class. Now initially, I wanted to react in frustration, make Sis feel guilty for breaking her word, get my pound of flesh. But I took 10 seconds and realized that grace is a thing. There was probably a good reason she wasn't there and I had to make a conscious decision right then and there to not act in anger. It was hard you guys and I'm willing to admit that! I had to repeat to myself and make the conscious decision to not be angry over and over again. And you know what? Seeing her reaction when I wasn't yelling at her or being all rude, it was good. It was so good in fact that I realized that showing her grace was even better than getting my pound of flesh. (She thought my class was at 12:20 for the record).

When you stop to examine your reaction to things and make the conscious decision to do the right thing, it really reveals to you how hard it can be! Seriously, every time I've done this now I realize that it takes some serious effort to do the right thing.

Try it. Next time you are faced with a situation where you could be mad or frustrated, stop, pause, and instead of just reacting, take the time to make the choice to act differently. Pay attention to how hard it can be to go against your sin nature! But also pay attention to how awesome grace is. I mean geez, I'm sure glad Jesus wasn't sitting there saying, "Well I really want justice to be served, they really should pay for what they did. I'm going to just be mad because I have the right to get my pound of flesh." GRACE, saving grace. Jesus was the ultimate example of that now wasn't he!?

Running a Marathon

October 7, 2015

I haven't been posting as faithfully as I was and I'm sure some of you have noticed! But here's the thing, this is the first time since I've had the blog that I get to go out and live! Not that I didn't have a life before, it's just that before my everyday life involved healing, resting, and waiting for the next thing from the doctor. Now don't get me wrong, that time was great, and the Lord did a lot for me and to me during that time. He still does! But that being said, I have a job now, I have school, and I am working on launching my photography business. So, there will be a few days that I miss, but instead of being concerned or bummed, please think of it as exciting. It's exciting to think that I get to go out and work toward goals for my FUTURE! I genuinely believe that I have one now, or at least more of one. I don't want to get ahead of myself but for now, the Lord has given me these opportunities here in Klamath, and I want to take them. I'm not disregarding or giving up the blog!

I know I've talked a bit about the power of prayer before, but as life becomes a little more "normal" I've noticed my prayer life weakening. I think it's kind of like that for a lot of people. During a season of trials or during a time where they need something from God, we tend to pray a lot more. Then when the going gets good, it's easy to kind of kick back and say, "Hey, thanks God for having my back, but I got it now." It reminds me of a marathon runner like at the beginning of the race it's a breeze. You feel like you could run for days, and it's super easy until you get more towards the middle. Then you work up a sweat, your lungs begin to tighten a bit, and you are wishing you had a car. Then the going gets really rough, you hit this rough patch, and you close your eyes and wish for a car, you NEED a car. The car pulls up, you hop in and lay in the back seat, the whole time thanking the driver for rescuing you. As you rest you begin to regain your energy, soon you have enough stamina to finish the race. So, you hop out of the car and start running again. This time it's so easy, you forget you ever even got a ride.

Now, I've never have nor do I ever plan on running a marathon, but that's the image I get when I think of how my relationship with God can be. I was just dropped off to keep running, assuming I can do this on my own, thinking that it's no sweat. I got it. God is not a magic genie! Praying is not to be used only for the times we need something.

The Lord showed me the other day just how powerful prayer is, and He set me straight in reminding me that during this time of "normal", I still need to be praying without ceasing. I still need Him. He is still powerful even when I feel like I have the stamina to do it on my own! Wouldn't you much rather hop out of the car and continue running but have the car driving next to you, cheering you on, giving you water, and there if you need to rest? I sure would!

Oh, I forgot to let you in on how the Lord reminded me how powerful prayer is. I mentioned that I was concerned about living in Klamath for three months. What was I going to do? How would I be productive? What's the purpose? Then I prayed for the Lord to give me direction, to open opportunities. Then Sara came along and gave me the chance to work at Impressions Design, and I believe it will change my life. Working combined with the classes I'm taking, is making me excited for my future! I've already jumped into designing, and I love it.

> *Then when the going gets good, it's easy to kind of kick back and say, "Hey thanks God for having my back, but I got it now."*

On top of that, I was praying for my photography. I knew that I wanted to respect Sara and my new job so if it was going to be a conflict of interest I wasn't going to pursue my photography while I was here. Instead of going to the Lord about it, I started worrying. I talked to my mom about it, and right then and there she prayed. The next day I spoke to Sara about it, and she was more than supportive about me doing photography! The Lord just gently tapped me with the car while I was running, to say, "Oh yeah, hey I'm right here, I only want what's best for you, no big deal."

So, PRAY. Pray right now as you read these words, pray about one small thing that seems silly, pray for a worry you have, and pray for a person that you love. Watch as prayer will transform and bless your life!

I'm Afraid

October 9, 2015

I lied. Well, I didn't lie but kind of. I posted on Facebook a couple of nights ago that I had "GREAT NEWS!!!" That's not false, but my excitement was false. To be honest, I was exuding this false excitement to please people, because I should be excited and it would seem right to be excited, but I'm not.

The Tuesday before the day we drove home from Seattle, I got my blood test to see where my antibody level is post-treatment. Let me explain antibodies. Cancer is a disease. He's part of the Mafia in my body, and he's trying to gather more and more members for his gang. The more members, the more police have to come in to save the day. Antibodies are the police, and when I was first diagnosed I had lots of Mafia members trying to do bad things to my body. There were tons of cops everywhere trying to fight the Mafia off. A normal person has about 75 cops in their body because they don't have many bad guys, I had 5,726 cops in my body when I initially was diagnosed. Anyway, think of surgery and radiation as the reinforcements to the police, like a grenade or a gas bomb or a taser, because the cops can't do this on their own. They take this test every three months as a form of surveillance. If there are more police then they know there are still Mafia members roaming the streets of my body. If there are fewer cops then they know the treatment did its job and the Mafia is slowly being taken down. So, I get this test, and my doctor told me we'd be delighted with a 20% decrease in cops.

I got a call two days ago, and my levels didn't drop 20%...they dropped by 75%! Seventy-Five Percent! Now comes the part where I lied, or whatever you want to call it. You see I knew that this was excellent information, exciting even, I mean that's progress! I tried to portray the same feelings that I knew everyone else should have, but when I got the news, I felt nothing. Then I felt fear. Then insecurity. Then confusion. I haven't written in a couple of days because I still haven't figured out how I'm supposed to feel. I mean for the last 4 months I have been fighting off the Mafia. It's like for real-life cops, if there were no bad guys then what would they do? They would be happy that there were no bad guys in the world, but at the same time, they would be out of a job, out of a purpose.

I fear that I will lose my sense of purpose, and I have fear because for the last four months I have had so many people love and care for me that I'm afraid of being forgotten. I have anxiety because they didn't tell me I'm cured, and I may not be done fighting. I have fear because cancer has brought me to the foot of the cross and I'm afraid that I will drift away. I'm worried because I've found identity in being "that young girl with a blog who has cancer," and I have fear because I'm getting excited about a future with my new job and I'm starting to get expectations that I will have that future. I have concern for planning because what if it comes back? What if I get a husband, or have kids, or have my dream job and it comes back to take that from me?

I haven't been excited. I haven't been anything, in fact, I didn't blog about it right away because I was trying to wait until I was excited, but you know what? Transparency is a fantastic thing. This is where I'm at. I'm afraid.

Brushing Teeth with God

October 13, 2015

I'm still afraid, and I still don't know how to feel. The doctors say that ending treatment is sometimes harder than starting treatment, and I get that now. In the meantime, I just prayed that the Lord would give me opportunities and things to keep me busy while I sort out how to feel. I understand that this could be a lifelong battle, battling the fear of cancer. My Mom explained it very well saying, "It's kind of like a soldier who has been fighting a war in Iraq every day for four months. Then he comes back to the states and is supposed to fit into a "normal" life again when really, everything has changed." I mean it's so different, but that makes sense to me. It's just weird right now, just odd.

Anyway, I mentioned praying for opportunities to come my way, and BOY did He deliver! So, I'm taking my media classes and working for Impressions, which are both giant blessings, but now on top of that, I have finally launched my photography business! It's so exciting to see my dream take form. I mean I used to think that photography would never be something I could pursue seriously. But it's serious now guys, and it's so fulfilling and it makes me want cancer gone! By the way, for those of you who don't have Facebook, my photography website is haydencrebbinphotography.com if you want to see!

I had a birthday yesterday. While 22 is an underwhelming age, I realized that I have a new appreciation for my birthday. It's more than just another wrinkle, or another day where I'm hoping I still get a present, this time it's a marker of another year to come. That's so promising and so awesome, I mean yesterday will never happen again. I'll never turn 22 again. I'm happy that I got the chance to experience turning 22, despite all the Taylor Swift references.

I realized that time with God can come during the times that you don't necessarily expect it. For example, brushing your teeth, that's an easy way to set aside time with God, even just spending 2-5 minutes.

Things have been busy, and that's a blessing. With that though, I have noticed how hard it is to make time for God. Well actually that's not true, it's not hard to make time for God, it's hard to make myself make time for God. I want to sleep every extra minute that I can, and then I want to go to bed or watch an episode of Grey's Anatomy when I get home. But I realized that time with God can come during the times that you don't necessarily expect it. For example, brushing your teeth. That's two times set aside where you spend two to five minutes, depending on the person. So listen to a sermon, or an audio Bible during that time! During my drive, I've tried to utilize that time to spend some time with prayer instead of listening to the radio. While you're doing the dishes or cooking dinner, or even while you take a shower, turn that sermon or audio Bible on! So really that excuse of "I'm too busy" is just that, an excuse. I'm going to purpose to get creative and make time. You try it, too, and let me know if you have any other suggestions!

Cancer Camp

October 27, 2015

I haven't blogged a whole lot this month, because I haven't known what to say. I'm still confused. It's like I was this girl before, and now cancer shattered that and as I pick up the pieces and put them together, they fit, but they form a different girl. It's difficult, it's confusing, and I still don't understand what to do with that.

I spent the last week in Spokane, a week that was supposed to result in packing up my apartment and closing the door on Spokane. The moment I got there I knew I wasn't shutting any doors, in fact, I feared that I might open new doors. The week was everything I'd hoped for last time I was in Spokane. The community filled me, I was pouring out and being poured into, I had fun, I got a glimpse of the girl I was last year, and I was truly joyful. I felt revived in a sense, and I just felt that peace again, like if I was going to die soon that I would be okay with it. I honestly don't know how to explain it, but I really missed Spokane.

While I was there, I wrestled with this fear of losing cancer that I mentioned in my last post. I came up with yet another analogy. I guess

...I feared that losing cancer would mean losing all that I should be crediting God! Cancer is just a tool that God used!

I'm an analogy kind of girl. Do you remember how summer camp as a kid was just a magical time? Like, you go for a week, it's super intense, and you learn so much and feel all this passion and purpose for God and you are surrounded by like-minded people, and you feel almost invincible? Then you leave, and for the next two weeks, you still have that spiritual high and all of a sudden you get back to the mundane life, and you find yourself longing for camp again?

I was at cancer camp guys. I spent five months in this intense, emotional, on fire time and so much happened and now I am at the mundane point, longing for cancer camp again. BUT, as I wrestled with this concept, the Lord brought something else to light. I was crediting cancer for the growth, for impacting people, for all the love, for understanding my need for God, for changing my perspective on life, for blessing me, for challenging me, and I feared that losing cancer would mean losing all that. I should be crediting God! Cancer is just a tool that God used! I don't have to have cancer to see God at work, I don't have to have cancer to understand my absolute need for a Savior, and I don't need cancer to have a passion for the Lord and a purpose here on Earth. I have to have God, that's it, and He isn't going anywhere.

I'm still confused, I still struggle, I still have fear, but through it all, God is here, and He loves me. He is walking with me even though I doubt Him and even though I don't always trust Him. I challenge you to examine who you give credit to for the blessings and changes in your life. Your church? Your pastor? Camp? Cancer? Yourself? Give the glory to God you guys! Boy, does He deserve it.

I Haven't Moved On

November 3, 2015

I don't know what to do. I feel like for the past six months I've been able to focus on the physical and spiritual side of cancer, and now the mental part is coming into play. Only this time I don't have someone telling me what to do, I don't have a doctor telling me who to see or where to go. No one prepares you for this part of the journey.

I'm going to my analogy again: a soldier goes to Iraq for six months. While he's there, he is under the command of the general, being told where to go, when to go, who to see, and what to do. For six months he does what he's told and fights as hard as he can to live. Then one day, they put him on a plane and send him back to the states. He's sitting on his couch staring at the TV, watching the war he just fought replay over and over again, only this time he is helpless, left with nothing to do but watch. They expect him to go back to a desk job and move on with his life as if a flip of the switch makes everything normal again. It may be normal for everyone else, but not him. What is he supposed to do? How is he supposed to move on?

I'm just here, going to school, back into work, and while those things are presenting excellent and exciting opportunities, I'm left wondering what the heck I'm supposed to do. People see me and say, "Oh my gosh Hayden, you look so good! If I didn't know you I wouldn't have even known you went through all that you have been through!" or "You look so beautiful, you can hardly see the scars." or "You're back at school and working? It must be so nice to be doing normal things again and getting back into the swing of life."

Something emotional, spiritual, and life changing. I have been face to face with death. I have been changed, and I am no longer the person I was before.

While those things sound nice, I find myself just smiling and nodding. That's what we all know to be true. When I saw cancer survivors I used to think the same thing. I used to think, "Wow they look so good, it must be nice to be normal again." I used to think they just move on as if nothing ever happened. So that's what I expected to happen. I mean, I know that I haven't been told I'm cured. In fact, I won't be told that unless my tests are clear for the next five years. But still, being in this limbo place with no doctors or surgeries or tests, I expected to blend back into my previous life.

That's not the case. I can't just go back. Something did happen, something big and traumatic and scary. Something emotional, spiritual, and life-changing. I have been face to face with death. I have been changed, and I am no longer the person I was before. And now I am just left here, I feel like no one understands and I feel helpless. Not hopeless; otherwise I wouldn't even talk about this. I have hope, and tons of confidence that the Lord will help me and send me resources to get through this phase, but I need help. I want to be transparent, and this should be a phase that people talk about. It's real, and it's happening, and I'm not sugar coating or being ashamed. I don't know how to move on, yet I refuse to just exist from test to test.

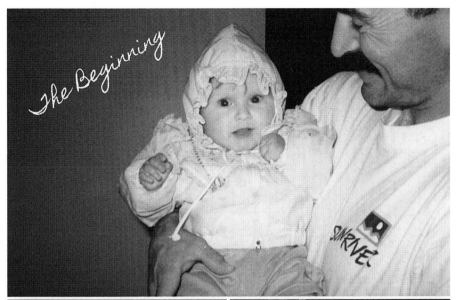

Camp Redwood Glen 2015

Palm Wedding
2016

Courageous Moments 2017

Death

November 5, 2015

I hate this. I hate not understanding, I hate being in a dry spot, I hate being afraid, I hate not being joyful, I hate it, and that's a good thing. I mean really, if I didn't hate the spot I'm in then I would be worried.

I sat at dinner today facing my reflection in the window. I stared at my face and I pictured that face under a veil getting married, I imagined that face smiling at her first baby, and I picture that face aging as she saw that baby off to college, I pictured that face surrounded by grey hair, but it wasn't my face. It wasn't my face because lately I have been terrified that I'm going to die.

It's crippled me while I'm driving when I'm watching careless teens out the window, or as I sit in class and listen to my professor, it's random. It's not even that I fear death. What I fear is dying here. In this town, with no friends, no ministry, no purpose, and in this "unjoyful" state.

Someone mentioned to me that reading my last post reminded them of that scene in Lord of The Rings where Sam, Pippin, and Merry move on with their lives and Frodo is kind of in another place. Then Frodo reveals that he is leaving to the undying elvish land and they don't understand. Then she mentioned that he writes in his diary, "Some wounds go too deep, some hurts too painful to mend." He was changed forever. I reflected on that scene (since I watch LOTR probably bi-monthly) and I immediately felt like for the first time I could relate to someone, and he isn't even real!

I am forcing myself to be transparent right now, and it's not easy admitting that I'm not okay. Through this whole journey, I've felt like I have trusted God and I have felt peace about the idea of dying.

It's not easy admitting that I'm not okay. Through this whole journey, I've felt like I have trusted God and I have felt peace about the idea of dying.

And I want to say, "I'm doing great" and fulfill people's expectations, but that's not what we're called to do. I can't get help if I'm not willing to admit that I need help. I want people to know about this phase of cancer, and I guarantee I'm not alone in these feelings and I know this is going to be a lifelong struggle.

I long and desire to be in Spokane. I long to serve in a church and be a part of a ministry, I long to have an authentic community that loves the Lord. During this time where I don't feel like I have much to say, I want to hear about what God is doing in other people's lives, I want to be encouraged by my brothers and sisters. But although I long for that, I want to be sure that I am not running away. If I have a heart issue, if I am going through some brutal sanctification, then moving to Spokane won't fix that. I am alone with God, and maybe that's precisely where I need to be.

Living Like I'm Dying

November 16, 2015

I've lacked the motivation and passion for blogging lately. I don't know why, I guess it's just hard to find that passion in the mundane. So, I've been praying that if the Lord wanted me to continue writing that He would re-ignite the passion and give me words. Boy, did He deliver. I had two people this week tell me that the blog helped them during a trial that they were going through, so even if I'm not necessarily blogging for me, I'm blogging for you, and that's just cool! We have those times sometimes. Our trials may not be to benefit, or grow, or change, or affect *us*, because they are meant for *others*. God uses our trials for the benefit of others.

I'm doing better about the whole death thing. I've been thinking, well it's more like I fear death less. Instead of living like I am dying in the negative, dwelling in a sadness type of way I decided to do the opposite - live like I'm dying in that I need to find joy and purpose in every day. Because really what's the point of this life if we don't find joy? Or we don't see a purpose, and if we don't live each day grateful for breath and for all that Jesus has done for us? We are supposed to live a life glorifying God and how do we glorify him if we just exist? If we wake up, go to work, come home, go to bed, and repeat, what's the point?

So, the practical steps that I've taken since my last blog are first of all thanking God for each day. I was really good about doing this at the beginning of my cancer journey, but as life has become a little less intense I haven't done a good job of finding ways to be grateful throughout the day. I like what Mame (my grandma) says, "Live like you can't take it with you." I haven't been as generous in "living like I'm dying" by blessing others with a gift or word or time or acts. I am turning that around too. Being generous has made me more joyful, as I bless others!

I am investing in people too. Instead of living like I'm dying in the negative way and kind of being like, "What's the point in getting to know them? It's not like it will be for long" or being offended that some people have fizzled out, I have lived like I'm dying in a positive way. I feel like that is all the more reason to invest deeply into people and allow God to use me in whatever way, and for whatever time, I have. None of us is promised tomorrow!

A friend of mine challenged my thinking the other night as I was sad, feeling like I don't have a lot to pour out right now. I wanted others to pour into me and waited for them to tell me what God is doing in their lives, but they weren't. He said, "What can you do about it?" I pondered that one for a minute and my response was, "Hmmm ask them what God's doing in their lives?" Then I started laughing as if the answer had been in front of my face the entire time!

So, I have been asking people that question instead of waiting for them to tell me. Let me tell ya, it's been so awesome! I challenge you to ask people that question this week in your conversations. It's a simple question, but it opens an opportunity to learn about our amazing God, to relate, to be transparent, to go beyond the surface, and to be a true sister or brother in Christ!

The truth is, we are all dying. We don't know when our time is. It's more in my face, yes, but we can all have this positive perspective to live like we are dying, it can challenge you and show you what is important in life. Getting wasted at a party. Is that your purpose in life? If you died right after would you feel like it was worth it? Going to work and being grumpy and mad all day because your coworkers are annoying? You can't change them so change you! Sleeping your way through college instead of soaking up everything there is to learn? Is that it? If you die is that enough? Anyway, the point is, examine your life through the lens of death (in a positive way) because we are all going to die. Find joy, glorify God, build relationships, have fun, be who you want to be NOW and live life to its absolute fullest!

Hola!

December 1, 2015

Hello strangers! You are probably tired of hearing me apologize for the delay in posts for the past month. I was reminded yesterday that this blog is beyond me and it is God's tool! I was in Big Lots, and this girl was helping me get something off the top shelf. She stopped and asked, "Are you that girl who posts things online, uh, Hayden?" I was surprised because it's been a while since the blog has been mentioned, especially because I haven't been writing weekly. She continued with, "My sister read your blog and called me one day crying her eyes out. She said that I have to read it because it's so inspirational!" It was an excellent reminder that the Lord has used and will continue to use my story. So, I have to keep writing it!

After my long and traumatic radiation treatment, Mom decided we needed a family vacation and she booked us a cruise to Mexico!!! We drove to LA and got on a huge ship to visit Cabo, Mazatlán, and Puerto Vallarta. We danced, swam, sunbathed, rode mules, saw sights, and we snorkeled. It was an over the top, brain resting, revitalizing vacation. You don't have to plan anything. You can eat whenever, whatever, wherever you want, and our room was so dark that I could sleep until midafternoon if I wished to. It was my dream!

It was also a brain break from cancer. I vowed the moment that I stepped onto the ship that I would forget that I have cancer, that I would forget all the stress and fear that I've been feeling and I would just relax and enjoy this vacation. It didn't work, you know why? Because cancer is a part of me now. But not in the way one may think. I mean sure it's potentially killing my body, but it's also a part of who I am now. It's my testimony, and it's a reminder to me that life is indeed precious and we have to use our time to glorify God, otherwise what's the point?

On the ship my sister and I shared a room, and like all sisters, we eventually got in an argument. I was taking everything my sister was saying personally. I was getting upset at things that never would have bothered me before. As we talked it out, I just started crying. I realized that I had cared way too much about what my family thinks of me. Because of my fear of death, I have been trying to leave them with a certain image of me. I want them to think I'm strong and that I'm ok, but

I vowed the moment that I stepped onto the ship that I would forget that I have cancer. It didn't work, you know why? Because cancer is a part of me now.

I'm not and I need to talk to them about my fears and about cancer and I've been afraid to let them down. We were able to talk about many things that were on my heart and holding me back. Cancer is still affecting me in ways I didn't even know.

With that said, I would ask that you pray for me because I have my test coming up in two weeks. I'm afraid of what I will find out, and as you all know Merkel has a high reoccurrence rate. It's been hard to know how to feel. I'm nervous, but then again, I have faith. I'm frustrated, yet I have peace. I've been in this limbo of "Maybe I'm cured, or maybe I still have cancer". This is the first time since radiation ended that I will see the doctors. I mean when you don't see doctors and you don't have tests and needles, and you aren't losing hair or getting burned, it's easy to feel normal. It's easy to slip into my old perspective on life. The attitude that I am an average 22-year-old with a bright future ahead and big plans, and I lose all sense of urgency. I don't ever want to forget that life is short and precious, that God is good and my life is for His glory. I don't want to forget to be grateful for every day, to find the wonder in everything, and to go for my dreams and do great things and not wait for tomorrow! To live my life.

Anyway, I challenge you guys to help keep me accountable to write! In my busyness, I lose motivation, and I want to write selflessly. If the Lord is going to use it, then I should be excited! Love ya!

I Remember

December 3, 2015

Today is my Mom's birthday and we had a lovely night celebrating her with a family dinner. She is an extraordinary person, and she has taught me how to be a better woman in Christ. I would not be the person I am today, and I could not go through this trial without her constant encouragement and care. So Happy Birthday, Mama! I love you!

But now I'm afraid that I'm ending my night on a different note. My Grandma is in the hospital, she just got a knee replacement surgery. It went well, don't worry! She is doing great, and she looks great. That's not why I ended my night in tears. I walked into the hospital for the first time since my surgery. It's amazing how our minds associate smells, noises, and scenes to specific memories.

All at once my mind flooded with images and memories of my surgery. I sat in the hospital room staring at the dripping IV bag, the buttons that control the up and down movement of the bed, the pull string for the nurse to come after you go to the bathroom, the hospital cup with lukewarm water. I haven't thought about my time in the hospital as vividly as I did tonight. I remember the fuzzy image of the nurse when I was coming out of 11-hour anesthesia. I remember how thirsty I was and not remembering where I was. I remember just praying that I would see my family and go back to sleep. I remember that first night, barely lucid as they filled my body with morphine and shoved a giant shot in my stomach every 8 hours. I re-

My Grandma is in the hospital, and she is doing great. That's not why I ended my night in tears. I walked into the hospital for the first time since my surgery. It's amazing how our minds associate smells, noises, and scenes to specific memories. All at once my mind flooded with images and memories of my surgery.

member the awful woman in the bed next to me, screaming and moaning about the noises and pain. I remember keeping my arms as straight as a board because I had double IV's and it hurt to bend them. I remember not being able to go pee, and the nurse had to watch me as I tried my hardest. I remember the silent celebration when I finally did pee, only to be embarrassed that the nurse had to clean up after me each time. I remember sitting up at night listening to the strange beeps and scrapes and thinking to myself, "I'm a cancer patient." I remember the pain as the nurse suctioned the drains going in through the back of my neck into my throat. I remember gazing into the mirror for the first time and seeing a black mass of stitches on a swollen face, and I didn't even recognize myself. I remember being humble and vulnerable as the nurse used towelette's to bathe me. I remember wondering if the days I spent in the hospital would be some of my last memories.

As I remembered I cried. I'm crying now. I don't know why, all I know is that I remembered.

Scan 1 of 20 (Claps from Strangers)

December 21, 2015

Update from Seattle! I want to start from the moment we stepped into the Collegiana. I mentioned before that our minds are amazing, the way a smell or sight can trigger a flood of memories, like when I went to the hospital to visit my grandma. We stayed in the same room that we stayed in when I did radiation. It was so weird stepping into the room and seeing the bed I lay in as I went through the changes and emotions from the effects of radiation. I looked at the chair next to the table where Mom and I made healthy food while "Cops" played in the background. It was a strange feeling. Not as emotional as the hospital was, but I had a lot of emotions swirling around my mind.

The first stop was at UW, Mom and I had only been there one time for my biopsy, but I spent a bit of time there with Traci, so that was quite a throwback for me! I went back to prep for my CT scan. Thinking that I'd get an IV for contrast, then the nurse hands me thing jug of pink liquid. "You have an hour to drink this." I went back to my seat and began to chug. Luckily, I'm a pro at this after chugging so much juice, and I had it down with no problem. I got the CT scan, and it was pretty standard; contrast still feels super funky. I left the test feeling hopeful, yet realistic. I used shopping and family to distract me from the lingering results. The next day I got a call, "I just want to let you know your CT results were clear". Relief was my initial feeling. But that relief was quickly overpowered with the reality that this scan was only one of the 20 I have left to clear. I found it hard to celebrate this small victory without letting the five years ahead drown my spirits.

My family and I were sitting in the food court when I decided to tell them. "WOOOOHOOOOO!!!!!" my Mom exclaimed so loud that the entire food court went silent and every head turned our way. Noticing our new audience, Mom shouted, "Her cancer scan was clear!" All of a sudden everyone in the food court and surrounding area started clapping for me. Then the tears came, and it felt like the entire mall was crying. After that people came up to congratulate me, and it was truly an awesome moment. The Lord gave me that moment to remember that this is a victory and no matter what might come, I have to take it one test at a time and choose to celebrate.

The following day was a day spent with the doctors at the Seattle Cancer Care Alliance. I want to mention that I am beyond blessed to have the team of doctors that I do. They care about me, they asked me about photography and wanted to know about graphic design, and they were excited to hear that I get to move back to Spokane. They have a notebook that they keep notes on more than just medical facts about me, and they are notes that make me a human in their minds, not just a medical case. What they had to say was not exactly what I expected...to be continued.

Mom shouted, "Her cancer scan was clear!" All of a sudden everyone in the food court and surrounding area started clapping for me. Then the tears came, and it felt like the entire mall was crying.

So, About My Accident

December 27, 2015

I was going to finish the part 2 to my other post, but then I got in a car accident, so I'm choosing to give you the inside scoop on that first.

On Christmas Eve I woke up to go to my physical therapy appointment. It was cold, snowy, and icy outside but I got in my car and proceeded to the route like always. It's funny how driving becomes like second nature and you don't have to think about pressing on the gas or clicking on your blinker. But I think people get into auto mode too often and choose not to think.

Anyway, I was driving down Shasta Way when an SUV slid past the stop sign into the road. It happened so fast yet it happened so slow. I had time to process what was about to occur yet I had no time to slam on my breaks. The blow came with great force, the moment my car hit the SUV my body jolted forward only to be met by two airbags. With my sight blocked by the blue of the airbags, I felt my car spinning, sliding across the ice like an ice skater, although much less graceful. Those few seconds as I spun into the other lane were the scariest seconds of my life. I knew what was happening, I was spinning into the oncoming traffic, yet I had no control.

I wondered if the next blow was going to cause my death. Was I going to get my legs pinned resulting in being paralyzed? Was I about to feel the glass shatter and the sharp pangs of glass stabbing me? Or was the other car going to swerve and miss me? I gripped the wheel, preparing myself for the next blow and I said a silent prayer for my family. The next blow came, hitting the front of my car and sending me into another spiral until my back tire hit the third car, jolting me to a stop. I felt no pain; I just felt shocked. I was frozen in terror as my body started shaking uncontrollably and a million movie car accidents flashed through my mind.

I remember the EMT's telling the people in the car not to move, in case your neck is broken. Was my neck broken? Could I move my toes? Was there blood? I didn't move to check. I stared straight ahead as smoke started to fill the car. The man outside kept asking me if I was okay, telling me to get out of the car because there was too much smoke. I searched frantically for my phone, praying that I could find it to call my family. I finally decided to get out, my legs were working, and I felt no pain. I started crying, uncontrollably. It was just a reaction, maybe from the shock. Maybe from the sight of my car smashed and mangled. I couldn't even recognize it as the car I just recently raved about. I felt numb, and I told the firemen and police and ambulance guys that I was fine. I just wanted to curl up and cry.

No one wants to stand around in the cold after that happens. But I wasn't hurt, even after all that, after my car was totaled. I walked away with some trauma and a few nice bruises. Once again, God protected me, He saved me. The other cars involved were okay; no one was hurt so praise God for that. After I was cleared from the ER I went home to celebrate Christmas Eve with my family, and I was so grateful that I wasn't in the hospital.

"It wasn't my fault, I didn't do anything wrong, and now I have to pay for a new car." HAHA, what a joke! The Lord's response to me, "Well, I paid for you, and I didn't do anything wrong. What about the cross huh? I DIED; I paid the ultimate sacrifice for the wrong that you do every single day."

The two days following the accident I had a range of emotions. I was grateful to be safe, and I was angry that I no longer have a car. I was frustrated that there is a long process to go through with the insurance. I have a huge problem with injustice and feeling like things "aren't fair." I didn't go through too much of this with cancer, but oh I sure felt this after the accident. The "Why ME?" The "Really God? After all I've been through!?" I'm still working through the anger I have. But in all this I still know and trust that God has a plan He sees the bigger picture, and He is working all things for my good. This is a part of that good, even though, gee, it doesn't feel good!

He REALLY humbled me in the midst of my anger yesterday. I was grumbling, shaking my fist at him saying, "It wasn't my fault, I didn't do anything wrong, and now I have to pay for a new car. Now I have to pay, and I didn't do anything wrong." HAH, what a joke! The Lord's response to me, "Well, I paid for you, and I didn't do anything wrong. What about the cross huh? I DIED; I paid the ultimate sacrifice for the wrong that you do every single day." Talk about a Christmas message that He delivered to me huh? Talk about the humbling truth of that if we are to live by Christ's example then I should react like Christ reacted, out of love. Out of a humble spirit seeking to glorify God. I have cancer, and I got in an accident, and at times I don't like it, and it doesn't seem fair. But at the end of the day, God knows what I need, and He never has and will never do anything to harm me. So I walk forward in that truth.

In that, please pray for me as I search for a new car! I am trying to move back to Spokane on the 6th and can't do so if I have no vehicle. I hope you all had a fabulous Christmas and I challenge you to remind yourself of the reason for the season. Love Ya!

Re-Diagnosed

January 20, 2016

I am weary. I feel discouraged. I feel weak. I feel frustrated. Merkel is back. I have two new tumors on my face and the biopsy results came back from the first one positive for cancer. Gosh, it was all like deja vu. At the biopsy the doctor claimed that it was just a cyst. I'd heard that before so this time I wasn't so quick to believe him. After the removal, he looked at me and sighed, "That didn't look like a cyst." I knew it. But they shipped a chunk of my face off to the pathologist, and I played the waiting game. There was hope this time since my CT scan and blood test were both clear. They wouldn't be clear if it were cancer, right? No. It can't be. Yesterday I sat there anxiously as I watched the doctor come in with the paper describing my condition in his hand. He looked up at me and told me that it was indeed Merkel. My heart sank; my mind began to buzz as I replayed this same moment just eight months ago, the first time I was diagnosed. The moment they told my 21-year-old body that I had cancer. It felt as though I was re-diagnosed and it hit me just as hard.

I can't do this alone. My human nature has already tempted me several times just to give up, to become cold and bitter and let this cancer kill me. I'm afraid of the road ahead. I'm so scared to go through this all over again. I'm angry. All those needles and electricity, the stitches and biopsies, the scraping, all that work to get my body even to function normally again and now I feel as though I'm pushed back to square one. Like you make it super far in that annoying leapfrog game only to get hit by the car and have to start from the beginning again. The only thing is, I was the kid that threw in the towel and didn't attempt it again. Or maybe it's like that athlete who loves to run. He's a great runner and one day he breaks his leg. He's strong though, and he fights

I am reminded that God is not cruel. He has known suffering as a man, He has empathy and He is crying for me. This time I do not have the strength to fight, God must be my strength, and I have surrendered it all to Him.

back. After months and months of trying, he finally can run again. He gets up on that track, listening for the sound of that gunshot beckoning him to move forward and, bam, breaks his leg again before he can even start. Does he try again?

Now I wait for the doctors. I wait for them to tell me what to do, where to go, who to see. I cried all day yesterday as I replayed surgery and biopsies and radiation and my skin melting off and my hair falling out, and tears came with every memory as I thought about repeating that nightmare. I don't want to, and I don't understand. But as I process through it all, I'm reminded that there was a tremendous blessing that came from all that pain. I am reminded that God is not cruel. He has known suffering as a man, He has empathy and He is crying for me. This time I do not have the strength to fight, God must be my strength, and I have surrendered it all to Him.

Dying

January 22, 2016

My laptop doesn't work anymore, and I am now forced to blog using my phone. I apologize in advance if there are more errors than usual, maybe I should start proofreading...

Anyway, I've been on a roller coaster of emotions the past few days. The day after my diagnosis was the worst. I spent the day crying, tears of anger, tears of frustration, tears of defeat, tears of surrender. Remember our friend the guttural cry? Yeah, he came back. Do you ever listen to yourself while you cry? Do you ever take a second to stop thinking and just listen? It makes me cry even more, as if I'm outside of myself. I think about how sad my cries sound, how broken this person is. I listen to my shortness of breath and the timid whimper as I inhale. The whole thing is just heartbreaking.

I've been in a battle with my human nature and God. That second day that I spent in tears, I was ready to give up. I was done. That's the first time I welcomed death, not just accepted death but embraced it. My thoughts scared me as I asked the Lord to end everything instead of making me start this all over again. I thought about heaven and how easy it would be to leave this Earth. I pondered the idea of just skipping treatment and letting cancer run its course until it killed me. Heaven. How often do we actually think about heaven? If I'm honest, I have been more excited to experience the earthly joys of getting married and having kids that I actually asked God not to let me die before that happened. I would rather have those things then go to heaven.

I'm reading this book by Tim Keller called, *Walking Through Pain and Suffering,* and he talks about how God has already given us the greatest gift; eternal life. I realized that I was thinking that the greatest gift would be for God to let me live long enough to have a family and I didn't even realize that He has already given me the greatest gift, the gift of eternal life, the gift of heaven. I had to fight to let my earthly joys go, I let my expectations die, and now I'm not afraid of death.

That second day something inside me broke, something inside me died, I was so tempted to become numb to it all. It would feel so good just to say "screw cancer" and give up. It's like in those war movies where you see the battlefield, like in *Lord of the Rings* when thousands of orcs surround their little army, yet they draw their swords ready to fight even though they have no chance. How come they don't just stand there and accept the blade? How come they don't just end it right there and avoid the whole fight? Why do they even decide to try?

That second day that I spent in tears, I was ready to give up. I was done. That's the first time I welcomed death, not just accepted death but embraced it. My thoughts scared me as I asked the Lord to end everything instead of making me start this all over again. I thought about heaven and how easy it would be to leave this Earth.

That day I replayed every event in my mind. The first surgery, the two biopsies, the 11-hour surgery, the recovery, the radiation, the burns, the electrocution, the needles, the scraping, and to think about hitting rewind and play it all over again. Why would I do that?

Then the Lord gave me a different perspective...

To Give Up or Not?

January 23, 2015

~~~~~~~~

It's interesting to me how cancer puts my faith on a fast track. When I think about who I was and where I was eight months ago, I am astounded at how much God has done. I mean that verse that talks about how perseverance in trials produces faith, it's so evident in my life. Today is only Saturday, and I have an entirely new perspective compared to where I was on Wednesday.

I left off on Wednesday's blog when I talked about wanting to give up. How I wanted cancer just to run its course and kill me. How I wanted to live the way I wanted, doing the things I wanted to do and then I could end it all without going through this all again. I mean that would be easy right? And comfortable, and selfish. So the next two days, I went through my day with the perspective of giving up. What did a seemingly fulfilling and satisfying life look like? As I went throughout my day, I realized that it was all kind of... disappointing. I went about the day wondering what my purpose was if I lived my life on my terms and for me? Everything became pointless and shallow as I saw it through the filter of "I'm going to die soon."

In the scope of dying, nothing seemed to matter. My new car, my makeup, what that one person thought of me, getting to go to a concert, getting a bunch of likes on Instagram, so what? If I die and turn into dust what does that matter?

I began to realize that a life without Christ has no purpose. What did it all amount too if we were only meant to live for ourselves and turn into dust?

I want to be the soldier that you can stand behind, the one that you cheer on to fight and the one that never gave up because it looked like the army was outnumbered. Besides, we have a pretty badass army with God on our side!

I pictured it all in my mind; these two paths that I could go down. The first giving up, letting cancer kill me. I would live the life I want to live, I wouldn't have to face this new battle, I would just die, and I wouldn't persevere. I thought about the message that was sending to everyone who is following my journey. How you would see this girl, who started out really well and then gave up. God would look like a cruel God who killed a 22-year-old girl, and no one would be encouraged to fight their own battle. All because I was afraid and too selfish to take the hard path.

Then I imagined the other path. The one where I fight, the one where I sing Gods praises and seek to bring glory to His name because that is my purpose in life. Cancer may still kill me, sure. But now you would see a girl who started out well and finished well because she realized that she can't do this. She never had the strength to fight this battle, but God gave her the strength, and because of that she fought and had faith that God has a perfect plan for her. You would see that God is a loving and merciful God that does not leave us to battle alone. You would then be encouraged in your trials to fight the good fight and persevere.

I don't want to be the soldier in a battle that willingly stepped into the Orc's blade. I want to be the soldier that you can stand behind, the one that you cheer on to fight, and the one that never gave up because it looked like the army was outnumbered. Besides, we have a pretty badass army with God on our side!

Mundane

February 5, 2016

I haven't been consistent in my blogging. It's something that you have all noticed, and it's something that I've seen, but I didn't take the time to think about why. Today several people told me about how the blog has helped them in some way, and I was just reminded that this is the Lord's tool, and if I don't write then I am not utilizing this gift! I think the main thing for me is that it's hard to find the motivation to write during the mundane. When big events aren't happening, or profound theological discoveries aren't being made, I don't feel like it's interesting enough to write. (Ha-ha not that I make them, but you know what I'm saying).

My Mom said something today that really stuck with me, "God is not mundane," Wow. How true is that? How often during my day does God show me how amazing He is by a beautiful mountain or a great discussion with a friend? So, I apologize for feeling inadequate, or for letting the insecurity of not writing an "awe-inspiring" post stop me from doing so.

I'm impatient. I hate the "hurry up and wait" part of this journey. The tumor in my face is growing rapidly, and now it's to the point where I can see it in my peripherals. Well, wait, if it's under your eye is it still peripheral? I don't know. Anyway, cancer is growing, and I'm sitting, and that's such a hard thing to do. I have an appointment for next Tuesday to figure out the details of my treatment plan, so I will keep you updated!

It's hard to find the motivation to write during the mundane. My Mom said something today that really stuck with me, "God is not mundane." Wow. How true is that?

I watched the old YouTube videos and cried today. Tears of joy actually, because God is SO good. I just meditated on His blessings as I sat and stared at my face, marred with black stitches, now bearing only the faint remnants of a mark. I felt refreshed with encouragement as I watched the video about the walkathon. I watched the video where I pulled chunks of my hair out, and I reached up to feel newly grown hair slowly but surely coming in. I reminisced on my depression in October, as I felt convinced that I was going to die before Christmas, as I was sitting in the living room at my awesome job in Spokane in FEBRUARY. Guys, God reminded me today that in this time of waiting and worrying that He is entirely in control. His plan is perfect, and it's never something that we would or could plan for ourselves. I'm going into round two of cancer, and I want to have the perspective that I get a second chance to be blessed beyond belief.

When I die

February 8, 2016

I've been thinking about death more lately. Not in a wrong way, it's just, death put's life into perspective a bit ya know? When you think about the fact that you're going to die, it puts your priorities and the people in your life in a new light. Anyway, as I was pondering these things the Lord gave me a really cool thought. When you die, you can't take anything with you. Success, knowledge, education, money, family, looks, material possessions, you can't take any of that with you. But what you CAN do is leave things behind. Every human around you is a soul, and you can leave something behind for that soul that will stay forever with them, even when you die. What a radical concept huh? I mean talk about living a purposeful and Christ-like life. When Jesus died on the cross He took nothing with Him, instead, He left EVERYTHING.

We have it all wrong these days, thinking that our lives amount to our success, or the knowledge we gain, or even the things we have. If you die and that was your focus and goal, then you will still leave the earth with nothing, and you will leave behind very little of value. Then what's the point? I want to live a life thinking about what I can leave behind. What can I give every soul that I come in contact with? How can I leave a little bit of Christ on the Earth?

C.S. Lewis says, "You don't have a soul. You are a soul. You have a body." I've been thinking about this a lot lately. How often do we view one another as souls? What even is a soul? According to the definition, a soul is the spiritual to immaterial part of a human being, regarded as immortal — the part of a human that is ETERNAL. Every interaction you have with a human is a chance to impact a soul. A soul that has an eternal future in heaven or hell. How does that change your perspective? How does that weigh on your heart? Does that affect how you see your students in a classroom? Does that affect how you look at your waiter?

> When you die, you can't take anything with you. Success, knowledge, education, money, family, looks, material possessions, you can't take any of that with you. But what you CAN do is leave things behind.

Does that change how you look at your co-workers? These aren't just bodies that merely exist; these are souls.

What a radical idea! We live in an agenda driven, selfish world. We care about what WE are doing or what WE want or where WE are going. We care about what WE have to gain, not what we have to leave behind. This has really challenged me lately as I struggle with taking the time to blog. This is what I can leave behind. The encouragement, the transparency, the hope, the words that God has given me. If I die, this is how I can leave a little something to each of your souls. I challenge you to think about that, think about what you can leave behind, and think about whether you treat people as bodies or souls.

I head to Seattle again tomorrow to get an ultrasound on the tumors in my face. They have to be at least 1 centimeter for me to be eligible for a clinical trial, so prayer warriors, please pray that I will qualify! Love you all!

Let's Go Round 2!

February 11, 2016

~~~~~~~~~

I feel good. I feel really good! I feel joyful today as I think about the tremendous blessings He's bestowed on me. One specifically that just floored me was a package I received from Tamara and some people from her bible study. They wrote me 50 notes of encouragement, and I just cried as I sat there in awe of the Lord's work through my journey. What an honor it is to witness His hand. He is so alive and real and at work in my life and the lives of others, so thank you Tamara and everyone who blessed me with those notes!

The Seattle update is that I really hate driving and driving alone especially, but I just prayed this time that the Lord would use that time to give me some peace, and He did! I listened to good preaching, good music, I stopped when I wanted, I prayed, and I just enjoyed the beauty of having some alone time on the beautiful drive.

The great news is that Seattle determined my current stage is Stage 3b, not Stage 4! The other spots in question were dismissed because they haven't changed in size. I formulated a plan with the doctors, although this is still a "hypothetical" plan because I have to pass all the eligibility requirements for the clinical trial. But I am hopeful! I go to Seattle again next week to get another CT scan, some blood work, labs, and an EKG. Once those results come back, if I meet the requirements then I will start the clinical trial the following week. For those of you who don't know, my clinical trial will be with an IV drug that treats my entire system. It's not yet

> *I received a package from Tamara and some people from her bible study. They wrote me 50 notes of encouragement, and I just cried as I sat there in awe of the Lord's work through my journey. What an honor it is to witness His hand. He is so alive and real and at work in my life and the lives of others, so thank you.*

FDA approved which is why it's called a trial and why there are so many specifications and special requirements. Being treated systemically is a HUGE advantage because I have a chance to get ahead of the cancer, rather than cleaning up the mess left behind. After two doses of the IV treatment I will then get surgery and then radiation. It's a little more involved than I expected, but one thing I have to remind myself of constantly is that it's TREATMENT, praise God that we even have options!

Prayer warriors, please pray that the screening will all be approved and I will be enrolled in the clinical trial! Thank you for the constant prayer and support, it truly has meant SO much to me throughout this journey. Love you all!

The Fire of Anxiety

February 19, 2016

I woke up this morning and looked at my face in the mirror. Yep, there setting upon my fair complexion lay two large spots, two ugly purple cancer lumps that have seen rapid growth in the last three months. I felt sick. Here I am playing the "hurry up and wait" game with the doctors and insurance, and while I wait for them to schedule my CT scan (with no sense of urgency I might add), I am just supposed to sit and watch my cancer grow. Man has it been a challenge. A challenge to my faith, a challenge to trust in the Lord, a challenge to rid myself of the anxiety that I have new lumps, a challenge to my patience, it's just challenging!

I'm in Seattle right now, and I feel as if I am a pawn in the cancer chess game. I have to follow the protocol to be enrolled in the clinical trial, so I don't have a choice. I need this CT scan. It was so encouraging to see my army of prayer warriors come together to cover me in prayer. I thought to myself, "With all these people praying all over the world, there's no way I won't get my CT scan!" but disappointment and frustration flooded my mind as I did not get the CT scan, how can that be?

The Lord did something for me in the midst of that frustration and anxiety. He reminded me that He is good and sovereign over everything. I reminisced on past events like having Traci at camp, Traci whose job before Salvation Army camp was to navigate CANCER patients through treatment. Then I remembered the disappointment I felt when I couldn't get into my surgery at Stanford on that Friday and had to wait until Tuesday, and how my surgery ended up taking 11 hours instead of 4 and they wouldn't have had time on Friday! I then remembered the time that I felt anxious about all the medical bills coming in, then through things like donations, bake sales, and the walkathon the Lord provided for our needs once again!

I then was reminded recently (thanks to Mom's post on Facebook) that I was getting anxious about the fact that I have to pay rent and utilities, but I haven't been able to work very much as I travel to and from Seattle. Then we received a call from Triad. The school secretary just happened to "find" $125 they forgot to give me after a bake sale they had. It so happens that the cost to cover my utilities for the rest of the year is $125.00. Then Maddie Hilyard organized a "miracle minute" at Henley and raised $900.00...the EXACT cost of my rent for the rest of the year. UMM WOW. And then, just today my church reached out and offered to pay for my CT scan! What a testimony to the Lord's goodness.

I could spend hours going through my journey and remembering the intricate ways the Lord has blessed me during this trial. Every blessing I choose to remember is a bucket of water poured on the fire of my anxiety. The Lord has comforted me with the promise that He will work ALL things together for our good. How can we not cling to that promise!? How can we not let that give us an everlasting peace? So my CT scan hasn't come together in MY timing and according to MY plan, but my God has a better plan, and I will choose to rest in that.

Thank you for your support and prayers! Please continue to pray for my CT scan to be available this Monday so I can get my first treatment on Tuesday, Lord willing!

I'll Keep You Safe

February 23, 2016

Today was one of the longest days I've had in a while. It started with an 8:30 meeting with the plastic surgeon to discuss my surgery post clinical trial. Then off to get some blood work done. Then on to the dreaded biopsy...

The biopsy is one of the most traumatic surgeries. Not only because I am awake, but also because everything is in my face directly next to my eye, nose, and ear. It's sensory overload like you wouldn't believe.

This particular time I had a lot of anxiety going into the procedure. We had trouble because I have built a resistance to numbing medicine and so I had to get 10 or more shots around my face, each one delivering a deep pinching pain. During the procedure, I closed my eyes to hold back tears, not because I was in pain but because I imagined myself as a "normal" 22-year-old.

I was thinking, "I shouldn't be here. I shouldn't be here getting my face cut up while a bunch of doctors hold out their containers, eager to collect my tissue like I'm just an experiment. I should be with my friends. I should be at a concert or work or in class. Not here Lord, not here." I started to cry as I tried to wish myself into another life, into another body not marred by yet another procedure.

"Hade I am using you to save people through this. Medically I am saving people by giving these doctors tissue to research and find a cure. Spiritually I am saving people through the testimony I have given you."

I tried to tune out the clipping of my flesh and the twisting of the knife. I put in my headphones to welcome the distraction of music, and the first thing I heard was, "I'll keep you safe."

The song continued, but I clung to the lyric, "I'll keep you safe" as if the Lord was holding my hand, as if He was wiping the blood off my cheek and saying, "I'll keep you safe."

Then, as my face was passed in pieces to each doctor, the Lord said to me, "Hade, I am using you to save people through this. Medically I am saving people by giving these doctors tissue to research and find a cure.

Spiritually I am saving people through the testimony I have given you. We can do this, let me be your strength and trust me, I have suffered too. I am crying here with you." And with that, I cried. I saved the guttural cry for the bath at home. Today was a hard day, it was painful, it was long, and the Lord is still good.

Oh, and I received my first infusion! So, the goal and hope is that this infusion with help shrink my tumors, so I don't have to get a huge surgery. Please pray that these tumors will shrink!

Only Hope

February 25, 2016

~~~~~~~~

Yesterday was a rough day! I woke up in Seattle and said good-bye to my parents. How blessed am I that they drove all the way from Klamath to support me during the biopsy and first infusion! And then I had to drive back to Spokane. Now I realize that I should be less annoyed by the drive and more grateful, my fellow Merkel fighter Rose has to fly from Kansas every two weeks! Who am I to complain about a five-hour drive!? Anyway, I persevered through without any complications, and it's an excellent opportunity to listen to preaching, practice my singing, and spend some time admiring the Lord's beautiful creation. At one point on my drive, the song "Only Hope" by Mandy Moore came on the radio.

For those of you who have seen *A Walk to Remember* you know exactly what song I'm talking about! I had a really cool moment, as I was singing along and thinking about the story (she has cancer in the movie), I looked up at the blue sky and I started crying. The lyrics were written by Switchfoot so I'm not sure if they are meant to be about God or not, but to me, at this moment, I sang the lyrics to the Lord:

> *"Sing to me the song of the stars*
> *Of Your galaxy dancing and laughing*
> *and laughing again*
> *When it feels like my dreams are so far*
> *Sing to me of the plans that You have for me over again*
> *And I lay my head back down*
> *And I lift my hands and pray*
> *To be only yours*
> *I pray to be only yours*
> *I know now you're my only hope"*

It sounds like a cheesy drama film when I say it out loud, and it was maybe a bad idea since I was driving, but all that aside I just love how it says, "I know now you're my only hope." It was a song of praise for me, praise as I admired the beauty of creation, praise as I drew breath, praise as I drove away from Seattle with the new medicine flowing through my veins, and praise as I found peace in the promise that the Lord has the BEST plan for me.

When I got home, I felt the day hit me like a semi-truck. I guess that's a bad analogy since I've never actually experienced that. Let me try again. When I got home, I felt like an actual cancer patient. I think it was a combination of the emotional stress, the traumatic biopsy, the new medicine, the long drive, and the stressful and sleepless nights. The doctors warned me that there was a possibility that I would have flu-like symptoms as a result of the new treatment. They were correct! My bones ached, I had chills, and I just felt blah. Praise the Lord that I had nothing on my agenda and I spent the rest of the day resting and drinking water.

Today I feel much better. I still feel a sense of exhaustion and my face is still pretty swollen, but I don't feel like I have the flu. Now we wait, once the swelling goes down, I should be able to tell within the next week if my tumors are growing or shrinking. Please, please continue to pray that they shrink! The doctors feel confident in this clinical trial and have seen overall good results; this time I am praying that I am not the 1% girl. BUT I am choosing to walk by faith because you know what, if my tumors don't shrink, God is still good. That is a fact that I want to have at the forefront of my mind always. I have a MOUNTAIN of blessings to prove that God has the best and perfect plan!

Thank you for your support. I have been humbled and encouraged by the comments, likes, shares, messages, and cards I've received! I came home yesterday after a hard day to find a stack of mail with letters of encouragement and even some cool gifts! What a cool blessing that comforted me in my time of feeling blah. Thank you to everyone who has taken the time to reach out to me, it has helped me stay motivated, and it helps me to remember that the Lord does have a purpose in all of this. Love ya!

Unexpected Surprise

February 29th, 2016

My tumors haven't changed in size. Now, this is a glass half empty or glass half full scenario. We can say YAY because no change means no growth, or we can say, Nay, because no change means no shrinkage. I'm choosing to stick with the good old YAY. It seems to get me further along. I had a good weekend full of friends and fun and feeling like a healthy 22-year-old. I didn't have any crazy fatigue, and I started working out! For those of you who don't know, I HATE working out. Or at least I used to. But for the first time in my life, I am working out to be healthy and to take care of my body. In the past, I used to work out only because I wanted to look like a Barbie and after three days with no results I'd give up and eat pizza. It was a daunting task that didn't provide instant gratification, so I hated it! I feel so much better now. I have been waking up early and doing my workout, and then I eat breakfast because I'm actually awake, and I have so much energy! I highly recommend it. Plus, it helps me make wise choices throughout the day because I will be tempted to eat a donut and a mini Jillian Michaels will appear on my shoulder and go, "DON'T you dare! Do you want to ruin all the hard work I just put you through? Move on." And I do.

So today was filled with many amazing blessings and surprises! Is that even a thing I should say? "And an unexpected surprise?" Aren't all surprises unexpected? Anyway, to start off the day I went to get an oil change which is usually a task that I dread because I hate feeling pressured to buy things that I know nothing about. I picked a place where I can drop my car off and wait in the lobby. I walked into this teeny room that smelled like stale coffee, and the background noise was from the T.V. playing a creepy children puppet show. I sat down after the man told me I would have an hour wait and I sighed. I quickly searched for my headphones and looked at my phone for entertainment. Then a girl from Moody and her mom walked in. Her mom had JUST been through a skin cancer scare, and we were all able to have a really amazing talk. We swapped encouragement and stories, and my dreaded oil change turned into a real blessing.

Then I was told by some students at KU that they would like to donate all the proceeds to this year's Mr. Pelican to my treatment! What the what!?! Oh my gosh, I was so humbled, and I am incredibly grateful. If you get the chance to attend, it's on March 11th and they always put on a great show. Then the Lord was like, "You know what Hade, I think I want to do some more for you." and I came home to mail, which you all know by now is one of my favorite things. I opened up some encouraging letters, I got a really thoughtful package, and then I opened a letter from a name I didn't recognize, and someone had donated $5,000. I blinked twice, three, four times thinking that I was crazy. No way, would someone be that generous? In no way do I deserve that blessing. In no way could I EVER repay all these people. I went from gratitude to a little bit of a panic. I was starting to think, "No, no, no Hade, you can't let all these people be so kind, you can't let all these people be so generous, you will never be able to give back, you can't accept it!"

I stopped, took a deep breath, and thought about the way I was ruining my blessings. At that moment I was robbing people of the chance to be Christlike at the opportunity to help. The Lord gave His LIFE for us, He gave absolutely everything, and He asks us to receive it for free! He asks nothing in return; in fact, we don't deserve it at all. I don't deserve your generosity or kindness, but that makes it that much better! You are all giving it because you love me. Jesus gave His life because He loves us. So how could I not be thrilled that what Jesus did is being modeled for me during this trial through you all! It's incredible and totally humbling, thank you. I have a new excitement as I am reminded today that the Lord has an intricate and good plan for me. Shrinkage or not. Cured or not. He is alive and He is working in all of us! The power of prayer is so evident to me. We were just praying for a financial blessing as I enter round 2 of this battle and the Lord has been more than faithful. Please be encouraged today my friends!

Baring Souls

March 2, 2016

The Lord has really challenged me to be transparent throughout this journey. To share my struggles, my praises, my sins, my strengths, to share everything with all of you. I am not only challenged to write it all down on a blog that I post for all of you to see, but I am also challenged to be transparent in person. This is not an easy thing to do. There are times when I really fight the Lord because I don't want to be vulnerable, or as some would say, "bare my soul." But as I have walked through this trial, I have realized the importance of being transparent.

It's sad to me to look at the church, at my school, and the Christian community in general and see so many people willing to say they are sinners but not willing to admit that they sin. There is a facade of perfection among us today, a wall that we put up so no one can see that we struggle. We say, "Hey, how are you?" and respond with, "Oh I'm doing well thanks" and we go on our merry way.

A friend of mine sent me a verse today, 1 Corinthians 1:10 and it reads, "I appeal to you, brothers and sisters, in the name of our Lord Jesus Christ, that all of you agree with one another in what you say and that there be no divisions among you, but that you be perfectly united in mind and thought." I know I have brought this up before, but I want to point out the word usage here. BROTHERS and SISTERS. I also want to point to the part that says "perfectly UNITED in mind and thought." This picture of a family, the family of Christ is to be united. How can we be united brothers and sisters if we aren't willing to share life, to be transparent and raw and real with one another? How are we supposed to support one another, encourage each other, mourn with each other, praise with each other, or even help one another if we all walk around with the, "everything is all right" mask on? We are all sinners. We are all the same sinners that deserve hell. I mean look at Paul, David, and Moses. These are men that God loved, that we respect, and yet, the Bible includes their sins! The Bible doesn't just show these men as people who went perfectly from point A to point Z. It shows the in between too! Why? Because it was no accident. Your struggles, your sin, their struggles their sin, it all serves a purpose. As brothers and sisters in Christ, our objective is to help

How are we supposed to support one another, encourage each other, mourn with each other, praise with each other, or even help one another if we all walk around with the, "Everything is all right" mask on? We are all sinners. We are all the same sinners that deserve hell.

one another become more Christ-like. Christ was the ultimate example of sacrifice, we need to sacrifice our pride, our facade of perfection, our need to be perfect, our hope to look pleasing to one another, and we need to become a united people. Let your walls come down and take the masks off.

I challenge you to go to a brother or a sister and initiate transparency. Be honest and talk about what is honestly going on in your life. You will be blessed and surprised by how much you will grow, and you will be in awe of how much God will do in others through you!

Down the Well

March 10, 2016

I'm sitting in my room gazing at the Christmas lights hanging over my bed. What is it about Christmas lights that can just make a room look ten times better? I'm not feeling too great, definitely better than yesterday but I still have the flu like symptoms from my last infusion. Last meaning previous AND LAST as in no more infusions for now! It feels so encouraging to have the new medicine in my body. The next step as you know is surgery which is scheduled for the 25th of this month. I have made the decision to not be worried, frustrated, discouraged, or anxious about my tumors until the moment before surgery because anything could happen between now and then! The Lord's will be done, that's all I ask.

I went to an awesome women's retreat this weekend. It's weird to say that out loud because I forget that I'm considered a woman now, it sounds so adult. The theme of the study was, "Having a Mary Heart in a Martha world" about the passage in Luke where it talks about how Martha was in the kitchen while Mary was sitting at the feet of Jesus. I'll get into that in another blog, and it was a beautifully convicting and challenging passage for me!

What I wanted to mention right now is that I felt so encouraged and amazed by this group of women that I got to spend the weekend with. For the last ten months, I've been here and there, and I haven't been able to invest long term in the community I'm in. At first, this bothered me, with the shallow kind of "hi and bye" relationships that I would form and I felt like there wasn't enough investment. But then as time went on, I realized that that the Lord puts people in our lives at the right time for the precise amount of time that we need them. Anyway, so going on this retreat was a refresher for my soul. I got to connect with women of all different seasons, and the Lord used each one to bless me in some way. As the weekend came to an end, I prayed that it wouldn't be one of those "camp" things where you share your heart with people because camp gets you in the spiritual mood, and then you leave and never hear from people again. And boy did He answer my prayer! I have received countless messages from the women, some of them brought me meals, I even got invited to Easter at one lady's house! That is family, you guys. These women hardly know me, yet they are coming around me like Aunts and caring for me. I just love this picture, and it's one that we are blessed to see in the family of Christ.

I'm going to butcher this saying a little bit, but my roommate told me that sympathy is staring down the well at your friend and saying, "I'm sorry you're stuck down there! It looks hard, but I'm rooting for ya!" And empathy is climbing down into the well to help your friend fight through the trouble. I have experienced so many of you having authentic empathy with me, and boy has it changed my journey. God is so good to give us each other. I challenge you to seek a brother or sister in need and climb into the well with them. Walk next to them and don't let their trial or heartache scare you. Don't run the other way or stand at the top of the well shouting your encouragement from afar.

Love you all!

Another Tumor

March 14, 2016

Well you guys, my tumors have grown. It's been interesting though, as I woke up and felt the size difference. I didn't have the urge to cry or to be angry, and my anxiety didn't paralyze me. I just kind of accepted it. Like I have peace right now and faith that the Lord will give me the strength to endure whatever happens on the 25th. I head back to Seattle on Sunday, and I get a CT scan on Monday morning. I have all the pre-surgery appointments on Tuesday, then Good Friday I head in for surgery. Just to recap, since my tumors seem to be growing that means the treatment hasn't worked (they could still shrink eventually!), and so I will have surgery to remove the tumors. The doctors will be removing so much tissue from my cheek area that they have to take fat from my stomach and do a fat graft so they can reconstruct my face. When I heard that I was like, "Please take all the fat you want! I won't miss it!" ha-ha. But in all genuineness, I am a little fearful. If it were anywhere else I wouldn't really care but, it's my face, the face that I've looked at for the last 22 years and it's already been through a lot.

So, I wrote that first part about 3 hours ago. After I saved it as a draft I sat down to work on my bible study about Job. As I was sitting there reading about Job's anguish and cry to God, I reached up to my face only to feel the small, familiar beginning of a new tumor. A 3rd tumor. My heart sank, a 3rd tumor means that the treatment didn't work. A 3rd tumor strips away the hope I had that although the tumors didn't shrink they could still be dead. I got in the car to head home and the guttural cry met me once again. I felt in that moment that the anguish that I just read about in Job was the same anguish I was experiencing right then. Fear flooded my mind as I felt hopeless. The tests, the biopsies, waiting for the trial while I let cancer grow in me only for it to fail? I felt terrified at the thought of treatment not working. What would that mean if I get it again? What would that mean for Stage 4? Then, as if that wasn't enough, Adam, the one person that I was looking to for comfort here, was diagnosed with the chicken pox today and cannot see me for ten days.

And on top of that, I've never had the chicken pox so there's a possibility that I will get it now. I am not in a processing place right now. I am at a loss. I am discouraged. I am frustrated. I am exhausted. I am disappointed. That's all I can say on the matter at this moment. I am just crying and seeking Gods strength to get me through. I am on my knees right now like Job saying, "Take this away, God. Please just take it away."

Another Surgery

March 25, 2016

My CT scan showed that I have a 4th tumor, and it's spread down to my neck. I'm sitting on the floor crying. I'm crying for the end of this day. It was a really wonderful day and if I go to sleep then I have to wake up to my world changing, yet again, tomorrow. So, I'm mourning the face that I see right now and the feelings I have right now. I feel like I just regained my confidence after the last surgery. Like I was finally starting to feel normal again, and now I'm diving into the unknown head first, and it's terrifying. I can't control anything about tomorrow, not the tumors, not the surgeon's hand, not the way my face gets put back together, not the future of the disease that is killing me. Nothing. Instead, all I can do is cry for today and know that I enjoyed every moment of it and go into tomorrow knowing that I have no control. Instead, I am putting my faith and trust in my God who does have total control. That's so hard though, and it's hard going into a day knowing that you will come out a different person. I gaze back and reminisce on the last surgery, and it was life-changing. The Lord used it for good, and with a lot of hard work, I am where I am today with confidence in my recovery. But I will forever be changed by the physical, emotional, and spiritual scars. So, I'm crying right now because I am afraid of who I am going to be tomorrow, and who I am letting go of today. Yet I know that the Lord will show me that my true identity is in Him.

My surgery is at 3:00 tomorrow, so please pray, please, please pray.

Post-Surgery

March 26, 2016

I haven't slept a full hour. Hospitals are absolutely the worst. AND I have another terrible roommate; remember I had that Pam chick last time? Why God, why? This new roommate has slept a total of 4 hours all the while talking and snoring in her sleep. When she wakes up she comes over to my side of the room to wash her hands every hour. At 3 this morning she walked over to my side to use the mirror to "clean out her nose because it was bloody." At four this morning she tried showing me her microscopic scar and in doing so flashed her entire breast. She laughs at the TV and at five this morning decided to call her family. She moans and groans and calls the nurse every five minutes, and currently she is wolfing down her breakfast which happens to be one of everything on the menu. All I want to do is sleep. Is that too much to ask?

Anyway, surgery went well, and I'm pretty sure it went longer than we expected because if I remember correctly, I got to my room at midnight. I don't remember much because when I am coming out of anesthesia, I am totally drunk. The doctors took off my head wrap this morning; sweet relief! Now I'm just so anxious to go home, but I have pulmonary edema and they have to make sure I'm okay. My face hurts and is pretty scary looking like last time. It was definitely more involved than I anticipated, but I am grateful to the Lord that He gave me enough strength to get through it yet again!

*"Do not grieve, for the joy of
the Lord is your* **strength"**

(Nehemiah 8:10)

Alone

March 31, 2016

I feel so much better today. I woke up feeling rested. My eye wasn't swollen shut, and I wasn't cloudy from the pain medication. This week has been a rough week for me, not physically but mentally. I rolled out of the hospital bed on Saturday afternoon, and Adam pushed my wheelchair up to my parent's van, I got in, and we drove straight to Klamath. My Mom has been a caring nurse, making sure I rest and pumping me full of good nutrition. Thanks to her I am on the fast track to healing! But even with all the care and love from my family here, I spent a lot of alone time.

Being still is super difficult for me. I realized this week that I am a planner and I like to feel productive. Staying home to "recover" and having alone time has been a scary place for me, a place full of anxiety and fear. If you have been a devoted follower of my blog you'll recall a similar time in November when I started feeling depressed because I felt convinced that I was going to die before Christmas. There's something about being home and not living my "normal" life, or maybe it's even just being home and watching as everyone else goes back to "normal" life. I start to get in my own head, and I start thinking about all the wonderful things in life that I will miss out on.

It's like I feel like I am a ticking time bomb, running out of time, and sitting at home "recovering" is just a waste of the precious time that I have. I convince myself that I am going to die here, laying in bed with my face cut open, doing nothing of significance or importance. I start to dream about a wedding and kids and what life would be like if I weren't ruled by the ticking timer of cancer inside telling me when I will be done. Alone in my room, alone with my thoughts, I start to feel the weight of my trial and suffering.

As I sit in the stillness and stare at the ugly popcorn ceiling in my room, it's like I imagine the cancer is eating up my body. You see the time I felt I was wasting by being alone, I could have really utilized that time to be alone with God. To be still and find peace in His presence. But I want to have control, and in the busyness and the mapped-out planner that I keep in my purse, I have the control, at least I feel like I do. I am doing the things that I want to do, and I am being productive, and the

Lord used this time to show me just how little control I genuinely do have. And when that is taken away from me, and I have time to see that, it's terrifying. It's scary because it forces me to give up the control and give it to God. To truly cast my burdens, to truly lean not on my understanding, but to rely on the God who knows the purpose He has for me and the perfect plan He has for my life. If I don't I will die alone, trapped in my fear and anxiety, and I will truly suffer.

It's like I feel like I am a ticking time bomb, running out of time, and sitting at home "recovering" is just a waste of the precious time that I have.

I look back on that time in November and think about all the events that took place up until this very moment. I got in a car wreck, I started dating Adam, I had a wonderful Christmas, I had a clear scan, I moved back to Spokane, I visited friends in Texas, I got a new car, I got re-diagnosed, and now I am in recovery from surgery number two. I could have never planned for those things to happen! In the midst of it all there were some really hard times, but as I look back on the tremendous blessings that came out of every single event, I just laugh at my tiny tunnel-vision view of my life. In November all I wanted was to live long enough to see another Christmas and move back to Spokane, and God did WAY more than that. So in these times of being still, I am challenged to meditate on the blessings, to look back on God's perfect plan unfolding, and to remind myself that I see a stitch in the giant blanket He is sewing.

Suffering Well

April 7, 2016

I'm so glad God gave us the book of Job. I'm finding myself continually referring back to his suffering as I contemplate my own. How remarkable is it that a story of a man who lived that long ago could be relevant to me today? The entire book and story are so interesting to me because you expect it to drive people away from God. I mean we finite humans don't want to deal with the discomfort of not understanding, and therefore we try to fabricate our answers. In this case, we read the book of Job, and most of us sit there and ask, "why?". And when we realize that the question isn't answered directly, we huff and puff and blame it on an uncompassionate God that allows bad things to happen to good people.

The beauty of the story is not that it answers "why" but answers "who." The story of Job points to Christ because ultimately, we will never know why we suffer. Instead, we can get to know the God who knows why. I mean sheesh the whole time Job was suffering, he had no idea that God was proving the devil wrong! He didn't know that there was a heavenly audience watching him and praising God alongside him. Job suffered well, and because of that, his suffering points us to God.

That so challenges me in my own trial. Lately, as I look upon the new marks marring my face, I have been asking why. I look at other girls who get to keep their lovely cheekbones or perfect complexion and wonder to myself why I had to be the one to get my face reconstructed not once, but twice, and as I go further and further into questioning why, I get more and more frustrated and depressed. I may never understand why I have cancer, but I can draw nearer to the God who knows why and the God who became human himself to experience suffering. As I look to God and my trial, I can suffer well and point others toward Him. So, don't look for the "why's" in your situation, I challenge you to look to the "who."

> *I may never understand why I have cancer, but I can draw nearer to the God who knows why and the God who became human himself to experience suffering.*

This week in Spokane has been very fulfilling and refreshing. It's so nice to be back at work and in the community. I'm taking it easy of course, but I feel energized! I head to Seattle next week for radiation, and my follow up appointments, so please pray that the radiation will do its job!

Being Hole-y

April 12, 2016

I like to have all my ducks in a row. I've been struggling with this need to control everything in my life, as a lot of us do. The Lord has been revealing to me that I am a very destination focused person and I don't enjoy the journey. I'm a "grass is greener on the other side" kind of person. The more I learn and grow, and the more life has its curveballs the more I realize that trying to control everything makes me frustrated, angry, fearful, annoyed, anxious, and hopeless. When I attempt to be in control, I don't suffer well. Heck, if I were in control I wouldn't suffer at all!

This Sunday my pastor said in his sermon, "Sometimes we are so obsessed with stopping the suffering that we don't learn anything from it." I had to meditate on that for a minute. That has been so true for me during this trial. The times when I want things to go my way (aka stopping the suffering) I start to desperately look for ways to reach my destination (being cured). It's easy when every day I get a new cancer cure sent to me. Eat this, spray that, avoid this, fly there, etc. The anxiety of the unknown begins to rob me of the joy in the journey. That is the cool thing about suffering though, it shows us just how little control we have. Instead, it takes our gaze off of ourselves, and our abilities (or lack of) and points is to God. Isn't there so much peace in that? God is powerful and mighty, and He is kind and all-knowing, He is empathetic and strong, He is perfect and wise. He is everything we aren't and most of all He is good, and He loves us. He even tells us that He is doing a GOOD work in us.

I can't stop this suffering, but I can control my perspective and focus on what I learn through the journey. It's like when you're on a road trip, if you are focused on the destination then time seems to drag on and you get restless. But if you focus on the journey, the beauty of creation, the good conversation, the memories in the music playing, then the destination doesn't become as important, and if you never arrive, at least, you made the most of the journey.

Suffering well means it's not about us and what we can or can't do or what we do or don't deserve. The moment you fix your eyes on you, man you will be met with a lot of self-pity and despair. But the moment you fix your eyes on God, you realize that the things on Earth don't matter. What God is doing for the eternal kingdom is ultimately what matters!

I get radiation tomorrow, and today I just had follow-up appointments from 7-4! It was an exhausting day. Oh, and they had to cut a chunk of my face out, hence the new gaping hole. Prayers that the hole will heal up nicely too would be appreciated! Love ya!

Whack-a-Mole

April 13, 2016

I had radiation today. It was so strange having that mesh mask squish my face again as I had experienced every day for six weeks. I lay there for an hour with my eyes closed, seeing only the flashes of light from the radiation machine and smelling that familiar toxic smell. It took me back to those days in Seattle. The person I was, even then, is so different from the person I am now. I reminisced on all that the Lord has done for me between then and now. How can I not look in awe at His goodness, faithfulness, and mercy! But I don't look back and think that of God because life went back to normal, or because it was easy or comfortable, I look back and think that because through tough times God made me a better person, a more Christ-like person.

Between then and now I was in a car wreck, I found a new tumor, I was re-diagnosed, I had two biopsies, I grew four tumors, I had major surgery, and today I got radiation. But God has been teaching me so much, things I wouldn't have learned had I not gone through all this suffering.

I know that you are good and faithful. You have given me the strength to overcome this suffering, and you will be faithful to continue.

For example, today after radiation my doctor looked at me and said, "We are playing whack-a-mole with these tumors right now. I want to prepare you that they very well may show up again on the right side." Shortly after hearing that, my right lymph node all of a sudden blew up to a golf ball size. Now in the past, I would have freaked out, I would have been angry, and I would have let my anxiety take over. This time it was different, this time I said, "God, you have brought me through this trial not once but twice now and I know that you are good and faithful. You have given me the strength to overcome this suffering, and you will be faithful to continue. If I have to face this a third time, please prepare me and allow me to see your goodness and your GOOD plan that is beyond my understanding. You know the reason why, and I will focus on the who." I have peace you guys, and man there is so much freedom in that. I don't know what this means yet, it could be a new tumor, or it could be a reaction from radiation, so please keep that in your prayers!

The Next 2 Months

April 21, 2016

I laughed when I first heard that my Bible study was about to dive into a 5-week study on the book of Esther. Esther? I mean how deep you can go with Esther? Heck, all I remember is the cute little Veggie Tales' story about Esther the singing asparagus. It's nice and all, but what is there to study? Oh boy, how finite my little brain is. Let me backtrack a little.

I'm back in Spokane, and my lymph node has gone down to a normal size, praise God! Now comes the two months wait period between all the treatment and the next scan and blood test. As I embark on my next two months of "normal life," I couldn't help but think about the last time I had this "recovery period." It was hard, and it was dark.

I remember the month of November, convincing myself that I was going to die before Christmas. I remember the depression that overwhelmed me as I thought about everything that I would miss out on. I remember coming home from a day spent at work and school and being frustrated that I felt I merely existed through the day and didn't live it. I remember feeling lost, feeling like I had just experienced months of trauma and doctors and people telling me where to go, who to see, how to live, and what to do. Then all of a sudden, they drop you off like nothing ever happened. They just expect you to go back to "regular" life as if your life hasn't changed dramatically. These next two months could easily be months that I spend in the dark.

> *I mean how deep you can go with Esther? Heck, all I remember is the cute little Veggie Tales' story about Esther the singing asparagus.*

As I read through the story of Esther, I was in awe at the divine providence shown throughout the story. It's almost too crazy to believe at times, the timing, the details, down to the simple fact that the King had to read the right page at the right time to be reminded of Mordecai saving him at the same moment that Haman was coming to ask the King to kill him! I mean what!? How could you read Esther and dismiss things as mere coincidences? I could totally relate to the story as I thought about the crazy ways God designed my own story, like Tracy being at camp, or getting diagnosed in California, or even the fact that this blog exists. In hindsight, it is undeniable that God's promise that He has a perfect plan for our good and His glory is one that we can take refuge in. But reading the book of Esther has challenged me. One thing you see in her character and that of Mordecai's character is that they didn't have to wait until the "hindsight aha moment," they trusted God regardless. They moved forward in faith even though for all they knew they could have been killed. They never had the opportunity to see every single little detail that God incorporated into His intricate design. With that being said, in hindsight, I can look back on the details of my own story, and I can without a doubt say that God has worked everything for my good and His glory, but I want to be like Esther and Mordecai and trust Him at the moment. I feel peace going into the next two months. I don't feel fearful that I'm not doing anything and I'm not looking to the doctor to tell me what to do. I am going to enjoy having a schedule, hanging my clothes in the closet, joining a Bible study, and doing things that I have truly missed! I am going to spend each day living and not existing, and I will move forward into the unknown, knowing that God is a good and sovereign God and He has an intricate design for my life.

Oh, I visited a naturopathic oncologist who advised me to put Manuka honey in my wound, it's strange, but it's healing!

Yummy Humble Pie

April 29, 2016

I am so, so, so happy to announce that I am writing this blog on a new laptop! Praise the Lord! It's amazing what God can do in your life if you commit to prayer and patience. He will always provide you guys, not in our timing, or in the way we expect it, but He is still faithful.

I feel like there has been a reoccurring theme in my sanctification lately. You know when God wants to get something in your brain, and it's brought up in every sermon you listen to, every book you read, and every person you talk to? Well, man, God has been driving home two points in my life lately:

1. I am so not in control, and He has a divine design that works everything together for our good.

2. Having a gospel-centered perspective will change your life.

I think I hit on the first point when I talked about my bible study going through the book of Esther, and how it caused me to reflect on my own life and see all the intricate and surprising ways the Lord has worked things together for my good. Apparently, that wasn't enough to get through to my prideful brain! I sat there with God, and I was like, "Yeah, okay, I gave up control God! I mean heck, I have cancer, talk about understanding just how little control I do have. Plus, I really do see how you've worked together every detail, isn't that enough?" I imagine He laughed, "Oh Hade, you haven't even scratched the surface, my friend." And I honestly haven't. You see, I don't have a choice when it comes to cancer, I'm pretty much forced to give up control! So, to humble me and show me that I don't have it all together, the Lord decided to use my relationship. Allow me to be vulnerable here and give you a taste of just how in control I think I am.

Adam and I have been dating for nearly five months, and I'd say we've been through thick and thin, but it mainly just feels like we've been through thick. Immediately after we made it through my second cancer battle, I got ahold of every book, article, podcast, and CD that I could find in hopes that I would find the formula to create the perfect husband and to create in me the ideal wife. You see, in my mind, if I could get all my ducks in a row, if I could just make the necessary changes in my timeline, then I could have the perfect wedding, the perfect marriage and I could do it all before I could potentially die. So, I (still claiming that I believe that God is in control) planned an August wedding, even though I wasn't engaged, and I fixed my eyes on Adam with every intention to mold him into the perfect husband in time for my perfect August wedding. If I could just read enough, if I could send him enough articles, if I could only find the right sermons, then everything would go as planned! With my eyes fixed on everything BUT GOD, I mostly attempted to become God. The only problem with that, well I'm an incredibly flawed human!

You know when God wants to get something in your brain, and its brought up in every sermon you listen to, every book you read, and every person you talk to?

Thankfully the Lord doesn't leave us in our flawed thinking, He humbles us, and then when we realize just how ugly our sin is, He transforms us, but not without some pain! So quickly my fantasy, my perfect little Hayden world, and my perfect Hayden relationship became not so perfect and definitely did NOT go according to MY plan...to be continued.

Yummy Humble Pie Pt. 2

May 3, 2016

Adam and I didn't break up! I didn't realize that my last blog came across that way! I was merely trying to paint a picture of my need for control. Sorry to those of you that had a small heart attack at the thought of us splitting up! Anyway, I was going to write a part 2, but as I sit here I realize that God is still doing serious work on my heart! But I will tell you this, a relationship involves two sinners, and two flawed humans. In my Hayden world that's not the case, I have really struggled with trying to be God and change and make Adam into the man I want him to be, which is pretty much Jesus! So here I was thinking that controlling every detail would be better than allowing God to be God and keep his promise that everything works together for our GOOD. Of course, the more I tried to control the more out of control things got. Ultimately, I gave up, I was like, "Okay God, everything I'm doing is just not working and I guess it's time I let you do something." As if He wasn't doing everything already. Then, after weeks of frustration and disappointment and dying to my selfish desire for control, Adam and I were driving to Leavenworth and on the way up we got in a little, disagreement let's say. I was about to tell him to turn around and take me home but I remembered the book, *The Meaning of Marriage* by Tim Keller (highly recommended read) and how they talk a lot about the importance of prayer and of a gospel mindset. I sat there ready to fight back. In my defensiveness I was ready to present my case and then I thought, "I am the biggest sinner in the room. I don't deserve God's grace, yet He gives it to me." And with that I chose to pray instead of respond, and after praying I picked up my current read, *The Silence of Adam* (another highly recommended book) and I opened to Chapter 9. As my eyes skimmed the page I felt as if the book was written for me for such a time as this! It was mind blowing you guys, God's divine providence was shown yet again. After reading the chapter to Adam, the Lord really did a lot in our hearts and relationship. I was blown away. I mean for weeks I tried to change things and failed, and here, at the very last moment, when I was ready to give up, the Lord had a much better plan. I guess all of this is to say, God has a PERFECT plan for WHATEVER you are going through. Trust that what He says is true and do not be anxious about anything! Pray without ceasing and ask the Lord to help you trust Him in the moment, even when it seems like it's hopeless. I am just in awe of God and I am so excited to grow in my faith, even though growing means He is going to give me more opportunity to practice…"If we knew what God knows, we would ask exactly for what He gives." -Tim Keller.

Pray without ceasing and ask the Lord to help you trust Him in the moment, even when it seems like its hopeless.

Anyway, I am feeling great physically! I am healing fast, and I am praying that my June scan will be clear so I can enjoy a treatment free summer. My labs from the naturopathic oncologist came back, and I had superb levels, thanks to nutrition! I was just Vitamin D deficient, no surprise there.

A HUGE prayer request would be for Adam. We are going to a doctor in Coeur d'Alene tomorrow to see if Adam has Lyme disease or not. Please pray that if it's not Lyme that we will get some answers, and if it is Lyme that the Lord would give us the strength and resources to move forward. Love you all!

The Faces of Suffering

May 12, 2016

I'm reflecting on the last 11 months of my cancer journey. Did you know I'm coming close to a year since my diagnosis!? And to think, I didn't know that I would live until that Christmas. Cancer has changed my life completely. I look at this series of pictures, the very first photo of the girl on the mountain. Man, I feel like I don't even know her anymore. I look at her and to think that one day, one diagnosis would change her life forever. She had no idea what was coming.

We don't have any idea what the future holds, I mean in Photo 1: I was a healthy 21-year-old. I had a beautiful smile that I wasn't satisfied with, I had a body and a face that I felt insecure about, and I was learning to love God more, but my relationship wasn't that deep. I was a planner, and I thought I had my life pretty well mapped out. I didn't even consider the possibility that my life could be any different.

Photo 2: I had just had my first biopsy. The doctor told me that she didn't know what the thing on my face was and that she couldn't even say it was benign, so I was moving forward with the possibility that I may have cancer. I was paralyzed in fear. I was walking in the dark just begging God that it was just a random weird tissue thing. I was working on my insecurity and was relieved that I just had a little scar.

Photo 3: My life was changed forever. I had to tell myself every day that I have cancer just because it didn't feel real. Life was all of a sudden not my own. I was ordered by doctors, whisked away to that biopsy and that PET scan and driving here and moving there. I was told that I had cancer all over the left side of my face and neck and that I would need radical surgery to remove it. My relationship with God became more profound than ever, and He became a real comfort and presence in my life. I began to let go of my control and take every moment as it came. I learned to be grateful for the little things in each day and not let the future worries drag me down. I let go of all insecurities, my face was altered forever, and I decided to post everything for the world to see. God used the blog in my willingness to share to do RADICAL things, and I even felt unworthy.

Photo 4: I was moved to Seattle to do six weeks of radiation. I watched as my summer days were filled with treatment, while my family and friends enjoyed camp and various summer activities. I began to get comfortable in the daily grind of therapy. Then I lost some of my hair. I had a moment of anger and moments of "Isn't this enough God!?" But then He would help me see the purpose in my suffering, and I would praise Him. My skin melted off, that was terrifying and painful. They don't warn you, ya know.

Photo 5: I was re-diagnosed the moment I moved back to Spokane. I was angry at God and I was weary. I was afraid because this time I knew (or thought I knew) what was ahead of me. I was now dating Adam, heck I never thought I would date anyone after Photo 3! The blog had nearly 100,000 views, and people from all over the world joined my prayer army. In God's mercy He allowed me to see that my suffering was bringing Him glory and growing the kingdom, what more could I ask?

He loves me, despite what the world says about suffering, He LOVES me. I am a changed woman, thank God for cancer.

Photo 6: I felt afraid, four new tumors. After two traumatic biopsies I was wheeled in for yet another face altering surgery. What would I look like afterward? Would I lose more of my smile? My eye function? My dimple? Would the scar heal nicely? Would Adam still love me? After surgery, I was shocked as I gazed into the mirror at a stranger again. What would be next?

Photo 7: The tissue in my face died. As I was healing, I noticed one black spot that just continued to look like zombie flesh. Thankfully I didn't lose any facial movement in my lip or eye, but I lost my dimple. That was sad. The doctor had to cut out the tissue until I had a gaping hole in my face. Really? Another thing? I prepared for the next two months, and I had a pretty positive attitude. I decided to enjoy the two months of peace rather than let anxiety rule like last time.

Photo 8: The Lord is GOOD. I look at the woman in Photo 8, and she looks nothing like the woman in Photo 1. Her physical appearance is different; she loves and trusts God more than she ever has; she is a cancer survivor of 11 months. She looks toward the future, and it's possible that cancer will kill her. It's possible that she will have to battle it again, and maybe even five more times. It's possible that she's done with cancer, and it's possible that she could have a family. While all things in the future are unclear and unknown, there is one thing she can say with confidence; "God is the same God He was when I was a healthy baby, and He's the same God He was when I was a rebellious teen. He is the same God He was when I went through the first battle with cancer, and He is a GOOD God that is never changing, and He will be the same God

I know in my future, whatever that brings. He has given me the strength to get through cancer not once but twice, and He will do the same for me in the future. He loves me, despite what the world says about suffering, He LOVES me."

I am a changed woman, thank God for cancer. Love you all.

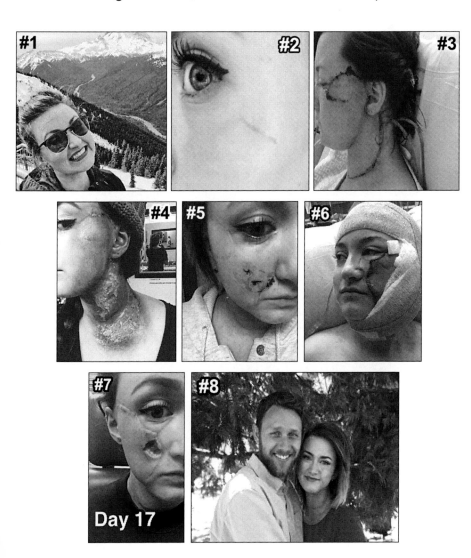

In Light of Eternity

May 14, 2016

I have been alive nearly 1-year post-cancer diagnosis. I am almost a one-year cancer survivor. I sit here and type that, and as the reality hits me, I want to cry. Yesterday I had a lot of alone time, which for me means reflecting time. I spent the day reading the book, *1000 Gifts* and thinking about the last year. In that book, the author talks a lot about the importance of having a heart of gratitude. She begins a list and writes down every little thing that she is thankful for. She also talks about how gratitude is cultivated out of remembrance, and as I remember this last year, I cannot help but swell with gratitude. I have not just scraped by this last year. I haven't just barely made it, no, I have lived another fantastic year, a fruitful year, a year that has been abundantly blessed.

Some may look at my year of cancer and say, "How can she be okay with this? She lost so much time, she lost so much money, she lost her smile, she lost some of her beauty, she lost her freedom, she nearly lost her life!" Sure, it's a temptation to think that way, but when I choose to have a heart of gratitude, to look at the cross, when I choose to have my mind set on eternity and on the truth that the purpose of the Christian life is to glorify Christ, I totally get Philippians 3:8 "What is more, I consider everything a loss because of the surpassing worth of knowing Christ Jesus my Lord, for whose sake I have lost all things. I consider them garbage, that I may gain Christ." Because while I may have lost some of the earthly things, in light of eternity it doesn't matter, look at what I have gained! I know God more intimately, and I have the opportunity to glorify Him with my life, and therefore God will bring others to know Him. So how can we say that I have lost?

Because while I may have lost some of the earthly things, in light of eternity it doesn't matter, look at what I have gained!

I encourage you to adopt the phrase, "In light of eternity does this matter?" Geeze, it has really given me a new perspective! It shows me that the things of this Earth, man they don't matter! Adam and I were driving and everywhere we looked there were these HUGE, STUNNING houses. Now initially, I envied the lives of the people living there. I would daydream about the rich and famous and wish that one day that could be me. This time as I caught myself becoming green with envy, I thought to myself, "In light of eternity, what does a big beautiful house matter?" It doesn't. Well if you aren't using it to glorify God, it means nothing. When you die it will just be left here, you can't take it with you. In light of eternity does (winning an argument with your hubby, getting that job promotion, taking that luxury vacation, dating the quarterback, you fill in the blank) matter? I totally get Philippians 3:8:

> *"What is more, I consider everything a loss because of the surpassing worth of knowing Christ Jesus my Lord, for whose sake I have lost all things. I consider them garbage, that I may gain Christ."*

It's Okay Not to Be Okay

June 1, 2016

I haven't been okay. There's something about this two-month wait-ing period in between scans that is hard for me. The past month I've been struggling with depression and insecurity. This time has been dif-ferent in that I don't have anxiety about the future as much as I am just dealing with the emotions from the past. I feel like a stranger, like an imposter. I look in the mirror, and I have a different face. The face that I was familiar with for 21 years is gone, not only is it gone, but it is never coming back. I can never go back.

There are times when I want to act like cancer is a broken leg, like it's just a season, and it will pass, just like getting your cast off, you then can move forward and look back and say, "Boy that was a crappy season of life!" But I realize that cancer isn't a season for me, there's no getting my cast off and moving on. I will never be rid of it, and I will never be told that I'm cured, I will never go back to the old and familiar me. I will always live with the possibility that it will come back, I will always have my scars, I will always have the memories, I will always have side effects of cancer. In one year my life has completely changed.

I cried all night as I looked through old photos of me smiling, teeth showing, skin radiant and smooth, eyes bright, and the guttural cry met me once again. I felt as if I was mourning the loss of the old me. I looked at that old girl and thought, "She was beautiful. If only she spent those years confident and not taking the fact that she can smile for granted." I can only take so much of the stares, of the lady at the grocery store gasping and asking what happened, of little kids pointing and asking their mom what's wrong with my face. I have fallen into the trap of com-parison. I am envious of the girl with the radiant smile, the one who lights up a room, whose laughter isn't held back by the paralysis in her lip. I am envious of the girl whose complexion is buttery and smooth, who can reach up and feel a gentle softness rather than the deep divots of a scar. I am envious of the girl who has beautiful cheekbones and a sym-metrical face. I am jealous of the girl whose biggest concern is finishing up a final and not wondering if she will get to enjoy her summer or spend it in the hospital.

I'm not okay right now. And for a long time, I haven't allowed myself to struggle. I haven't grieved. I've experienced trauma, and I have been through a lot in the last year. It is difficult for me even to type this out because I feel ashamed, I immediately tell myself, "How could you do this Hade? How could you think that? How could you say all these things when there are people who can't see or walk or talk?" How could you talk about how hard this is when Jesus gave you the ultimate gift of eternal life?" And when I am lying in my bed sobbing, I think that God is saying the same things to me. I don't picture Him holding me. I picture Him scolding me. You see, I'm not seeing God as an empathetic God, as a caring and compassionate God, as a God full of grace and as a God whose "strength is made perfect in my weakness." I haven't allowed God to hold me and say, "It's okay not to be okay Hade, I understand, and my heart hurts for you."

There are times when I want to act like cancer is a broken leg, like it's just a season, and it will pass, just like getting your cast off, you then can move forward and look back and say, "Boy that was a crappy season of life!"

If I See Another Needle...

June 13, 2016

Hello, and I know it's been awhile, I know I've kept you all eagerly waiting to see what's next in the life of Merkel girl! I went to Seattle last week for the dreaded monthly scan. Man, what a rough week. I often look at the things that happen in my life and wonder if I'm the only one who feels the theme of life is, "If it can go wrong it will go wrong," or "does it ever go right?" or "why can't things just go smoothly?". I started my week of appointments with my regular blood draw, eight vials of blood, chatting briefly with the nurse, (usually about how my favorite vein is just so plump and juicy) and then I went on my way to the next one. The rest of the day was pretty basic—radiology check-up, the CT scan and then home.

Tuesday, I saw the team and discussed my CT results, they also discussed what the next three months look like for me and all that good medical stuff. Off to the lab again because they forgot to order three of my blood tests (they could have had it done the previous day). The nurse was a nice woman, chatty as all get out but nice. She found my treasured vein and had no problem drawing my vile of blood. She cleaned up, and as she threw away the needle, she looked at the table with a horrified expression. "Oh, honey! I am so, so, sorry, but I forgot to draw the other two vials of blood! Here I was chatting away, and I forgot." I didn't even have the energy to react; why should I be surprised? Once again, she hit the good vein, drew more blood, and sent me on my way.

The next stop that day was the hospital. I had to get a special test done to see if I qualify for this T-Cell therapy so next time if I get diagnosed I have options. I lay on the bed and direct the nurse to my juicy vein. Usually, they gawk and awe over how easy it is to get an IV in there, not this time. This time she told me that it's shot, overworked, and messed up. This has never happened to me before, so I don't have a "Plan B" vein. She looks around and for some reason decides that the side of my elbow would be the best decision. The straight needle goes in and hits nothing, so she wiggles it around hoping to have success. After moving and shoving and coming up dry, she yanks it out and tries the other arm. At this point, I mentally checked out. There was no use in getting upset or focusing on the pain or even caring. With the straight needle in the left arm and an IV on the right, my blood began leaving my body. Four hours and 12 vials of blood later the test was finally finished. I was exhausted, frustrated, and ready to go postal as I sat in traffic for 40 minutes. In the back of my mind, I was clinging to the tiny bit of hope and relief that ahead of me I had only two appointments and they didn't involve needles!

I bet I'm not alone in questioning whether this life is worth it or not. I mean, cancer aside look at the world we live in. Suffering and heartache, death, shootings, insecurity, self-hatred, self-harm, bullying, drugs, having to put a freaking steering wheel lock in your car. It's enough to make anyone question!

The next morning, I had a visit with my plastic surgeon. Things were going well until he realized that my scar tissue was super tight. "I think we should inject some steroids to help the healing process." I'm sure I went dead in the face. Of course, why not, why am I even surprised? We walked to another room, the room where he cut a chunk of my face out, and he got the needle out. I leaned back and 1, 2, 3…7 shots to the face later, and I was holding back tears. Not really because of the pain, mainly in absolute frustration.

That night I went home defeated. I reached a serious breaking point. I walked into my room, closed the door, and cried that long, deep, cavity-shaking guttural cry. I told God that I was done and that I didn't want to live this life, this cancer life. That I was tired of the doctors and needles and tests and results and people and statistics and changes. That if I couldn't be a healthy 22-year-old with a normal life then it wasn't worth it for me. I told Him that I tried my best, that I did everything He wanted. I wondered what dying would be like, and I thought about ending it all. Would it be that bad just to be done? Would it be so terrible if the Lord just made my heart stop, so I don't have to do this anymore? It may sound extreme, but I'm willing to be transparent and vulnerable here because I bet I'm not alone in questioning whether this life is worth it or not. I mean, cancer aside look at the world we live in. Suffering and heartache, death, shootings, insecurity, self-hatred, self-harm, bullying, drugs, having to put a freaking steering wheel lock in your car. It's enough to make anyone question!

As I wrestled with this, I was reminded that we were not made for this Earth. Suffering is a promised part of this Christian life, and this is not "our best life now." I know we're supposed to look to Jesus for our hope and strength and continue to trust God's plan for our lives. But today I just can't.

Oh, and in case you're wondering, my scan was clear! So we celebrate for another small victory.

Is Hade Still Alive!?

August 10, 2016

Wow, well you guys, I am still alive! In fact, I'm more than just alive, I'm alive and well! This summer has been a breath of fresh air, a cold drink of water, and I have spent the last two months feeling like a "normal" 22-year-old. God has been so gracious to give me a break from doctors and tumors and cancer. But bigger and better than all of that is, I'm getting married! Yes, you read it right. For those of you who don't follow me on Facebook, Adam and I are getting married in 17 days.

We've been planning on an August wedding since April, but we set the date in June and got officially engaged in July. It was kind of backward, but who would expect anything different from me?! We set the date before the engagement because unlike "normal" people, we have to plan around scans and treatment, so, August 27th seemed to be the perfect day before the medical chaos.

Let me share my engagement ring story with you. My ring is beyond beautiful and everything I could dream. It's unique and was worth the long wait! Let me explain:

Sometime in June, I posted a picture of Adam and I announcing our engagement. Many of you didn't notice that I was covering my left hand! Hahaha, and that was because I didn't have the ring yet, and I wasn't sure when it was coming. Week after week passed and I was going out of my mind. You see, I thought I already knew what ring I was getting — more explanation needed here. About five years ago, Adam had purchased a ring for this girl that he used to date and decided not to propose, so she never even knew a ring existed. He tried to sell it and had no luck, so he kept it through the years. When he told me about it, I wanted to see this ring. It was a beautiful ring, and it fit me and being the bargain-brained person that I am I told him that if we fall in love, and he ever proposes to me that he could use that ring and save his money. I had no idea that we would actually get engaged at this point.

Time continues, and Adam is the man of my dreams. He graduates from Moody Bible Institute in Spokane in May, and Adam packs up his stuff to move to Klamath Falls. He got a job with my aunt and uncle working at their zip line, and he moves in with my grandma Mame and lives with Chandler's future husband, Alec. It was the most wonderful time for all of us.

It's June now, and Adam asks my dad if he can marry me. Dad says yes, and we set a date in August at my parents' house. I assume Adam will ask me to marry him any day now and use the ring he had from years ago. So I wait, and dream, and wait some more. I don't like to wait. I'm a mover and a shaker so I'm having a freak-out. What's he doing? Dad said yes, we have a date and now we're getting our engagement photo taken—but NO RING. Torture.

Fast forward to July, and it was so hard for me because I was telling people I was getting married but had no ring on! I found myself sticking my hand in my pocket or conveniently running it through my hair, anything to avoid the glance at my left finger and the look of confusion. Adam felt so terrible, he didn't want to give anything away, but he just told me to trust that that the day will come and he is working on it. But I was thinking, what's there to work on!? You have a ring!

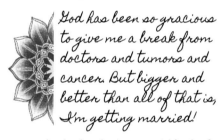
God has been so gracious to give me a break from doctors and tumors and cancer. But bigger and better than all of that is, I'm getting married!

The day was upon us, July 25th. I knew it would be the day because Adam asked me to take work off. He picked me up in the morning after cleaning my car, and then we drove to Ashland. The whole time I was trying to plan a reaction. I mean, I'm a control freak you guys, but also because I kind of suck at reactions to gifts and surprises and I usually practice in the mirror. We get to Lithia Park over in Ashland and Adam takes out a complete picnic set. We found this beautiful secluded spot by the creek and lay out the blanket. Next thing I know rose petals are being scattered around me, and I wonder who made that a thing, you know, rose petals being the essence of romance? Anyway, we then enjoyed a picnic lunch and the whole time I kept trying to stall. I had been waiting for this moment for weeks, why was I now trying to stall!? Well, I guess I was trying to savor the moment. If you're like me, we dream about this moment. We watch YouTube proposals and long for the Bachelor proposal, we romanticize the Nicholas Sparks moment, so I wanted to savor it.

Finally, it was time. Adam read a letter he wrote to me, and I held back tears - I mean makeup people. Can't have mascara everywhere LOL. Then he cleverly had me open a gift while he got the ring out and BAM! He's down on one knee. The truth is the actual down-on-one-knee part lasts for a second. I mean in movies and stuff it seems like that is an everlasting moment, but maybe that's because I practically said yes before he could get the words out!

When he opened the little black box, LIGHTING STRUCK THE EARTH, AND ALL HUMANS WENT BLIND. That ring though! It was the most beautiful thing I had ever seen in my life. It was more than I could have dreamed!

It turns out, it wasn't good enough for Adam to give me an old ring. He wanted me to have something personal and extraordinary. He wanted to show me how much he loves me by putting in time and effort to creating my dream. He sure did accomplish that. The ring is a halo set that was custom built by Holliday Jewelry. The middle diamond is from Adam, but the outer diamonds are from a ring that I inherited from my lovely grandmother Mame. Adam had the jewelers put my grandmother's diamonds into a ring that would be a keepsake to me. It couldn't be more special to me, and to think that I have a piece that also reminds me of Mame, I have no words. It was well worth the awkwardness, and the wait!

So, I'm engaged, with a ring beyond my dreams and a man that is my hero and the love of my life. It's the stuff dreams are made of.

I'm so excited to marry the love of my life! Thank you, God!

Hayden Palm

September 24, 2016

Hello blog world and virtual family! Man, where to even begin. The last month has been packed full to the brim, and I mean overflowing with news and happenings.

To keep from writing a book, I will give you a general overview of life lately. Number one thing is, I GOT MARRIED! Yep, married the love of my life Adam Palm on August 27th. It was fast and furious. But hey, when you know you know. After all we've been through together, it was the perfect next move for us. Then we went on a ten-day honeymoon to Costa Rica, man what a blast! It was a beautiful trip and such an excellent way to relax and recoup after the wedding craziness. Then we had one day before we left for Seattle. In that one day, we looked at what felt like a bazillion houses. Feeling discouraged at Klamath's rental market we left for Seattle thinking we'd never find a home.

In Seattle, I had my routine scan and blood test, although this time we got to attend the Merkel dinner. Man, what an awesome event. To think that I attended last year as a girl amid radiation treatments, and I got to return as a married woman and a survivor of 1 year. God is GOOD. The dinner was awesome. I adore seeing my Merkel family like Rose, Jim, Steve, Phyllis, Carol, and Don. It's a fantastic feeling to look around the room (even though it's mostly old white guys) and see people that know exactly what I'm going through. It's a room full of hope. Hope that we can all fight this, hope in that we have all fought this and as long as we sit at the dinner table we are winning. Everyone remembered me as the "girl who spoke last year." I mean I kind of stand out, being the youngest and a woman. My scans came back clear! Man, what a huge weight lifted. Tumor-free for another three months. When the doctors left the room, Adam leaped up in excitement, and it's so cool to have my best friend by my side for life.

So now I am in Klamath Falls, man it's just a black hole! It's the town you vow to leave but always come back too. Adam and I ended up finding the cutest little rental. Well, cute now. It's an old house with some, let's just say "character." But it's a good starter home. Adam is starting work as a substitute, and he starts EMT classes at the end of this month. I'm not quite sure what I'm doing yet. Photography is in full swing, and

God has blessed the business a lot! It's so nice to be doing "real" life. Having three months of peace is the best feeling in the world. God has been so gracious to us during the first month of our marriage. People have been extraordinarily generous and very helpful. I will never cease to be amazed at how God uses a community to enrich my life. Thank you for being there for me through EVERYTHING. And for hanging in there as I let the craziness of life affect my blogging. God is showing me that it's important to share what is going on in our lives with each other. The good and the bad. Every part, and so I want to challenge myself to share the good with you guys. It's easier for me to write about the bad and the hard times. But boy, right now the times are good, and I want to PRAISE God with you all!

Here's to the next chapter of the Merkel Miracle, starting as Mrs. Palm. Love ya!

Round 3

September 27, 2016

Round 3. I can't believe I'm even writing this blog. Cancer was a far-off memory, a nightmare that I haven't thought about. The summer was pure bliss. A little slice of cancer-free heaven. I felt so much peace and joy that I forgot about the evil little disease floating around my body, searching for the next cell to attack. A wedding, a honeymoon, and a clear scan. Talk about excitement, and then this weekend as my hand caressed the bottom of my chin, I felt a familiar, round, lump. A tumor.

My mind went into a whirl, directly outside of the faint little scar, right next to the area fried by radiation, a small tumor has staked its claim.

Round 3.

That's the thing about Merkel, it's not a "one and done" kind of cancer. Each diagnosis, each battle feels like I've been diagnosed with cancer all over again. I keep repeating "Round 3" in my mind. In less than two years I will have battled this cancer three times. I hate it. I hate the dread paired with finding a new tumor. I hate looking in the mirror and wondering what new scar this will add to the collection. What new terror will this behold?

I had to tell my husband and my family. That's probably one of the most hurtful parts of this entire ordeal. Walking into the house knowing that I was about to deliver the worst news to them. Turning their ordinary, happy day, into one of despair. Seeing the look on their faces, the gaze you recognize as their heart just dropped into the pit of their stomach.

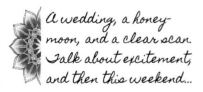
A wedding, a honeymoon, and a clear scan. Talk about excitement, and then this weekend...

Seeing the tears involuntarily rush down their cheeks and seeing them experience the guttural cry. I gazed around the room as I looked upon my mom and dad, my sister and Alec, and my husband. In the midst of all the pain, I couldn't help but feel so much gratitude. These people are the soldiers on the front line, and yet I can't imagine how many warriors back them up. How many prayers will go up when I post this hard news? How many people will cry out to God in despair on my behalf? How many people will be more grateful and cling to the Lord? That I'll never know.

When Adam and I were sitting on my couch, I paused crying for a moment and thought, "What can we do this time? How can we fight better? How can we glorify God more? How can we trust more? What do you want God?" See even though my heart is broken because I have another battle ahead of me, I have an advantage. I serve a warrior God. A God that couldn't love me more and a God who doesn't waste a moment of my time or leave one of my tears unaccounted for. The 3rd time is the charm they say. I can't wait to see how will God use cancer to bless me this time. I love you all!

Frustrating Fly

September 28, 2016

I went to a little BBQ last night at my parents' house. I usually love being social, people fuel me, but not last night. I just wanted to go home and curl up in my fluffy white comforter, in my safety. I asked myself why I wanted to seclude myself, and I know that being alone in my mind is a horrible place during these times. Once again, I came up with an analogy...

We are all running on the grass, running the race of life. Somewhere along my race I tripped on a little tiny pebble (my tumor) and fell into the mud. Now, this is nasty, sticky mud that's nearly impossible to get out of. I'm stuck in the middle of the grass, in this mud pit. I can't move, but I can watch everyone around me run freely on the grass. At times people will stop and wave to me and shout, "I wish we could help you!" But their race continues. Mine doesn't, and it's paused. Whether it's a temporary pause or a permanent pause, I'm not sure. But it's hard for me to be around people during this time. I'm envious. I was running in the grass. My path was marked. Marriage. Job. Family. I got married, and I had several job opportunities in line. I was set to be a "normal" person again. I even had kids on my mind. After all, I just had to be clear for a year before I could get pregnant. Four months down. And then this tiny lump appears in my neck.

How can such a small thing cause so much damage? That's been my question lately. I mean a little bump threatens my life, it wrecks all my plans, it causes so much pain and despair. This tiny lump that feels as though I could pluck it out and move on with my life is actually enough to kill me. It's frustrating. It's like that fly in your house. That big, juicy fly that makes the loudest buzzing. Life is beautiful until you see it one day. Then it's all you can think about. It's all you can hear. It distracts you

I had a plan. And at this very moment, I don't see how God's plan is better. I am forced to think about Job. He and I are becoming terrific friends. The hits just kept on coming for Job (like Merkel keeps coming for me), yet God had a much bigger and better plan.

from everything you're doing. You lose sleep. You follow it with your eyes. You use every household item to kill it. A fly swatter, a towel, hairspray, a cup, and yet it escapes you every time. It could have been there for weeks, but now that you know about it you are obsessed. There's a fly in my neck. In fact, I just found out; there are two.

I'm having a hard time trusting God. My plan seemed so perfect. I was going to work part-time to help Adam and allow him to go to school. I was going to learn to be a good wife. I was going to cook more. I was going to take a photography class. I was going to join the worship team again. I had a plan. And at this very moment, I don't see how God's plan is better. I am forced to think about Job. He and I are becoming terrific friends. The hits just kept on coming for Job (like Merkel keeps coming for me), yet God had a much bigger and better plan.

I'm going to Sky Lakes Hospital in Klamath Falls for an ultrasound-guided needle biopsy at 8 a.m. tomorrow. I'm honestly dreading it. It hurts. And in a way, it brings back awful memories of my first diagnosis. They jab this giant needle in your neck and plunge it back and forth. But I am trying to be grateful that God gave me an appointment so soon, especially since a second tumor has already emerged. Sheesh, Merkel is aggressive! Thank you for all the prayers and support already. If you could lift up my biopsy to God in prayer I would appreciate it so much. And pray that it doesn't hurt or that I fall asleep or something! Love you all.

I Want the American Dream

September 30, 2016

Last night I panicked. I panicked over finances, I panicked over change, I panicked over being a new wife, I panicked over not being able to work, I panicked over the biopsy, I panicked over the next battle I am about to face, I panicked over the unknown.

As Adam and I sat in the car in front of our house, I began to cry for the 30th time since my recent diagnosis. He asked me what was wrong. It was hard to be honest with him, but through tears I told him that if I trust God all the panic and anxiety wouldn't be there. But I don't trust him, and I refuse to be humble because right now I'm mad at Him. He then asked me if I've complained to God yet? He reminded me of David in the Psalms, crying out in anger to the Lord. What an amazing husband God has gifted me with. So as worship music filled the car, I closed my tear-filled eyes, and I complained.

It felt odd at first, not that I haven't been mad at God before, but telling Him about it directly was kind of a new thing. As I started my prayer, "God, I'm super mad at you. I'm frustrated and confused and I don't want to do this. Why me? Why me again? Why me a third time?" I froze.

A question plagued my mind. Why am I so mad at God? I didn't want to answer. But as the Holy Spirit probed further my only answer was, "I'm mad at God because He took away my comfort." Immediately I cried "Yes, because He took away my comfort." I mean if I'm honest, honest to the depths of my soul, I want to be normal. Take that further, and I want to be what our world says is comfortable. I want the cookie cutter, I want the American dream, I want the white picket fence. I cringed at the thought. For the last four months I've been comfortable, and in that comfort, joy came easily. Now that... all this crap has hit the fan...it's hard to find joy. Therefore, I'm mad at God. I'm uncomfortable, and that makes me angry.

Suddenly I was tempted to feel ashamed. I know that God is an empathetic God, I'm learning that at least. He wasn't sitting there as I complained to Him going, "Well Hade, you know what? Just suck it up and glorify me already. Why do you have to be so stubborn and difficult all the time?" Nope. He said, "I know my sweet daughter, cry, be frustrated, be in pain and anguish, I am too. I hate evil and the disease in this world. I hate that you are suffering." After a long while, I paused to wipe the tears from my eyes, and I smiled.

Then JOY.

I could smile at that moment because God is the constant source of our joy. Or He should be. So, in the comfortable or the uncomfortable, in the beautiful and the ugly, in the stability or the chaos, He is unchanging. And I sit here, after a long, exhausting day. After yet another biopsy, after another IV, after another hospital visit, and I'm still frustrated, I'm still scared, I'm still confused, but I'm not mad at God for allowing me to be uncomfortable. I choose to seek joy, and I choose to seek God. Love you all!

HOG (House of Gratitude)

October 4, 2016

The English language is odd. Like how the word LIMBO can mean "an uncertain period of awaiting a decision or resolution" but it can also refer to the "How low can you go" stick game. In this instance, I'm not referring to the stick limbo, although now that I think about it, I feel as though I'm being forced to go lower and lower. You start out standing up, then you're squatting, and before you know it you're barely off the ground, trying with all your might to stay up. I'm in the medical limbo. I've played this game before, and it's a hurry-up-and-wait kind of thing. My biopsy results were inconclusive. I'm supposed to watch the lump for the next week. Sit and watch to see if it disappears or gets bigger. It's an odd thing, to sit and watch. To wait as a life-threatening beast either grows or decides to disappear. But here's the thing about waiting, you're forced to rely solely on the Lord.

I can't do a thing about this lump. I can't remove it, and I can't go to the doctor, I can't take a pill, and I can't drink a particular tea or eat a certain root, I can't sniff a specific oil or sleep a certain amount. I am not in control. The things I can do, the things I am in control of are my perspective, my relationship, my dependence on the Lord, and my attitude. I intend to do the best I can in those areas.

A tremendous help in controlling my perspective during this time is to focus on all the blessings in my life! It's hard to do at times, but it's easier these days because my ENTIRE house is filled with blessings. It's a house of gratitude no doubt. Allow me to walk you through it.

When you walk up to my HOG (house of gratitude, now referred to as my HOG), you see two cars in the driveway. Each vehicle was given to us graciously. Inside our home, you walk into the living room. Each couch was given to us, the old window hanging on the wall was given to us, the rug was given to us, the coffee table was given to us, the lamp was given to us. Heading into the kitchen in my HOG you will see a cute dining room table that was given to us, and the kitchen itself is filled with gizmos and gadgets...GIVEN TO US. As if that isn't enough to convince you, in our bedroom, the BED was given to us, and the dresser was given to us. There is not one area, one room, one square foot of space in my house that I can escape gratitude!

My HOG (house of gratitude) got me thinking, isn't that really the case EVERYWHERE we go? Isn't every house a HOG? Isn't every breath, flower, kiss, raindrop, grain of sand, a thing to be grateful for? Everything has been given to us, and we deserve none of it. The intense Irish music play-

...my entire house is filled with blessings. It's a house of gratitude no doubt. Allow me to walk you through it.

ing in this coffee shop, the laptop I type on, my ten fingers, a husband, all given to me. How often I forget to be grateful, but how essential it is for our souls. You can't have an attitude of gratitude and be an angry, bitter, or sad person. Sure, you are allowed to have your moments, even your days, but as I am tempted to demand that I have the life I am told by the world that I'm entitled to, I will take a moment to look at all that I have that I don't even deserve.

Thank you all for helping me during this time. Your kindness and generosity, your words, they all help me keep a positive perspective during this waiting! Please pray for this week of waiting, but even more please pray for my husband, Adam! Next week we head to Spokane for his Lyme treatment, and I am begging the Lord that it will work. Love you all, and I'm grateful for you ALL.

Going to War

October 14, 2016

I'm tired. I've become too familiar with this term in the last two years. Lately, I feel as though it's a permanent state. Fatigue. An abnormal amount of it. I guess that's not crazy considering my body has been fighting a life-threatening tumor. It annoys me though. Maybe it's also the fact that I just turned 23 years old...Nahhhh. But I can say that I am so incredibly grateful for another year of life. 23 blessed years. Thank you for all the birthday wishes and encouragements. It was tempting to douse the celebration of my birthday in the worry, anxiety, and stress of Adam's treatment for Lyme disease and my upcoming treatment. I'm grateful for friends and my husband who help me focus on the present and the excitement of the celebration of life.

Adam and I head to Seattle on Tuesday, and I get a bunch of tests done on Thursday. They want to try a new clinical trial on me before we go to surgery and radiation. It's a gamble. Last time my body didn't respond to the trial, and three tumors grew in the meantime, but if it works, GAME CHANGER. We could get ahead of this thing instead of the old game of whack-a-mole. It's a risk I'm willing to take if it means skipping surgery and radiation.

My heart has been in a healthy state of peace. Adam and I were talking about it the other day. We are different warriors, this time. This is my 3rd battle. No, this is my third war, I've had a dozen or more battles now. But I have two wars under my belt, and I'm wiser because of it. I'm not stronger, nor am I more capable. I am still David with his slingshot. But, imagine if David was able to fight Goliath three different times. The third time he would be able to reflect on the last two battles and have a wave of calm and trust as he saw God's strength and power come through for him. He would approach the third battle boldly, and with less fear. He would have more confidence that the God he serves is powerful and good. He would doubt less, and he would learn from the first two battles. He would look back and see that He is just as weak and still wields only a slingshot, but he would see his God who is more than capable and uses something better than a sword.

It's a hard decision every day to wake up and remember that I GET a third chance to fight this war better, instead of being angry and bitter towards God saying that I HAVE to fight this a third time. I want to look back on the mountain of faithfulness, and I want to look back at the wars and see God's strength through me.

"I can do ALL things through Him who gives me strength."
Philippians 4:13

Clinical Trial Fears

October 21, 2016

I have this devastating guttural cry, woe-is-me, I'm done, this isn't fair moment every time I get diagnosed. Yesterday I had that moment.

A clinical trial. It seemed like it would be a straight forward, almost easy road, but there is no easy road with cancer. I sat in the REI garage crying and contemplating the different paths I could take. I could go forward with the trial, I could do surgery and radiation again, or I could skip treatment altogether. The latter sounds so enticing, to just be done, to go back to normal until cancer runs its course. This isn't the first time I've explored the idea, but the truth is, all roads have sacrifice. So then after I realize that there are no easy roads, I feel trapped. I feel like cancer has me trapped; there is no escape; I have no choice. Then amid my self-smothering, I panic.

The clinical trial is a systemic infusion every two weeks for the next year.

The next year! Uuuugh...

The very words make me squirm. I long for home, no, I long for stability, for calm to this chaos, for a schedule. The last year and a half I've been a gypsy, going from one place to the next. I've barely been able to hang all my clothes in the closet, and now I have to make the trek to Seattle every two weeks for a year. After eight weeks and two biopsies, they will determine whether I am responding well to the drug. If I don't respond, there is a risk that my tumor will continue to get bigger and spread, leaving surgery, radiation, or chemo as my only options. The tumor has already grown to the point that it's a painful lump pushing against my throat. That possibility scares me so much. I'm the 1% girl remember? Stats bring me no comfort; neither do others' success.

But what if it works? What if my tumors dissolve into nothing and cancer slowly fades from my body? From my life? What

> I could go forward with the trial, I could do surgery and radiation again, or I could skip treatment altogether. The latter sounds so enticing, to just be done, to go back to normal until cancer runs its course.

if? And it's in the what if's that we can make ourselves crazy. I've been telling people that being diagnosed for the third time makes me feel kind of like I'm living out Groundhog Day, but the cancer version. Every time that I begin to go into panic mode, every time that I ask the Lord to just kill me now and be done with it, every time I doubt His plan and insist that mine's better, every time that I start to look at other 23-year-olds and envy their freedom, in these moments, when I feel all loss of control, the Lord lifts my downcast face to meet His gaze. He says, "Look at me daughter." When I look up, I imagine Him staring back with tears in His eyes, because He hates this too. Then I look back on the first diagnosis, the devastation, the wondering if I'll live past Christmas; then I reflect back on the second diagnosis, the anger, the wondering if I'll ever get married. And as my gaze shifts from poor me, from the weak, feeble, and untrusting human to the all-knowing, kind, merciful, and GOOD GOD, I remember...

Greater things are yet to come. I will make it. I will be okay. Not because I'm good, or brave, or strong, but because *God* is good and brave and strong. He has brought me through two battles with cancer, and He is gearing me up for the third.

Greater things are yet to come. Love you all!

20 Vials Later

October 30, 2016

The first Avelumab Infusion is officially flowing through my apparently non-existent veins. It pretty much feels like the last trial did. I feel achy, nauseous, feverish, exhausted, and I have a headache. So the flu without the flu part. Last time it only lasted a full two days, I'm hopeful that this is the case for this trial!

My most recent visit to Seattle was terrible. I mean other than the fact that my Sister and Mom were able to come with me, which made it all worth it!

I started out the night before we left with a really positive perspective. I felt encouraged and ready to fight this battle. I felt a peace in letting it go and giving God control of my life. I felt as though He gave me this new inspiration and a warrior spirit. The drive up was easy and wonderful. The night before my appointments was enjoyable. My appointments, however, started off on a sour note.

Twenty vials of blood are a tall order, even a vampire would think so. My one good vein pumped out a solid 12 vials until I begged the doctors to go away as it dried up. Now we enter foreign territory — finding a new vein. You see, I have always been able to depend on my ONE good vein. It never fails me. So, the nurse feels around on my opposite arm. Nothing promising but she finds one to "give a try." For those of you that get blood drawn a lot or get IV's often you know the terror paired with "give it a try." This means digging, digging under your skin, digging in your veins, and it's disgusting and painful.

So the nurse pumped another four vials out of some random vein deep beneath the surface. Finally, they found a third random vein to "try" in my hand and barely got four additional vials filled. After that discouraging event, they then went on to tell me that I won't be able to receive my T-cells until December. Now while that's scary in that we are waiting another month, it was more disappointing to learn that the one week in my life that actually matters to me is the week I HAVE to receive the T-cells, the week of Sis's wedding. I broke down. I cried my eyes out in front of my new team, in front of my mom, and in front of the nurse. I couldn't help it. I exclaimed to them, "I'm 23, and cancer just ruins everything! Why do I have to do this? Man, I'm just so frustrated." And they all looked at me and agreed. "Cancer Sucks," they replied. Then I went from that embarrassing and frustrating appointment to the biopsy...to be continued...

Have You Ever Lost Your Mind?

October 31, 2016

ffffffff

Who can know the mind of God much less understand their own mind at times?

I had every intention of continuing my story of how everything went wrong. The biopsy was painful, the next day it took three digs to find a vein for an IV, we got pulled over on the way home...yadda yadda. But I'm not going to say more than that, because God had a different plan for today's blog.

I don't know how to navigate this. Cancer. Life. Loving God. Loving myself. Just everything. It's one giant rollercoaster. One day I'm great and confident, the next day I'm begging God to end it all. Today I had one of the worst break downs since my diagnosis. I started the day feeling so encouraged at church, and I was singing, laughing even, and just recovering from the frustration of my last visit. I was sitting at my computer trying to figure out alternatives for Sis's bachelorette party since I will be in treatment. I started thinking about how much cancer ruins things in my life. I became envious of the girls, my family even, that they get to go. The only obstacle they have is work. It made me enraged to think that cancer will keep me from fully participating in the most important week of my only sister's life. It's more than just missing a bachelorette party, though obviously.

Then something happened, and I can't explain it, and I don't know; I cracked. I don't exactly remember what happened to be honest. It didn't even feel like me; it felt like I was a stranger from a movie — one of those terribly sad movies where you cry for the girl on screen. I started screaming. I started screaming and shaking. My mind was cloudy, and I even thought I was going crazy. I screamed, exclaiming that I can't do this anymore, that I don't want to do this. Right there in front of my family. Have you ever been so angry that you actually want to harm yourself? At that moment I just wanted to smash my head through a wall or pull out my hair. I wanted a distraction from the sudden range of emotions I had just let go. It was one of the few times I've let it ALL go. I didn't think. I didn't analyze. I didn't try to be strong. I couldn't stop if it I wanted to. It was my last straw. It was just raw emotion. My only thought – Jesus, help me, help me, help me.

I hate that vulnerability, and I think it's because I know there are no magic words, there's no 4-step process, there's no pill. It's just, there. It's much easier to contain it, to act like it doesn't exist, to busy yourself enough never to give it a thought, and to maintain control. That's what I like, control.

The Lord is perfectly okay with just being there. He shows us that in Psalms when David is just pouring it out to the Lord. I can imagine that he was shaking, screaming even, just like me. Or Job. The Lord didn't condemn them, and He doesn't condemn me for it. I rebuked myself though. I don't give myself a lot of grace I'm realizing. Mainly because I don't understand God's grace well enough, nor do I accept it. I am a weak, feeble, lost, confused, angry, flawed, human. I have no "inspirational strength" outside of the strength that God graciously

Today I feel like I lost my mind, genuinely. But the crazy thing is, God loves me the same as He did yesterday when I was praising His name.

gives me. Every single day is a battle. I have very down and low days where I want to lay in bed until I'm dead, where I exclaim, "Take this away God, I can't do this again!". I have better days when I can keep my eyes on the Lord and exclaim, "God you are sovereign AND good, thank you for the blessing of life itself."

Looking Beyond This

November 17, 2016

I'm still here. I took a little break from blogging. To be honest, the last few weeks have been difficult.

To catch you up, I just had my second Avelumab infusion, and the next one is on the 28th. The last infusion went well, one poke, and a few hours later I was done! I flew to Seattle this round, and boy it is just a thousand times better. Flying is less stressful, it takes less time, and my body feels so much better afterward. I wish it wasn't so dang expensive! So, I'm exploring the alternatives, this coming trip I'm taking the train.

I haven't felt very good. The tumors in my neck are continuing to grow which is scary already, but now I'm experiencing a lot of odd feelings. I'm light-headed, I have frequent headaches, I have fogginess, I have trouble focusing, I see black spots more often, and I feel more exhausted. My soon-to-be EMT husband thinks it may be the second tumor pushing on my carotid artery and making the blood flow to my brain slow down. I decided to test his theory by pushing on my tumor. Hah bad news, I nearly passed out!

It's hard to sit here and watch my body freak out. Knowing that cancer is actively eating away at my body makes me feel like I'm slowly dying. It's an odd roller coaster to be on. Some days I welcome the thought, some days I feel devastated. I mean, I know that technically we are all dying, but how many of us actually think about that?

I'm terrified that I'm never going to be able to have children. I had a dream the other night that I was pregnant. Do you know those realistic dreams that feel so real? It was magical. I mean in my dream I wasn't sick, I didn't have super fat cankles, or the pain of carrying another human, just the magical mommy feelings. I woke up only to the fact that my chin is the only thing that looks pregnant. Such disappointment.

In those times where I'm frozen in fear that cancer is going to kill me before I get to put a little Hayden here on Earth, I'm reminded of the time last December where I thought I was going to die. I started to panic, thinking that I'd never get to experience the joy of being a wife. And here I am. But what if I don't get to be a Mom? This is the place when eternity has to come to my mind. This idea that "greater things are yet to come," or "we are not made for this world."

Heaven. How often I forget that heaven is my reality because I've placed my faith in Jesus. How often I neglect the beauty that I get everlasting life in HEAVEN. While Motherhood is something I pray I will experience, and while it's such a beautiful gift here on Earth, how much better will heaven be? I think the idea scares me a bit, to be honest. I mean, it's hard to fathom, so I don't like to go there. I want the tangible, realistic. But gee, to think that this Earth is the best there is? How's that for a sad reality.

This idea that "greater things are yet to come," or "we are not made for this world." Heaven. How often I forget that heaven is my reality because I've placed my faith in Jesus. How often I neglect the beauty that I get everlasting life in HEAVEN.

It's easy to take hope for granted. But man, look at our world. Look at the chaos, the hatred, the terrified souls that think that this is it? We need to hope, and we need to remember that our suffering, our President, our marital status, our kids, our jobs, this isn't all there is. Thank the Lord for giving us hope, a hope to look beyond the evil in this world and know that one day we will bask in the glory of heaven. To know that we will not end up as merely a pile of bones in the dust. To know that this is not the best there is. I don't marvel in the wonder of that enough.

Please pray for these tumors to stop growing and for the medicine to works! Also, please pray for me as I plan my travel. I have to be in Seattle every single week of December. So, prayers for my attitude and perspective as I travel a lot, and prayers for travel to not be too expensive and not booked up! I also have a PRAISE. Adam got a new job!!!

Unfortunate Update

December 19, 2016

The Collegiana, the mesh mask, Cross and Crown Church; it's odd how I've made so many good and so many terrible memories here. If you haven't followed my story for long, last August and September after my giant 11-hour surgery, I lived here at the Collegiana for six weeks and had radiation every day. For those of you who have followed my story since the beginning, I'm sure your heart sank at the mention of those things.

They pulled me off the clinical trial.

It was some of the hardest news I've had in a while. I had so much hope that the trial would be my miracle. My tumors kept getting bigger and bigger and so finally they decided to do a scan, that scan revealed another five new tumors in my neck. With a sense of urgency, my doctors discussed all the possibilities and, in the end, settled on radiation. So here I am, entering week three of radiation. This time though it is twice a day, every day until the middle of January. I haven't mentioned anything because I didn't want cancer to ruin the joy and perfection of my sister's wedding. And it didn't!

It's always such a range of emotions for me. I am terrified that I have seven tumors now. Devastated that the trial didn't work. Thankful that they caught it before Stage 4. Sad that I have to be in Seattle, away from my family and husband. I am scared because I know the horrors of radiation. And currently, I'm very frustrated because radiation is burning the inside of my mouth, therefore, resulting in severe blisters all over the right side of my mouth. It hurts to talk, eat, and drink.

Once again, I'm reminded of things we so quickly take for granted. While you're reading this I want you to swish some spit around, and you feel that moisture? It's there for a reason, so thank God right now for spit, because it's something I miss having. Now do me a huge favor and take a few seconds to savor and chew on your next meal. Enjoy the spices, the textures, the crunch, the sensation of biting into something solid without really having to work too hard, and thank God for the ability to eat and enjoy it. Right now, I have to forfeit solid food, and it's not enjoyable at all. It's work to make sure my sores don't scrape against my teeth or that salt doesn't penetrate one of them.

Now that wasn't a moment to have a pity party for me! Because as I tell you to be grateful for the things we easily take for granted, I am learning through this new trial to stop focusing on all the things I don't have or get to do. Because that makes me cry. Instead, (the lesson I seem to learn every other week) I need to find reasons to be grateful. That is a heart and an attitude rooted in the gospel, rooted in the knowledge of what God has done for me, which is the ultimate thing to be grateful for.

So, as I take a sip of water every minute to relieve my desert mouth, I will challenge myself not to be angry that I now have to rely on water but to think about the fact that I have easy access to water everywhere I go. See the difference? It's such a simple change yet it is the difference between me spending my next six weeks depressed and crying, or laughing and finding joy.

Once again, I'm reminded of things we so quickly take for granted. While you're reading this I want you to swish some spit around, and you feel that moisture? It's there for a reason, so thank God right now for spit, because it's something I miss having.

NOT that it isn't okay to struggle! Man, the struggle is real, and I am learning to allow myself some serious, guttural cries. And I'm sad, and I'm devastated to be in this situation yet again. And that isn't wrong.

I also want to point out that this perspective struggle is a choice that I have to make every other minute! I don't just flip a switch and move through this cancer skipping and whistling, and neither will you.

This is hard; it's so incredibly hard. Going through my third round with this is exhausting, and every time I feel like I can't take another swing, the Lord continues to give me enough strength to keep on keeping on. Please, please pray for me. Pray for relief from the pain I'm experiencing. Pray for this to work and kill this stupid cancer. Pray for the Lord to work through my weak and flawed human nature to bring glory to Himself. Pray for my family as I'm separated from them for six weeks. And praise God for the things we take for granted that He blesses us with!

Love you all.

Cried over Eggs

December 20, 2016

ᖴᖴᖴᖴᖴᖴᖴ

I bawled my eyes out this morning during breakfast. It's funny; they say "Don't cry over spilled milk" but is it okay to cry over an underwhelming bowl of eggs? I could barely eat the scrambled eggs my mom had made me. It was a very humbling moment, to lose something you rely on and enjoy so much. This thing we call eating. I know its main purpose is for nutrition and survival, but man we have made it into an art! An art that I am learning now that I really enjoy. Anyway, back to the eggs. I started crying out of frustration that it was so much work to have a simple breakfast. The blog I wrote last night (in that moment) completely went out the window and my perspective on the situation was that in my boxing match with eggs, the eggs were winning. Eventually, after too many tears and a bunch of water, I won.

After my discouraging breakfast battle, I went back into my room and decided to take a bath. A bath and my book makes everything better. As I was going back and forth between changing my perspective on my situation or dwelling in my anger toward my current eating disabilities, I received two separate messages.

Now, I won't go into detail for the sake of their privacy, but two different people reached out to tell me how the blog post from yesterday specifically affected them. It was mind-blowing how God timed it just right. I was able to get yet another glimpse at how God is using every little aspect of this cancer trial.

It's not for nothing.

Blisters in my mouth, not for nothing.

Radiation burns, not for nothing.

Surgery and scars, not for nothing.

Biopsies and failed treatments, not for nothing.

Blood draws and leaving home, not for nothing.

Cancer, not for nothing.

IT'S ALL FOR THE GLORY OF GOD. Boy, isn't that something?

So, in my bathtub, as I read the messages, eggs started to become much less important. The burning sensation in my mouth, or the difficulties talking, or the tumors in my neck, they serve a higher purpose, way beyond me and way beyond what I'll ever know on this Earth. Does it still totally suck? YES! And God even knows that! He isn't even mad about me crying over eggs! In fact, He cries with me. But then, He, in His sovereignty and wisdom, takes this gross cancer and does good with it. GOOD things people, from cancer! *and the crowd gasps at the mention of the big bad "C" word and the audacity that I'd say good can come out of it!

Two different people reached out to tell me how the blog post from yesterday specifically affected them. It was mind-blowing how God timed it just right. I was able to get yet another glimpse at how God is using every little aspect of this cancer trial.

It's those messages and that truth that encourages me to continue. To know that God is doing work beyond my little tunnel vision focusing on eggs.

With that, I encourage you to share your struggles with people! You don't have to put it on blast on a blog, but share it with someone because otherwise, how will God get any good from it? (I mean He's God and can do whatever He wants but, you know what I mean). And also, share with people how God specifically uses their struggle in your life. Be bold!

It's almost Christmas, and I refuse to let dumb cancer affect the wonderful celebration! Also, if you have any suggestions on food that doesn't have any spice and that's soft let me know! So far, canned, bland, chicken noodle soup and yogurt are what I've had success in eating. Love you all, and I am so grateful for so many prayer warriors.

Is it a Wonderful Life?

January 11, 2017

I know it's been a hot minute since I've posted, but hey here I am! Alive, breathing, mostly in one piece, and COUNTING DOWN THE DAYS! Saturday the 14th is, (Lord willing) my last day of radiation. After that, well, we know how it goes. I will, and I'm sure you will, pray, pray, pray that I heal well and don't have to have surgery in the next few months!

I want to backtrack to Christmas. I spent my Christmas at home, thanks to your generosity and kindness, and it was exactly what I needed to refresh. While I was home, my husband asked if we could watch, "*It's Wonderful Life.*" Now I'm not gonna lie, when I saw that it was a black and white film, I totally fought him on it, insisting that it was doomed to be boring. Anyway, it was one of those films that hit me in a very unexpected way.

For those of you who haven't seen the movie, consider this your disclaimer. It's about this guy named George Bailey. Stuff goes all wrong in his life, and nothing goes as he planned. Hmmm, sounds familiar already. He gets to this point where things are out of control, and he seriously thinks about just ending it all. Again, I relate! Anyway, as he is about to jump off the bridge, an angel appears and takes him through what his life would be like if he didn't exist. Does that make sense? George says that everyone's life would be better without him so the angel shows what it truly would be like without him. It's kind of a rad scene because there are so many details that you'd never even think about. Now, I won't walk you through the entire thing, you should just watch the movie. But I will say that after George sees how much his life affects everyone, he has a change of heart. He goes back to real life and is now joyful and grateful.

There was this scene where his uncle lost all the money needed to keep their bank open, and George is depressed thinking that he will never fix it. Anyway, when he goes back to real life, his wife had asked for the townspeople to help. They start coming in and setting any spare change they have on the table while George stands there in awe. Phew! Okay, that's all I wanted to say about the movie, now we are all on the same page.

Now, there was a God-ordained parallel happening between my life and the movie. As I watched George's life become chaotic and out of control, I thought about the last two years of my life. How I had so many plans and how essentially my life got turned upside down. Then as George spiraled down, eventually finding himself standing at the edge of a bridge, I thought about the various times I stared at my pill bottle or thought about driving my car into a tree, the times I thought it would be easier to end it all.

But the next part, the part where George sees the impact his life has had, that part was eye-opening for me. I mean think about this for *Your life is not just about you. You have an impact on every single person you meet. EVERYONE.* a second. Your life has a ripple effect. I mean, try to imagine if you weren't alive. If you never existed, what would be different? And if you can't think of anything, ask the people around you. Your life is not just about you. You have an impact on every single person you meet. EVERYONE. It's a ripple effect, it all matters. It's kind of mind-blowing really.

Life is so detailed and complex, and we could never plan any of it. God has woven purpose into every little detail of your life. I picture it like we all have a unique color of, let's say ink. Every time we interact with someone, whether it's someone we know and love, the grocery clerk, the person you walk past and you make eye contact with, your kids, you leave a little bit of your color on them.

Stay with me here, let's take the example of the person you pass on the street. If you take a moment to dissect just that simple interaction, it's incredible! So, you could have walked past that person and smiled at them, but little did you know that they just had a family member die and they are just trying to hold it together. Since you were thoughtful in that small interaction, your smile made them smile, and since they were able to smile then, I don't know, it helped them feel something in that second. And who knows, maybe they went home and told their Mom about it and she felt encouraged to reach out to her brother that she's been fighting with, and then they do something and on and on it goes and you have a ripple effect. I feel like I'm rambling, but I'm just amazed, you guys! Our lives are NOT all about us, even if we try our hardest to make it that way. Every choice you make will have a far-reaching impact. So, make them count.

Lastly, George stood there and watched his community come to his aid, there I was standing in my living room, staring at a once bare tree, watching it fill up with beautiful ornaments of encouragement delivered by so many of you, and I thought, "It's a wonderful life." Thank you!

I Thought I Was Poisoned

January 19, 2017

So, I just realized that I haven't kept you guys in the know as far as how radiation round 3 has been. This is mainly for your curiosity, but also for those of you who will ever have radiation and want to know what it's really like. To be honest, the doctors aren't always the best at preparing you. They use vague terms and can't give any specifics because these days maybe because they don't know, and maybe because Americans will sue over any little thing.

The first weeks I had few symptoms, mainly just fatigue. Then as you know I got the intense mouth burns, ewww. After my doctor tweaked my treatment, my mouth started to heal, praise God! Then the dry mouth started, only this time not only did my mouth get dry, but any spit I produced was as thick as molasses, no exaggeration. Because my spit was so thick, I would get super nauseous and I didn't eat. Turns out losing weight in the radiation world is a big no-no so, they sent me home with a bunch of, ENSURE. Yes, Ensure, the protein shake that I grew up believing was only for Grandmas.

Backtrack a few days before nausea set in. I was alone in Seattle at this point, and a little bit anxious after watching some crime show. My fault I know. Anyway, I decided to make a cinnamon bagel with butter and cinnamon sugar (this is relevant). The Collegiana, which is the place I live, has a shared kitchen, like a college dorm, and often people will leave random food and things behind. Now I'm not one to eat people's leftovers, mainly because I can imagine them scratching body parts and then reaching into their bag of chips, the same bag of chips that they left behind marked, "free." Not free of germs!

Anyway, so I made my bagel and realized I didn't have any sugar. To my dismay, I was forced to grab a few of the restaurant style sugar packets left on the table. I took my bagel back to the room and took a bite, only to be met with the bitter taste of pure cinnamon. Confused, I poured more sugar on the bagel and took another big bite, still not a hint of sweet. Now at this point, I had three sugar packets poured onto this bagel, so this time I stuck my finger directly into the sugar, placed it on my tongue, and felt only the texture of sugar grains with but no taste. Okay, I'm assuming that a reasonable person would just shrug it off and throw it away...remember how I mentioned I was anxious? I immediately started thinking maybe it was poison, do people even use poison anymore!? No, maybe it's drugs I thought. Maybe someone hid their drugs in the sugar assuming no one would use it and now I have drugs or poison in me!?! I seriously debated calling someone. I checked my eyes, not that I knew what to look for, they looked normal. I felt my heart, and it's not about to explode. So after probably half an hour of panicking, and texting my family and telling them I loved them in case I never woke up, I thought it might be a good idea to get a drink of juice. After taking a swig of juice it hit me. This juice has no taste because I have lost my sense of taste. That's a side effect of radiation that my doctors didn't warn me about, but I happened to overhear another patient talking about it—the ability to taste sweet, POOF, gone. Hurray, at least I'm not poisoned or drugged. LOL

I eat for nutrition only, not pleasure. So please, next time you eat something that sounds good to you, take a moment to savor all the flavors, pay attention and enjoy it!

Losing your ability to taste sweet throws you off. It's incredible because I realize now how so many things have sweet notes that I would have never noticed. Biting into pizza only to be met with texture, some oregano flavor, saltiness, and the subtly of cheese, but not the sweetness of tomato sauce!? Terrible! I went to one of my favorite Portland ice cream shops, as I sampled flavor after flavor and I couldn't help but grimace at the savory notes that showed up, but ice cream without sweet is just gross. It was incredibly discouraging at first. You pick food based on what sounds good. You have an expectation based off experience or knowledge that your food will taste a certain way. It's a habit! So it's frustrating when you go to take a big ol' bite of spaghetti because it sounds good, and it smells like spaghetti, it looks like spaghetti, but when it meets your tongue, it tastes nothing like spaghetti. Food is dull right now like everything has been watered down. I have to add salt to everything. It's getting less discouraging now because I'm used to it. I eat for nutrition only, not pleasure. So please, next time you eat something that sounds good to you, take a moment to savor all the flavors, pay attention and enjoy it!

Okay, moving on. I don't know if it's just the power of prayer, or if it hasn't hit me yet, but I feel pretty good! I don't have my skin melting off, like last time, it's more like a peeling sunburn, and it's hot. So I am praying that I'm catching a little break! Woohoo! Thank you for praying. Love you all!

Why Should I Fight to Live Anymore?

February 3, 2017

This round of radiation has been...a thousand times better than last time! Praise God! I was kind of waiting for that awful moment where I wake up with hot skin melting off my neck, and here we are nearly a month later, and the worst of the worst was some crispy peeling! Eww. Using those words to describe skin, uh kind of horrible sounding. Anyway, the mouth is still dry as a bone, and my taste hasn't come back. I only have a few pesky sores on my tongue and throat, and I still have tumors. Yes, unfortunately, they haven't magically dissolved.

To clear things up, I know a lot of you saw my post about wanting to go work in an orphanage. I was so hopeful that radiation was going to get rid of my tumors. I mean heck, I had 60 treatments! I was encouraged to see that my golf ball tumor went down to a grape tumor so I thought that maybe, just maybe, I'd have some time off. So, as I prayed about how to use my free month, the Lord brought a mission trip to my heart. I guess it was just, I mean for the last two years I've been poured into. I've been a "charity" case. People have served me and done kind things for me, and I feel like it's time for me to pour out, to serve, and I know that I do that in some ways through my blog. I also just LOVE kids, and I love culture, and it just seemed like a good move!

Anyway, through the course of a week I had reached out to 10 orphanages based on your recommendations (thank you). It was coming together and I was getting pretty excited! But there was one issue, as my hand reached up to assess the pesky little, life-threatening lump in my neck, it was bigger. It was bigger and it was hard as a rock. We all know by now that this is a bad thing.

Radiation didn't work, all the way. I refuse to have the heart-crushing thought that radiation was all for nothing, so I'm choosing to believe that radiation was just meant to shrink the tumors. I mean, surgery on a grape is MUCH better than surgery on a golf ball! But I'm not going to pretend that I wasn't devastated. It's so hard to hear that yet another thing didn't work. This also means that I won't be going on a mission's trip, which was also very sad for me. Instead, I will make my way to Seattle on Monday for a scan and a new plan.

Surgery doesn't work, radiation doesn't work, chemo doesn't work, and the clinical trial doesn't work. I have to admit that these facts have terrified me during the last few weeks. I feel as though I have no back-up plan. Like they are just keeping me alive, not that I'm going to live. I am afraid that this cancer is going to kill me. I know we are all going to die, someday. And as I think about death more and more I have to ask, if you don't have God, then what are you living for? What would you say to me, a 23 year old woman with possibly not long to live, who, in the last year and a half has been through 12 weeks of radiation, two major surgeries, one clinical trial, seven biopsies, and is now looking at another face altering surgery that may not even save my life. Why should I persevere? Why should I keep fighting?

God is the only thing that is outside of myself, that I can choose to live for that will never leave me or forsake me.

As I wrestle with the desire to live for me and the desire to live for God all that I can say is that I should keep fighting because this life isn't about ME. It's not about being happy and comfortable; it's not about being the prettiest or the most successful, because nothing in this world will sustain. Not if I choose to live for my husband or my parents, not for my photography or my white picket fence dreams. Those will all fail me, they will all perish, and they are not a guaranteed constant. God is the only thing that is outside of myself, that I can choose to live for that will never leave me or forsake me. He will never fail me or stop loving me, He will never stop fighting by my side, He will never stop wanting the best for me, He will cry with me and He will bless me, He gave His life up for me, HE DIED FOR ME, and that my friends, is someone to live for.

Waiting Again, Ugh

February 11, 2017

~~~~~~~~~~

Hello, my blog-reading friends! Well as most of you know, or have heard, I had to go to Seattle earlier this week. I think I have the traveler's curse, seriously, or God wants me to learn a lesson that I'm just totally missing! I booked a train ticket to go from Salem to Seattle on Monday morning at 6:41. I woke up nice and early, zombie walked my way to the station, only to have the ticket man tell me, "Oh, did you not get the email, the train to Seattle was canceled" ...well obviously not because otherwise, I'd be sleeping! So, my kind and gracious and extremely even-keeled husband led me back to the car and drove me from Salem to the Portland airport at 6 A.M. Fifty minutes into our drive I am trying frantically to book a flight and get ahold of the airline. The random elevator music that they force you to listen to when you're on hold looped for a good 20 minutes before the operator stated, "We're sorry, due to a high call volume the wait list is three hours, please leave your number and we'll call you back." Three *HOURS* people! And you know that's not even accurate! So, we turned around and drove back to Salem. Oh, apparently there was a freak snowstorm in Seattle, and the city shut down.

Later that day, I was able to reschedule all my appointments for the next day. I booked a flight out of PDX for the next morning and after Adam got off work, he drove me back to Portland (yes, he wins best hubby award, he never once complained!) where my friend Clare so graciously let us stay.

Tuesday morning at five.I don't know how many of you are like me, but I'm an anxious wreck when it comes to morning flights! I never sleep well, and I wake up hours before my flight to make sure my phone is still working and to make sure I clicked AM instead of PM on my alarm. So at 5 in the morning, I hear the text ding on my phone, "Alaska Airlines apologizes for the inconvenience, you will receive a voucher in your email." What does that even mean!? I look on my app, and sure enough, my flight was canceled. It turns out that all the flights that got canceled the previous day got rebooked on our flight and we got bumped to the night time. Now, I'm used to things never going right, I mean, I'm not even being dramatic. If you're a frequent reader, you know that things just get complicated when it comes to my life. So, you'd think that by now I'd be as chill as an island lad, go with the flow ya know and remember that things always end up working out for me. Nope, still, haven't learned that lesson.

So, at 8:50 on Tuesday night I got on a flight and made it to Seattle. I had my CT scan which was like the other bajillion scans I've had, and as I was heading back to Salem, there was a NATIONWIDE SYSTEM OUTAGE at the airport. RIGHT when my flight was supposed to depart! I'm sorry, but WHAT WILL HE COME UP WITH NEXT!? The zombie apocalypse? That's gotta be the next thing! I made it to Salem, not super delayed thank heavens.

Now what? Well, now I wait until my meeting with Dr. Nghiem on Tuesday. I plan on driving, so please pray that there's no freak thing like someone hacking into the zoo system and releasing all the animals, causing the highway to close for safety, ya know because those apes can smash your car in... The scan showed no distant tumors which is GREAT news. So those little buttheads haven't moved past my collar bones, they prefer my face I guess. The only problem is, I know that my tumors are growing again. I can feel them. But the only scan the doctors had was one I did mid radiation, so the scan they recently took doesn't do a lot of good since they can only compare to the mid radiation scan, and compared to that of course, my tumors have shrunk. Does that make sense? Anyway, I'm hoping a physical exam will offer more clarity. Until then, our favorite waiting game.

Now, I'm used to things never going right, I mean, I'm not even being dramatic. You know that things just get complicated when it comes to my life. So, you'd think that by now I'd be as chill as an island lad, go with the flow ya know and remember that things always end up working out for me. Nope, still, haven't learned that lesson.

Surgery... I Hate that Word

February 16, 2017

I haven't cried that much in the last week, I've wanted to. Oh yeah, I've wanted just to let all the emotion out, but it hurts right now. Like, physically. Why do you ask? Because two days after my CT scan last week I woke up to this throbbing pain in my neck. The tumor under my jaw, not the golf ball to grape tumor, but the other one, was about twice as big as it had been the previous day. It blew up like a balloon. Swollen and firm, painful, and large this tumor decided to make its appearance. I mean this sucker even robbed me of my sleep! Every time I'd roll over on my right side I'd wake up.

Fast forward to this Tuesday in Seattle. I had a follow-up with Dr. Nghiem, and I showed him my new balloon tumor. He always almost laughs when I come in because there's always something new, something he's never seen, something he doesn't understand; he's always baffled. I'll spare you the medical details and the ins and outs of that appointment and skip to the important part. I have to get surgery.

Surgery, again. As I write this I get this chest flutter, like that feeling you get right before you cry—kind of a flutter in your stomach and chest and then that tingling in your eyes and nose. But then you try to keep the floodgates shut, so you almost get a stomach ache, you know that feeling? If it didn't hurt, I'd be bawling all over my keyboard as I tell you that I have to have surgery. When they told me that it didn't really hit home. I mean, I figured it would be in a few weeks until yesterday when I got a call which confirmed my surgery for next Friday. Next Friday. A week, I have a week to prepare to get cut open again. Aw man, here they come; the tears. I can't help it. Ow.

> That feeling you get right before you cry—kind of a flutter in your stomach and chest and then that tingling in your eyes and nose. But then you try to keep the floodgates shut, so you almost get a stomach ache, you know that feeling?

I'm not afraid of the pain to come. I'm afraid of what I'm going to lose this time. The other half of my smile? My spit? My neck mobility? My taste? What scars will there be? How will I look different? There are so many what-ifs in surgery, and it never goes as planned. Like the first surgery being 11 hours not 4, or the second surgery resulting in dead tissue and a gaping hole in my face, what will it be this time?

I'm afraid, I'm frustrated, I'm tired, and I need your prayers.

February 24th I will have surgery in Seattle. February 24th I will wake up in a hazy anesthesia fog again and gaze into the mirror seeing someone I don't recognize.

Deliverance

February 23, 2017

Three days. Three days until life as I know it changes again. A neck dissection is my next venture. My first surgery was a radical neck dissection, and this one will be similar. The goal is to leave everything be except the tumors, but since I had radiation first, it's hard to know how ugly things will be on the inside. Last time they removed everything, muscle, and glands, everything...I mean everything but the very vital elements to make my neck function. So, a neck dissection is no walk in the park.

I wrote in my last blog about how this was all sudden like I didn't have a lot of time to wrap my mind around it all. Then the Lord did something truly amazing.

On Sunday my church had a prayer night where they dedicated a portion of the hour to pray for me. Initially, I was uncomfortable at the thought of all that attention, which sounds kind of dumb as a write it considering it's prayer! Anyway, I need to start from the beginning of my Sunday. The day started out with my Dad guest preaching at the First Church of God. He preached on suffering, a subject we are all quite familiar with by now. So, I won't explain the whole sermon, but if you can you should hear it! One thing stuck out to me, "God will deliver you from your suffering." If you are a believer in Christ, then you WILL be delivered. Now for me, that can mean deliverance here on Earth through the miracle of being healed, or that can mean deliverance through death and my suffering ending because I'm in heaven. Either way, I will be delivered from my suffering. This brought a lot of comfort to me, and there is already a victory, what feels like a lose-lose situation has in fact already been defeated by Jesus. I WILL BE DELIVERED. There will be an end to this suffering, and there is a light at the end of the tunnel. What peace and hope this idea can bring! The church service ended with the congregation praying for me.

Then came the prayer hour. Sidenote on prayer. I know there are thousands of people praying for me. I read the comments, get the messages, see the texts, you guys are everywhere, praying! It's just so different for me to have a visual, to be there while people pray. It's surreal almost. Anyway, it was an amazing night. It was emotional for sure, but watching everyone around me, though they were crying and begging

God to heal me, it wasn't a depressing sight, it was a sight of worship, of glorifying God. We were all speaking to Him together. I heard this song "Sovereign Over Us" by Aaron Keyes:

"Even what the enemy means for evil
You turn it for our good
You turn it for our good and for Your glory
Even in the valley, You are faithful
You're working for our good
You're working for our good and for Your glory"

And I couldn't help but feel in that moment, that those words were true. Cancer, sickness, and suffering, God has turned it for my good and His glory. It's undeniable. It was undeniable as I looked at my brothers and sisters praying, crying out to Him in faith. Proclaiming His name. I

...that can mean deliverance here on Earth through the miracle of being healed, or that can mean deliverance through death and my suffering ending because I'm in heaven.

even found out later that there was a church in China with 13,000, yes that is the correct number, 13,000 people, who were praying for me at the same time.

So, this surgery may work, and it may not. I may be healed from cancer on this Earth, and I may not. And if not, He is still good, because I WILL be delivered either way.

The Lie of Ugly

March 10, 2017

I've only had a guttural cry three times since surgery. Let me rewind though.

Surgery went well. The surgeon told me that they cut out all the cancer they could see, and, "There was a lot of it all clumped up in there." It took closer to seven hours, so my prediction was close! I got a private room which was one of the biggest blessings ever, and I spent three nights in the hospital. Monday morning, they yanked the tube out of the front of my neck, which was such a disturbing feeling, and then sent me home. Adam wheeled me out to the soccer mom van and I conked out on the bed they made for me in the back. The drive home was terrible, it took a long time, and there was terrible weather. My poor family, they had to endure it while I dozed off in a drugged-up stupor! I've been staying at my parent's house for the last two weeks since Adam has work all day and we have no WIFI at my home! It's been good for me. My Mom has taken good care of me, and she makes sure that I'm staying healthy like usual!

The wounds. Let's address the gnarly. I have a nice cut from the bottom of my ear going down my neck to meet the old scar from the last dissection in the middle, like a scar necklace. I have a medium incision under my chin, a hole above my collar bone from the drain, four incisions on the inside of my thighs, three incisions in my stomach, and five stitches on my right cheek. So, needless to say, it's been a slow recovery! I got my stitches out a week after surgery. I lost count, but every single mark had stitches, so it was a process. It always feels better though, like a freedom of sorts. It's been painful, I've had swelling everywhere and bruising, and it hurts to move my neck, it especially hurts to sleep, so I haven't gotten much. Today it feels a little better, the swelling has gone down a bit, but I'm still in pain, which annoys me! Two weeks later I want to be back to real life. It's affected my back a lot. I can feel the tension, and my shoulder is very weak. So weak that I can't lift or move it as much, so that's hard to overcome! But the pain will lessen, healing will come, and I will be able to function and persevere.

My soul. I did well in the hospital and the first week home. The drugs can take some credit but not much for my soul. It seems always to be somewhat easy the first week, and I can't pinpoint why. Maybe it's just that I don't have the energy to think, let alone cry!

Cry #1: So this week was my week. Adam was over at the house, and I was brushing my teeth. I had just washed my face, and he was looking at me in the mirror, I looked in the mirror too and hated what I saw. I hated even more that my husband was gazing at the same image. Ugh, I'm crying right now as I type. I looked in the mirror and saw a swollen, chubby chin and cheek which made the other side of my face look even smaller and unproportioned, I saw scars and red and yellow and blue discoloration on my neck, I saw my lip as it droops on one side, making brushing difficult, I didn't see myself. And I for sure didn't want anyone else to see. So I cried. I cried, and Adam held me and told me that I was beautiful and that he loved me, how is he real life?

> *So I cried. I cried, and Adam held me and told me that I was beautiful and that he loved me, how is he real life?*

Cry #2: I got some kind of sickness mid-week. I felt achy, I had the chills, I had no appetite, ya know that bug. On TOP of everything else. So, it was night time, and Adam was about to go home. As I was saying goodbye I just burst into tears, again he held me. In between the guttural gasps and cries, catching my breath and trying to calm down, I told him that I was tired of being sick. I was tired of not feeling normal. I was tired of hurting and dealing with the side effects. I told him that I was discouraged, that I felt like I was back at square one. I told him I felt defeated knowing I can never take these things back that I will deal with this for the rest of my life. I felt weary, alone, frustrated, sick, hurting, and ugly.

Cry #3: I started a new "business." I won't say the name on here because I don't want to use my cancer for advertisement. If you're curious, you can ask me. Anyway, so I went to film a video of myself, and as I watched, I started bawling. Seeing myself on video, seeing myself the way others see me, it made me feel ugly, and it made me feel discouraged. I don't know why you look so good in the mirror, but the moment you change to the camera, you see yourself through different eyes. I almost didn't post the video. How could I when I look so bad? I told myself that no one would support me when I look like this. But I did. I posted it. I posted it because I will not let the devil rule me with lies, I posted it because I want to challenge the world's standard of beauty, I posted it because the way I look now is the look of a warrior fighting for her life, and I posted it because God loves me and although I don't always believe it, that's the most important love there is.

With God's help, I WILL get through this one.

Crying Over Burnt Chicken

March 30, 2017

I bawled my eyes out yesterday. I'm talking guttural cry, swollen eyes, deep gasps type of cry. How very sad you say, but what was I crying about? Burnt chicken. I know. SMH

I read this cooking blog that said you aren't a real housewife until you know how to cook a whole chicken. I went out and bought my first whole chicken, and found the perfect Pinterest recipe, I spent a half hour cleaning it, making the ideal potion of seasonings, and covering every inch with oil and spices to create the perfect baked chicken. I set the oven to 425 as the recipe said, and I waited patiently for an hour as the bird baked. Every 20 minutes I even burned the hairs off my arm trying to cover my masterpiece in the boiling juices. At the chime of the timer, I excitedly pulled the chicken out and compared it to the golden bird in the Pinterest photo. Only, mine was two or three shades darker than the golden perfection photographed. I stared at (what I thought was) the burnt chicken. In my mind the blog statement, "You aren't a real housewife until you can cook a whole chicken" haunted me. So, I set the bird on the table and collapsed on the couch crying.

Now we all know that the burnt chicken wasn't the real issue; it was merely the "straw that broke the camel's back." What's really been going on then?

Let's backtrack a couple of weeks. As you know, I'm recovering from surgery, that's a battle in itself. But I also have been having issues with my shoulder and back. At first, I was told that five of my ribs were out and I have bursitis in my shoulder. Then it changed to my dorsal scapula's nerve was damaged, and now they are unsure whether a nerve is damaged, or severed beyond repair. The result of all this being that my scapula has slid out of place and my muscles won't hold it up. I have a lot of pain in that area, I can't move my arm in certain ways, I get tired early and can't do things at the pace I'm used to, and we are again venturing into the unknown so I don't even know if there is anything I can do about it. I've done my best to stay positive about the whole situation. I have spent a lot of time praying and asking God for strength, and I thought I was doing well. Until the chicken.

Adam came home to a bawling mess of a wife, a dark chicken in the kitchen and a bag of brussel sprouts cut in half and then given up on. As he held me while I cried, he asked me what was wrong. Initially, I said through tearful sighs, "I spent so much time on that dumb chicken, and now it's burnt! And the blog said that a true housewife could cook a chicken!" As the words escaped my mouth, I realized that it was much more than the chicken.

Earlier in the day, my tax accountant told me my LipSense business - an MLM (multi-level marketing) won't make money and are pretty much useless. Then earlier than that I was told that there might not be anything

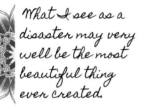

What I see as a disaster may very well be the most beautiful thing ever created.

I can do about my sagging and painful scapula and all I can do at this point to save my posture is wear a brace. Earlier than that I did six weeks of radiation, and it didn't work. Earlier than that, I did two months of a clinical trial, and it didn't work. Before that, I had a surgery, and it didn't work. Earlier than that, I did six weeks of Proton Therapy, and it didn't work, and the list goes on. My tears were a result of a whole two years of, "It didn't work."

Now, this is the part where my husband is a God-given miracle to me.

"Why did you start LipSense?" he asked? "For fun," I told him. "Oh, not to make tons of money?" he said. "No," I answered.

"Do they know for sure that your scapula can't be fixed?" he said. "No," I said. "Are you doing everything possible?" "Yes."

"If surgery and radiation and all those things didn't work, would you still be alive?" He asked. "No," I said.

Then he walks into the kitchen and cuts off a piece of chicken. The inside, to my complete amazement, was juicy and tender and perfectly cooked. As it entered his mouth, he told me that it was the best chicken he has ever tasted, and it was.

The moral of the story? I'm still trying to learn. I guess one take away would be that things aren't always as they seem. The burnt chicken was a reminder to me that I see only a little perspective in my fragile human mind. What I see as a disaster may very well be the most beautiful thing ever created. The last two years look like a burnt chicken to me, but God knows that on the inside is a beautiful, juicy, perfectly cooked plan.

Skater Girl Problems.

April 9, 2017

I listened to an excellent talk by this woman, and I wish I could re-member her name to give her credit but...oops. Anyway, she talked about this concept that purpose drives contentment. She starts out by talking about Pinterest, which automatically grabs my attention because I LOVE Pinterest. She talks about the joy in creating different boards and planning out your dream life. I could totally relate! I planned my entire wedding on Pinterest. I scrolled through photos of the perfect brides in the perfect dress at that perfect angle. I pinned snapshots of those little details, like delicate lettering, or cute little succulents. I pinned photos of the groomsmen with their beaming white smiles and chiseled jaws. After hours of dreaming and scheming, I left with a whole new set of expecta-tions for my wedding. After the speaker leads you through her Pinterest boards and dreams she then mentions that she becomes very discon-tent with her life after spending hours on Pinterest. As much as I wanted to say, "Well that's her problem." I found myself relating to that as well.

Discontentment. I feel like that is too familiar to me. I spend a lot of my time being discontent. I can trace this back to being a little 5th grader. I was constantly discontent. My best friend Kayla had everything I wanted at the time. She got the name brand pink VANS while I got the off brand brown suede ones. She got Toaster Strudels for breakfast while I got Honey O's (not even Cheerios), I was always comparing my life to hers. Fast forward to last week. I was discontent with not having a job while everyone around me went to work. I was discontent with how surgery has left me scarred while I see so many beautiful people in the media. I was discontent with our little rental when I see the stunning houses that my friends and family own, and on and on and on it goes. It's a sneaky one, and I often don't catch my discontentment in the moment, it's usually in hindsight. But after that woman mentioned that PURPOSE drives CONTENTMENT, I started to wonder, what's my issue?

My issue, I've found, is that I don't have a firm, unchanging purpose. Does that make sense? Let me show you by taking it back to my 5th-grade year of elementary school and jealousy. See, my purpose was found in being identified as a "skater girl." I mean really, I wanted to have the skater girl image. I wanted that identity, so my number one purpose and priority was my style. And because of that, I was always discontent. As long as someone else was being a better skater girl than I was, my purpose was unfulfilled. Now take it back to last week. I was seriously struggling with finding my purpose because I don't have a job. So, at that moment I was discontent because everyone around me was working and therefore I wasn't finding my purpose because I didn't have a job. I see that it's the hardest for me right after I fight another round of Merkel. I mean for months at a time my purpose is clear: FIGHT FOR YOUR LIFE. And I do, and I pour everything into radiation and surgery and healing, etc. But then it all ends, and they just drop me off at home, and I find myself feeling incredibly lost. I start searching for some kind of purpose, and I am often left feeling empty. Are you tracking with me now?

...if you find your purpose in living for God, you will always be content.

So, there is a simple solution here, I've known it all my life yet it is a CONSTANT struggle for me! The ONLY unchanging, constant, firm purpose is to live for Christ. I mean really, that's the only thing in this world that won't change. No matter what happens to you, no matter what you look like, no matter what brand of shoes you wear or what you eat for breakfast or what job you work, if you find your purpose in living for God, you will always be content. Man! As a person who finds herself longing for the Pinterest dream, or crying over not having the life I want, I find this solution to be radical. I want to be content, and I want to have peace with my life and with who I am and what God has for me. It's not easy! But I have to dwell on this, "That we are not our own, but belong, body and soul, both in life and death, to God and our Savior Jesus Christ." Our purpose must be to live for Him because we belong to Him!

Anyway, just a thought for today. I head to Seattle on Easter (sad about that), and I have my CT scan to see how I'm doing. Thank you for your continual prayer and encouragement!

You're Going to Be Sad

April 28, 2017

~~~~~~~~~~

"Why?"

"But why? I don't get it?"

"It doesn't make sense."

"I just don't understand? What the heck!?"

"That wasn't enough time!"

Many of you will say something along these lines when you see this post, and I want you to know that I said the same thing.

Before I explain to you why you are about to say these things, you need to know that it's okay to say them. To feel the hurt, the confusion, the frustration, and even the heartbreak. God feels that way too. And that's something that is so hard for me to remember, or even grasp. I often kick myself for asking those questions, knowing that I will not have the answers that I seek until I get to heaven. So, I encourage you to feel all the feelings but don't get hung up on questioning God. Don't go looking for answers here on Earth because truthfully, nothing will satisfy except this:

> "For I know the plans I have for you, declares the Lord, plans to prosper you and not to harm you, plans to give you a hope and a future" (Jeremiah 29:11).

God is not unaware of my situation, and He is not calloused and uncaring, His plan is not to harm me, or inflict pain on me, or punish me. He is in control, yes, He allowed this, yes, but He has a plan to give me hope and a future. Some of you doubt that I have a hopeful future, and sure, on Earth, my future looks more and more impossible. I often don't have a lot of hope that I'll have much of a future, here on Earth. A lot of times I do feel like cancer is going to kill me. BUT because He has saved me, I have a HOPE for an eternal future in HEAVEN. So, think about these things as I tell you what's next.

I have three new tumors. Yes, already. (Now you enter the exclamations from earlier). These tumors are completely out of character. The first one I felt is on the left of what would be my Adam's apple, if I were a dude. It's large already, and I had a tiny bit of hope that maybe it was *A lot of times I do feel like cancer is going to kill me. But because He has saved me, I have a HOPE for an eternal future in HEAVEN.*

scar tissue since it appeared in a previously treated area. You see, we thought we had an advantage, we felt that cancer wouldn't come back in an area that's been treated with surgery and radiation. Knowing we were wrong makes my heart break. It makes me fearful and discouraged. Will anything keep this cancer away?

The other two are on the left side of the back of my head, right where a headband would sit. They are two peas in a pod, snuggled right next to each other, again, a tumor placement that we haven't seen before.

So what now you ask? Well, I head back to Seattle to start the clinical trial again. This time we have T-cells frozen and ready to inject. The prayer is that the T-cells will be the game changer or a miracle. Only time will tell, but please, PLEASE, pray, pray, pray. I need it desperately. I also have to fly to Seattle quite often for the next couple of months so if you can help in any way there, I would be extremely grateful! Thank you again to all who read this blog. I am humbled by the way God has used this in your lives and in my own life, love ya!

I Should Be Sleeping

May 4, 2017

I should be sleeping. I should be curled up next to my husband in my bed, my freezing toes tucked underneath his warm legs. I should be home, and I should be doing wife things and thinking about what I'll make for breakfast or who I'll have coffee with.

I should be sleeping, but I'm wide awake. Partially from the nap I took after my 10th biopsy, and partly from the fact that I'm experiencing another guttural cry. It comes and goes, the emotion of it all. Tonight, it came after seeing a video I took of myself after my recent surgery, too recent if you ask me. It's odd, and sometimes I think I almost forget or block out what I've gone through. The videos and the pictures allow me to see everything from the outsider's perspective, your perspective, and I cry. I can't help but cry for the girl in the pictures; the stitches everywhere, the bloody red mess, the swelling, and the tubes. I feel so sorry for the girl in the picture. There in the hospital gown, bearing various scars and deformations, showing all that she's endured, and then it hits me, that harsh reality hits me in the midst of my brokenness for the girl in that picture. That girl is me. So, I'm crying. I'm crying as I sit in a bed that's not my own, alone, with freezing cold toes, a throbbing in the back of my head where they poked a prodded today,

There in the hospital gown, bearing various scars and deformations, showing all that she's endured, and then it hits me, that harsh reality hits me in the midst of my brokenness for the girl in that picture. That girl is me.

and the images of the past two years swirling through my mind. I'm thinking about the upcoming medical appointments I have instead of what I'm going to cook my husband for dinner. I should be sleeping, but I'm crying. And that's okay.

Praising Him through Frustration?

May 9, 2017

God is amazing. Seriously though, He continually baffles me in His goodness, and I am always reminded that when He says, "Ask and you shall receive" He means it! Not in a genie way, don't read this and then pray for a Mustang expecting that it will POOF! into your garage.

Two examples stick out to me of God providing for me this week. The first one, and one that I never want to take for granted is the kindness of God to motivate people's hearts to care for me. I have received an abundance of cards, words of encouragement, meals, airfare donations, and prayer. These things are not a given when you get saddled with the big 'ol cancer. These things are a blessing, and I'm humbled and so grateful for every person who has cared for me in some way.

Another example from this week happened a couple of nights ago. I was having a hard day, just struggling with those pesky questions of, "Why God?" "Where are you?" "How is this what's best for me?". I normally try to avoid questioning God. I find it easier for me at times to accept that this is my life. I try and find harmony amidst this calamity. To just "deal" with it. But eventually the tension and the outburst of, "this isn't how it's supposed to be!" resurfaces. So once again I was laying in my husband's arms just sobbing, nearly guttural. Side note you guys, as I'm sure you've gathered by now, my husband is amazing. Take notes here on how to handle someone who is suffering. LISTEN. He does that the best. He listens, he is patient, he is grace-filled, and he is selfless. If he hadn't taken the time to ask me what's wrong and truly mean it, I wouldn't be writing this blog. I would be stuck in the same rut of apathy. So, he chose to listen rather than sleep, rather than judge, rather than lecture, and after I poured out my heart, he encouraged me to read. See I have tons of books that people have sent me, but I tend to avoid them mostly because I felt like I'd feel bad about reading about others who are going through way more than me and handling it way better. But then he challenged me, "Why don't you read about someone else to be inspired by them, not to be condemned by them."

So, I listened.

The next morning, I picked up a book sent to me by friends in Spokane called, *"Rejoicing in Lament."* It was one on the top of the pile of books about cancer, ones that I was definitely avoiding. I already live out cancer, why do I need to read about it? That was honestly my initial thought. So, I flipped open to an old bookmarked page of mine, and the pages to follow were a direct answer to my cry. Did I mention that God was amazing!? And alive!? It's a sad world to live in if you dismiss everything as a "coincidence" or "lucky." No. This was planned and ordained by the Lord. The fact that I picked THAT book, the fact that I turned to THAT page, it was no coincidence, my friends, it was an answer to my prayers, it was a comfort to my soul because God CARES about me. Whoa.

Side note you guys, as I'm sure you've gathered by now, my husband is amazing. Take notes here on how to handle someone who is suffering. Listen. He does that the best. He listens, he is patient, he is grace-filled, and he is selfless.

So, I won't word vomit the last three chapters I've read, but I will talk about one sentence that gripped at my heart. "Even the most shocking psalms expressing outrage, fear, and despair are doing so before God, and that is praise." How radical is that sentence!? When I bring all my questions, all my cries, all my hurt, and all my frustrations before God, it's PRAISE! What the what!? How many times have I tried to manicure my prayers? How many times have I felt ashamed for feeling frustrated? How many times have I just decided not to pray at all if all I am going to do is cry? And all along, as it shows in the Psalms, I would have been praising the Lord, because I am coming to Him. RADICAL you guys, and man that one sentence was so freeing to me. I have been holding back in my relationship with God lately if I'm honest. I've been hurt, confused, frustrated, and unsure of how to even approach Him. I still feel all those feelings, and I still don't know what to do with it all, but one thing I do know, I can take them freely to the Lord. I can give it all to Him in its raw and flawed state, and it's praise. That's the God we believe in, that's a loving God, that's a God that, like my husband, will hold you and LISTEN.

I head back to Seattle tomorrow, I get a port put in on Friday, so if you could pray for that procedure to go smoothly I would appreciate it! Praise God that because of your generosity Adam gets to go with me for part of the time. I will be there until the 19th. T-cells with be on the 16th which is a BIG DEAL, so prayers for that as well, please! Love you all.

Tumor Flashbacks

May 25, 2017

It's been a very difficult past two days. As most of you already know, I received my first dose of T-cells last week. This is great news because they are actually floating around inside of me now! The infusion made me pretty sick and put me out for a good three days, and hopefully, that's a good sign.

But anyway, back to the present.

The night before last I was washing my face when my hand ran over a familiar lump. Yes, another tumor. This one is on my face, again, right under the scar where I got a hole cut out. It's the worst feeling when you discover a new tumor. Defeat, anger, confusion, heartache, disgust, despair. I think this one hit home especially because it's nearly in the same place my original tumor was, which brings back haunting memories and feelings. I just stared at myself in the mirror, and then I broke.

My poor husband. I wonder what went through his head as he is about to fall asleep and hears me in the other room, all of a sudden, bursting into a guttural cry. I've never seen him run to me so fast. Then we both just sat on the floor, sobbing.

I don't know what this means, and the doctors don't know what it means either. Was it growing before T-cells? Did it show up after? Do T-cells work? Will they work? So many questions and no answers.

I have seven tumors now. Seven tumors that can kill me. And I have spent the last two days wondering if I am going to die from this. I told Adam that if I do, I don't want anyone saying I "lost my fight with cancer." I hate that. Because of Jesus, I have won my fight with life! I will go to a place where I will suffer no longer, and I will live in a perfect, glorious place forever! Talk about HOPE, which is why I will continue forward.

On a side note, I want to remind you all that your actions MATTER. I was having a hard day yesterday, just thinking about the new tumor and dying and all that. I had to get some blood drawn for the clinical trial protocol. Instead of flying to Seattle for a blood draw, I decided to get it done here. I don't want to bore you with the details, but it ended up being this big ordeal. I was sent from place to place, told different things, the order was wrong, and then they couldn't even draw from my port, etc. etc. I was so stressed out that I started crying in front of the phlebotomist. Then one of the nurses there took me aside, (I know her name, but I won't mention it, she'll know who she is) and she just hugged me and told me that she has been praying for me. She said to me that I'm her little sister in Christ and that I'm not alone. In the midst of all the stress, while feeling isolated and frustrated, she reached out and comforted me. It was a seemingly simple thing, but it made a world of difference for me at that moment. It took two minutes of kindness you guys, and you never know what's happening in someone's life. Just be kind. Just do it. Take the time to care and to love, even the unlovely. So thank you for doing that for me yesterday Nurse S.

I head back to Seattle on the 1st. Please don't ask for further details on the trial because I have no answers at this point. Please pray for me and do something kind for someone okay? Thank you all and love ya!

About Death

June 12, 2017

I love when you guys come up to me and tell me that you read the blog. It helps to see you face to face, it makes it even more real that God is using my story to reach WAY beyond me. Lately, the Lord has used so many of you to bless me beyond belief! Everclean car wash did a fundraiser for me, Henley football did a fundraiser, Tashi Soaps did a fundraiser, and even Umpqua bank! I am incredibly humbled by your kindness and generosity so thank you all.

I have been giving this blog a lot of time and prayer. I know a lot of you have questions and I have some answers. This week my Mom and I head back to Seattle for another round of T-cells and a new trial drug. Yes, a new one because the most recent trial hasn't been working. I am up to 10 tumors, three in my face, three on my head, one on my throat, and two under my ear. The T-cells also haven't been working. The tumors are aggressive and defeated any T-cells that infiltrated them. It is NOT because my body is in bad condition and this isn't because my immune system is terrible, there is no explanation, except that it didn't work.

Initially, the news was extremely discouraging and devastating. I was counting on this to work. It's been our backup plan for so long that I almost felt invincible heading into surgery and radiation. In the back of my mind, there was always, "Well at least we have T-cells," and now T-cells are used up. The backup plan is done. This leaves us in an un-known spot. This is the scariest it's been for me. Plan A, B, and C are over. So, we move forward to plan D, and that will be a new trial drug.

I'm not invincible. None of us are. But I have to admit, it is hard to real-ize our mortality when modern medicine offers you so many resources to stay alive. For the last two years that I have had cancer, I have thought about death. But it always seemed so far off, it seemed so avoidable, and so in our control. I've never really experienced a lot of death in my own life either until my cousin took his life a few weeks ago. He was 21 years old, and it brought about the reality of my mortality. The fact that life is short. The reality that we aren't in control, as much as we try. Then, they told me that Plan C isn't working, and slowly but surely, I realized that my options are running out. So, I thought about death.

It's been amazing really, because as a Christian person death is not the end. I've been thinking a lot about Paul when he talks about longing for heaven and grieving for Earth. As the reality of mortality sets in, I have felt a longing for heaven for the first time in my life. Like you read all over in the Psalms, I have experienced the guttural cry of lament as I tell the Lord that I'm afraid to die. I have also experienced immense peace and joy in knowing that I get to live forever in heaven, in paradise. I get to live in a place where I will not be suffering, and I will never cry, and I will not have cancer.

My heart breaks knowing that there are people who will never experience that peace. They will live their whole life terrified of death. I am learning that you can't grieve for the earth without longing for heaven. You have to strike a balance. If you mourn for the earth with no hope for heaven then you can become bitter and angry. Jealous, you can start to justify why you shouldn't die and others should, and you can become miserable and panicked. When the longing for heaven comes in then, it forces you to meet death with a certain gratitude. Longing for heaven takes you back to the cross because without Jesus you wouldn't have the option of heaven. So, your heart is looking to the cross, and you meet grieving for leaving earth with gratitude for what God has given you, not what death is taking away. This has allowed me to say, "Oh death where is your victory, Oh, death where is your sting?"

So, your heart is looking to the cross, and you meet grieving for leaving earth with gratitude for what God has given you, not what death is taking away.

I'm dying, but really, we are all dying. I am so grateful to God for saving me, and I will not die and just become a pile of ashes in the dirt, THIS IS NOT IT. This life isn't as good as it gets for me, and death is not the end. As I cry and mourn over the thought of life ending here on earth, I also cry tears of joy as I thank God for being so loving, that He sent His son to die so that I may find joy in my suffering knowing that this is not the end.

~~Iso~~*lated*

July 6, 2017

This is hard. Suffering, pain, death, disease, it's just hard.

The last few weeks I have been able to do some really fun things with my family: no complaints there, only pure joy. But during the best of times, it's also been the worst of times. I have new tumors, a lot of them. My old tumors are growing rapidly, two of them being in my face. Every day I wake up and feel like something has changed. That centimeter of growth in my face tumor that makes it so now it pushes on my eye. That new tiny, familiar bump on the back of the other side of my head, the one behind my ear is now turning purple, etc. It feels hopeless and defeating.

I had a guttural cry in the car the other night with Adam. It started earlier in the day when I had a meeting with this woman. She was just so stunning and "normal" and all I could think about was the large tumor on my face or the fact that my smile doesn't work now, or I was worried about my hair moving to reveal these large red lumps. Insecurity ate me up inside. It shut me down. When fear plants a seed, it's amazing how it can filter the rest of your day. I went to a family barbecue, and I noticed the seed of insecurity inviting in the seed of envy as I watched my family laugh and talk about their future. They all seemed so unchanged, so "normal"; and then there was me.

It's isolating. I struggle a lot with not feeling alone. There's nothing that anyone can say or do except, "I'm sorry, and I'll pray for you." Sometimes I want someone to say, "I get it" or "I woke up with a new tumor today too" or "My face tumor is making my lip function not work too." But there is no one else. No one else knows exactly what I'm going through, and therefore, I feel alone.

I told Adam, in between deep gasps and streaming tears, that I picture my situation like this: I imagine one of those old movies, I'm running, and I fall. For some reason, maybe my leg is stuck, or perhaps I'm in a hole (I haven't figured that part out yet), but for some reason, I can't get up. Then this fiery, human eating ant starts to crawl up my leg. I'm able to swat him away. But then three come, and I can still defend myself. But then eight come, then 10, then 20, and I watch as I slowly see my body being engulfed by these ants. Meanwhile, everyone is standing there watching me. There are a few attempts to fight the ants off, but there are too many. So finally, everyone just watches, and I scream and cry for help. They tell me that they are so sorry and that they'll pray for me. They tell me that they wish they could do something. They say that they can't imagine what I'm going through. But they can't help me. I'm alone, slowly dying as these ants take over. (The ants, by the way, represent my tumors. If you didn't catch that.)

It's isolating and terrifying being alone with these ants. Watching as they destroy my body. But one of the things I've noticed lately, and one thing that I didn't mention in that story, is that, while I can't control the ants taking my body, I can control them taking my soul. In the midst of the lies of insecurity or envy or loneliness, I can run to the Father to shepherd my soul. To protect my soul, to nurture my soul, to heal my soul. My soul is already saved, and it's untouchable by fiery ants and lethal tumors. So instead of urgently trying to save my diseased body, instead of using everything I have to fight off the ants, instead of being angry as I look to the humans around me to save me, instead of isolating myself in the lie of loneliness. I am going to have the courage to go to God as my Savior, to thank Him for saving my soul, to spend my time not being angry with people but loving them, and to remind myself that we are NEVER ALONE. God has never left me nor forsaken me, He has never quit on me, He has always loved me, and I am not alone.

> *Its isolating. I struggle a lot with not feeling alone. There's nothing that anyone can say or do except, "I'm sorry, and I'll pray for you."*

I go to Seattle on July 10th. I'm not sure what the next steps are, but I could use a lot of prayers. Things are not going well for me. Physically that is. Please pray for wisdom for my doctors, for discernment for myself and my family, and for the faith that God is a good and sovereign God.

Chemo Here We Go

July 13, 2017

A few days ago, I got a call from my doctors asking me to come in ASAP to start chemotherapy. Chemo. The dreaded poison that I've been able to avoid all this time. I barely heard the words as they came through the telephone with urgency. The next few days I prayed, begged God for discernment and wisdom, and I asked Him to help me decide what to do.

Here I am at the end of my options, with more tumors creeping in and growing every day. I know that I don't have a lot of time left. Well, I don't know that for sure, but I do know I'm at the end of what I, as a human, can do against this cancer. Chemotherapy is a terrifying concept. The idea of nearly killing yourself to live. All the suffering I've seen it bring, the pain, the hair loss, the whole thing, and yet so many people have been healed from it. The few days after I got the call my heart was in turmoil. Do I want to try yet another thing that "might" work and yet fail me again? Do I want to spend what little time I may have left being miserable and poisoned? Do I want to skip it all and live out the rest of my days as best I can? These are the questions that wrestled around in my heart and mind.

Yesterday I met with my doctors. Man, I have been blessed with an incredible team. To see a dozen brilliant, scientific minds enter the room and shed tears over my case. I mean, I'm a person to them, they care about me, and they care about saving my life. That's just outstanding to me. Anyway, they reviewed my CT results with me. It's scary. I have 20 or so tumors, one of them is pushing my windpipe so hard that it's out of place. One tumor is pushing against my eardrum, so my hearing goes in and out, but nothing has breached any vital organs, so that's a blessing. But it's not looking good. We have no idea what to expect next with this cancer. Will it invade my windpipe? Will it creep into my brain? It's so hard not to let those thoughts rule over my mind. Like if someone told you that you're going to get in a fatal car wreck shortly but they don't tell you when. Man, how do you live with that!? I have to choose to trust God's plan and His timing. I have to give that to Him and let Him rule rather than be controlled by fear.

ANYWAY, after we discussed the CT results and had an in-depth conversation about how serious it is, they discussed chemo with me again. Essentially this is the deal, chemo will not cure me. It hasn't had long term success with Merkel patients. BUT the hope is that it will shrink the tumors to buy us some time to find another therapy. They are working hard on testing all different tissue samples, and I have one of the BEST doctors doing extensive research to find out what is wrong with my immune system. So, IF chemo works to shrink my tumors in the short term, then they might have an opportunity to try one last thing.

I will most likely lose my hair. Hair and I have had some tough times during this battle. I'm not going to feel bad or apologize that I am really devastated to lose my hair. It's a comfort to me. It makes me feel feminine and pretty, it disguises some of my ugly tumors, and I am scared to let it go.

A lab in New York is testing some of my tumors to see if I have a mutation that another drug might combat. Those results will take about three weeks.

So right now, the prayer is that (1) chemo will shrink my tumors and (2) that they will have some fantastic discovery that will lead us to a new drug option. Obviously, you and I both understand that if chemo doesn't shrink my tumors, I'm running out of time. And that's the harsh reality of it, you guys. But don't lose heart, that means I'm closer to a heavenly paradise!

In the meantime, I received my second dose of chemo today, and so far I am tolerating it well. I have some severe fatigue, a bit of nausea, and a significant lack of appetite but other than that I'm okay. Next week is supposed to be the hard week. My white blood count will be very low, I have to be super careful and watchful for any infection, and I will most likely lose my hair.

Hair and I have had some tough times during this battle. I'm not going to feel bad or apologize that I am really devastated to lose my hair. It's a comfort to me. It makes me feel feminine and pretty, it disguises some of my ugly tumors, and I am scared to let it go. Mom and I are going to go try on wigs tomorrow, and I can already feel that the Lord is helping me and giving me the strength to accept this new battle in my war with cancer. If you have tips on wigs or head wraps or scarves, let me know!

Thank you for being such faithful prayer warriors, and please never stop praying. Love you guys.

I'll Fly Away

July 26, 2017

Here I am, two weeks post chemo, and so far, it's been pretty okay. I was pretty sick the first week. The second week I felt relatively normal besides some extreme fatigue, and this week, just when I expected it would all be out of my system and I'd be back to "normal," I was sick in bed for two days. I just saw a gal that I used to work with on Monday, and I told her that chemo has been better than I thought, I mean I didn't even lose my hair! When I was a little kid (I think I've told you guys this before), I used to pull big balls of hair out of my head when I showered. It was just the normal shedding, but as a kid, I used to get nervous that I had cancer. Well, the morning after I told her that I'd kept all my hair, I relived that moment when I was a kid, but this time, I have cancer. I just sat in the shower, staring at my fist full of hair in shock. No one said it would hit me two weeks post chemo when everything seems to be getting better. It's been extremely discouraging.

When I'm super discouraged or feeling scared about dying, I listen to Negro Spirituals. I have learned so much in listening carefully to the lyrics. I encourage you to check them out. It will challenge your perspective on death. I mean here in America we have so many resources, so many options to "escape" our suffering. I get a new "cure" sent to me every single day. We have modern medicine, and we have all these special diets, we have essential oils, we have pills, we have clinics, I mean the list is astronomical! Only in America can we be overwhelmed by all the resources and "cures" and documentaries and research. While I am grateful for the abundant resources, I think it's created a certain expectation in our culture. Have you ever noticed that we have this expectation that we should die at a specific, comfortable, old age? If death comes before then it's not fair, or it's unjust, and we do everything we possibly can to prolong our lives and escape death.

As I struggle with this sense of entitlement, I listen to Negro Spirituals because they are baffling to me. Here you have a suffering people. These people were slaves, living with death being prevalent in all ages. Much of the death they experienced would be unjust and horrible, and yet, their songs are some of the most joyful and inspiring songs I've ever listened to. They are songs of passion, gratitude, and a genuine joy in longing for heaven, despite their circumstances.

I mean check out some of these lyrics you guys:

"Swing Low, Sweet Chariot"
If you get there before I do,
Coming for to carry me home;
Tell all my friends I'm coming too,
Coming for to carry me home.

"I Don't Feel No-Ways Tired"
Oh I'm seeking for a city, Hallelujah,
For a city in to the Heaven, Hallelujah,
Oh the brethren travel with me, Hallelujah,
say will you go 'long with me, Hallelujah.

"Listen to the Lambs"
Come on sister with your ups an' downs,
Want to go to Heaven when I die;
Angels waiting for to give you a gown,
Want to go to Heaven when I die.

I mean that's a teeny sneak peek. So, as I listened I thought to myself, "How do I, during this trial, in my suffering, as I wonder if I'm going to die, get to the place where I can sing joyous songs of heaven rather than complaining that I deserve more?". Well, the answer is, keep my eyes on Heaven.

All the Negro Spirituals are about the excitement of going to a better place, of meeting the Savior, of spending eternity in a world with no suffering. I mean this is NOT as good as it gets folks, and coming from a girl who has been fighting for her life for the last two years, who has had 11 biopsies, face changing surgeries, failed immunotherapies, burning radiation, and now chemo, I can say I'm so grateful that this isn't it. When my eyes are on heaven I am forced to reflect on the goodness of the gospel, I am forced to thank Jesus for saving me so that this isn't the end for me. I am forced to be grateful for what

As I listened I thought to myself, "How do I, during this trial, in my suffering, as I wonder if I'm going to die, get to the place where I can sing joyous songs of heaven rather than complaining that I deserve more?" Well, the answer is, keep my eyes on Heaven.

He has given me rather than all that I feel that He's taking away. And that's the key, that's what the slaves knew, they had an understanding and gratitude for what Jesus did for them so that they could sing songs that look forward to the promise of eternal life in paradise. AMEN.

I go back to Seattle for chemo round two next week. I will also hopefully get some results from some various tests that I can get into later. Please pray for my symptoms and me as I lose my hair. I appreciate all the support you've given me and some gorgeous head wraps too! Love you all.

The Truth About Being Bald

August 17, 2017

"Daddy where's her hair?"
"Hey look, that girl is bald!"
"You have a very nice shaped head."
"Well, at least there's no lumps!"
"You look like GI Jane."
"Mr. Crebbin's twin!?"
So, I lost my hair. Most of you know this by now. But I want to share the experience with you, the truth about losing your hair.

The moment you realize you are going to lose your hair is traumatizing. I mean at first, the experience is kind of what you'd imagine, or what you see on TV. Everything you do makes your hair fall out. When you sleep you wake up with hair all over your pillow, when you put clothes on you have hair all over your front, and back, when you try to brush it or put it up, you end up with fistfuls and a sink covered in...hair. It's annoying, it's terrifying, it's devastating, and you can't control it. I watched as my hair went from luscious, thick locks, to Sméagol stringy strands. Bald spots came through and it aged me. So, I decided to shave it off.

I had a certain numbness as I watched the hip hairstylist shave away the remnants of my hair. I didn't cry, but I wasn't okay with it. I stared at myself in the mirror, once again unable to recognize the woman sitting in front of me. I posted a photo immediately after stating that I was free. I must clarify though, I was free from the agony of losing my hair in giant chunks throughout the day, but I wasn't free from the insecurity of being a bald woman.

The first few days without hair were spent at the doctors. I felt, for the first time, like I belonged there. I felt like an actual cancer patient. I walked the halls feeling this weight of illness, like everyone saw me as I honestly am, a sickly, weak, dying cancer patient. I immediately put myself in the box that we all put every bald cancer patient in. I felt a new identity, and I felt pitied.

It only got worse when I went to public places like the airport. I could feel the heat of strangers staring at me. I imagined what they were saying in hushed tones. I stared at the floor, I made no eye contact, and I only focused on my furry new head. I hated how I looked, and I hated seeing myself in the mirror. I hated passing by my reflection and seeing a space where my bouncy curls used to be. I hated that I had no choice; that no matter what I did my hair couldn't be saved.

I tried a wig. I wore it on the second leg of my flight to try and blend in. I felt almost worse. I felt like I was wearing a disguise and everyone knew it. I didn't feel like a badass secret agent. I felt ashamed, more like a criminal wearing a different identity to escape. I know it must sound crazy. I mean here I have had countless surgeries leaving me swollen and scarred. Here I have had angry red lumps and nasty black stitches, and I was okay.

I'm not sure that I can pinpoint why this was so different for me, maybe because it seems so pointless. Perhaps because it feels like I was robbed whereas I agreed to the scars. Perhaps it's because the scars were symbols of healing and losing my hair just seemed like it only symbolized sickness. Maybe because it's true that hair is a woman's pride All I know is, it's hard.

So how did I get to where I am right now? Being able to make jokes about being bald and choosing that over my wigs and scarves? How can I look in the mirror now and not burst into tears? Or speak to someone with confidence without looking down?

It started when I was preparing to see my husband. I was terrified. We had been apart for two weeks and I was shaking at the thought that our reunion would be me sporting my new "cancer do." I imagined all

When I took my wig off to expose my bald head to my husband, I broke down in a guttural cry. He looked at me with tears and said, "I love you so much. You are a true beauty."

the things he would think, and I imagined him being disgusted and un-attracted to me. I knew of course that he'd never make me feel bad or say these things outloud, but I imagined what would happen in his mind. So, when I first saw him, I wore my wig. But the moment I had to pull off my disguise, to reveal the real me, it was like a picture of the gospel. My oh my. Bear with me. Here I was covering what I thought was a HUGE flaw. I was terrified to show it because I felt unlovable. Well, lemme tell you something. When I took my wig off to expose my bald head to my husband, I broke down in a guttural cry. You know why? Because he looked at me with tears and said, "I love you so much. You are a true beauty." And I knew in my soul that he meant it—all those things I made up in my mind, all my reasoning and justification for being unlovable. The ugliness and hatred I felt toward my flaw, was entirely accepted by my true love—what a picture of the Gospel.

Doesn't this remind you of how we act with God? Try to present ourselves in this lovely little disguise? Put a wig on our sins or flaws or past because we feel unlovable? Because of the unconditional love that Adam showed me when I felt my ugliest, I get the unconditional love that God shows us when we are our ugliest. When we take off that wig before God, He doesn't look at us with disgust, or think we are so ugly and beyond lovable. No, He looks at us and says, "I love you so much. You are a true beauty. My beauty and I have purchased you through Christ."

So it doesn't matter what the world thinks, or says, or what whispers I hear, or what lies I tell myself. I am loved, and I am loved despite my ugliest parts. I AM LOVED PEOPLE! I am loved by the creator of the flipping' universe! So, I will flaunt this bald head of mine, and I will walk in my true identity, as a daughter of the King! Heck yeah! Take that!

What's Next???

September 9, 2017

I've been a little MIA lately, so I know a lot of you are begging for an update! Well, the update is, the pill isn't working. I've slowly but surely been getting sicker and weaker and my tumors, them nasty tumors, are growing and rearing their ugly heads in new places. Man, I hate those things. Adam and I always joke around about wishing we could pop them right out. Now that I'm visualizing that, I'm glad that's not possible, ew! Anyway, I feel the effects of my cancer more than ever. I'm not sleeping but a few hours at night, I'm in constant pain from my tumors pushing on nerves, I have a harder time swallowing because of my throat tumor, I've lost a bunch of weight and can't seem to keep any of it on, and I'm so dang tired and have low energy all the time. It's not good, and it's not fun.

Lately, it's been kind of awkward because I feel like I don't recognize myself. This weak, sickly version of me is kind of new. My family has noticed my slow deterioration as well, and it's been especially hard on them because they feel like helpless spectators. It's hard for me because I so badly want to say, "The old Hayden is still here, she's still the lively, bubbly, adventurous, giggly person, the cancer Hayden is just overshadowing her."

I have to fight feeling almost guilty for not feeling like or being "me." But this is my new normal, and it's not my fault, and it's not in my control, and I have to give myself grace for that. It's kind of like when someone has the flu, and they aren't themselves and you just kind of dismiss it because you know they aren't feeling well, only this time it feels more permanent.

I head back to Seattle tomorrow with Adam, and we will attend the Merkel Dinner! I'm so excited to see old friends and make some new friends, the dinner is always so wonderful, even though I'm always the youngest Merkel Cell Patient, and super bonus - this year I'm a speaker for it! My doctors asked me to speak because they think that I'm inspiring, which is just so humbling.

After the dinner I will get an infusion of immunotherapy. I have to be honest, I don't have a lot of hope in immunotherapy anymore. In fact, I struggle with having any hope at all these days. It seems so impossible to envision myself healed. I have over 20 tumors, and as they grow, I feel less and less hopeful for a cure. But God is teaching me that instead of expecting him to do the things that I want or the things that seem like they'd be right, I should expect more of Him. Like, instead of sitting here placing all my hope in healing and waiting for Him to perform a miracle I want to have Him.

I want to expect that God is a powerful God, capable of miracles, I want to expect that He will never leave me or never stop loving me. I want to expect that He knows what's best for me, etc. It's not about WHAT He will do, but WHO He is. I hope that makes sense. I expect things of God's character, not of His actions because who can know the mind of the Lord? I have an understanding that He is powerful enough that He CAN heal me, but I also accept that if He chooses not to (on this Earth), then that's because it's not what's best for me.

> *I have an understanding that He is powerful enough that He CAN heal me, but I also accept that if He chooses not to (on this Earth), then that's because it's not what's best for me.*

Oh, side note, actually kind of a big side note, ADAM and I ARE GOING TO EUROPE! It was a very last-minute decision, but I figured, if these are potentially my last days, weeks, months of life, then I want to have my last hurrah. I've always dreamed of going to Greece and Adam has always wanted to go to France. So, the Lord opened the door, and our last hurrah (maybe) will be a trip from Seattle to Frankfurt to Athens to Thessaloniki to Paris, to Nice where we will rent a car and drive the French Riviera/Coast. Then back to Frankfurt, and home! We leave Tuesday the 12th and get back on the 25th. I am so excited you guys! Please pray for supernatural energy for me and also for me to give myself grace and patience because I'm still sick and won't be able to do a million miles a minute like I used to. I am so beyond blessed by this, and I can't wait to share the moments with you all!

The Not-So-Glamorous Part of Europe

September 27, 2017

We made it back from our Europe trip! Well, nearly. I'm still in Seattle receiving chemo. But we are back to the states and kind of sad, but also, we were kind of ready to be home.

I tried to keep you all kind of in the loop via Facebook, so I know that you guys know that we had a wonderful and exciting time! It was such a blessing. We had so many cool experiences, we got to see some amazing sights, and the time we got to spend together was much needed after a year of spending so much time apart. I'm not going to go into detail about the trip as far as all that we got to do and see. At least not right here right now! But I do want to thank all the people who were so generous in giving to our trip and giving advice and prayers and all that good stuff!

It's incredible to me how misleading social media can be. We can make something seem like it's outstanding, or make it look like we are the happiest we've ever been. I'm so curious how much goes on behind the mask of a cute photo and a witty caption. Well, because I've been transparent with you throughout my journey, I want to lift the mask off our Europe trip and tell you about the not so glamorous side. The side that I was frustrated by, heartbroken by, saddened by, and the side that I wanted to escape from so bad. The cancer side.

Yes, it's true, even a seemingly perfect trip to paradise will not allow you to escape the frustrations of suffering. It can often seem that way. You know, like in movies when the dying people make a bucket list, drain their bank accounts, and live out their days in paradise. Seems like a very tempting idea and I will admit, I wondered if Europe would be that for me. Unfortunately, the movie version of dying and the real-life version are very different, so I'll share with you what it's really like (keep in mind that I really DID have fun and I had some wonderful experiences, and I'm not making this to complain in any way, I'm merely allowing you behind the mask to see the truth).

The first couple of days in Athens I had a burst of adrenaline and energy and was able to start with a four hour walking tour. I had this false sense of, "Wow I can conquer anything, look at me go." I started forgetting about being sick as I gazed upon the sights like the Acropolis and Mars Hill and as I blended in amongst the tourist crowd. My tumors were giving me a little pain, but they weren't too big, and they were still easily concealed with a bit of makeup.

Yes, it's true, even a seemingly perfect trip to paradise will not allow you to escape the frustrations of suffering.

The first day in Thessaloniki I woke up to exhaustion as I've never felt before. My body felt like it was full of sand and my mind was cloudy. I could hardly function, and I lay there wondering if I could even do anything that we had planned for the day. I also noticed that my left ear had officially gone deaf thanks to the tumor pressing up against my eardrum. Thankfully, my husband is gracious and knows me so well because he insisted that I rest. It was a humbling moment for me, resting in Europe!? No way did I want to do that. I had a plan, I had a list, and being sick was not welcomed there. It was necessary though, and I knew that. We were able to spend the next day at a beautiful island and enjoy some fantastic food.

In Paris, I started to experience some pain in my rib cage. It was a new pain to me but not one that I could ignore. It was sharp and made it hard for me to walk around without taking a break. As we made the trek from train to train, to bus, to sight, to flat, I would feel weaker and weaker. That's when I started losing sleep. I would go to bed at night to be woken up my extreme pain in my face tumor and rib cage. It alternated so that I couldn't win. I would sleep for an hour and be up for three. Pain meds did little for me, and my poor Husband did everything he could to help soothe me to sleep, resulting in sleep loss of his own. I was so low on energy that Adam had to push me in a wheelchair around the Louvre. It was disheartening, and it affected my strength, my perspective, my positivity, and my "paradise vacation."

By the time we made it to Nice, my tumors had started rearing their ugly heads, amongst all the other issues I was experiencing. I had about four new ones, and my older tumors began to grow and become an angry red shade quickly. That was difficult not only because of the pain and the side effects they bring, but because Europeans are the WORST about staring! My goodness, the gawks and stares made me feel like a circus or a zoo creature. And the worst thing is, even when you make eye contact back, they still stare! They don't even try to break your gaze or try to go, "Oops, she caught me staring." It was mortifying, and it made me not want to go anywhere. I eventually got back to my roots and ended up taking it a step further by not wearing my wig, haters gonna hate, right?

So our trip down the French Riviera was much easier because we had a car, so that was a nice break for my energy. But as my tumors got bigger I was experiencing new side effects — one of those being not being able to swallow. We were driving from one French Village to the next when I went to take my ibuprofen pill, and it got stuck, and as it dissolved, it started burning. This is NOT how I pictured our paradise stroll through the French countryside. Before I knew it, we pulled over so I could make myself throw the pill up. I leaned over to puke with the view of France blurred through the tears of my frustration.

I spent the rest of our trip staying up almost all night from the pain in my tumors and rib cage, unable to catch a break. I would sit up and cry and try to let Adam at least get some rest. The tumors continued to grow and spread, making my face numb, making my eye protrude, pinching my throat and moving my nose. So, there you have the not so glamorous side of Europe, the unmasking, the truth. The truth, as I found out, is that I can't escape this cancer.

But what element did the suffering bring to my trip that I wouldn't have experienced otherwise? It helped me realize that if life is centered around me and my happiness and my wants and my bucket list, it will fall short. I had my paradise vacation all planned out, and nothing went as planned and if it were all about me, then that would have been one of the most devastating trips ever. But because of my suffering, I was reminded that it's not all about me, and it forced me to think more deeply about what it is about.

Instead of trying to find identity in being the most fashion-forward person in Paris, or trying to be so cool for getting to be in Greece, or for living my Notebook moment in the French Riviera, I was able to focus on the quality time I had with my husband. Yes, even the middle of the night crying sessions, or getting lost in the Louvre because there is no wheelchair lift. I was also able to focus on the majesty of God's creation through the intricate design of the Notre Dame or the clear blue waters in Greece. I also realized that instead of rushing to fulfill a bucket list or spending my last moments at the most beautiful places on Earth, I want to be home. My bucket list is spending as much time with my loved ones as I can. My bucket list is experiencing the richness of relationships and leaving behind memories with them. My bucket list is allowing God to use me in these times and experiencing his wonder through the beauty of creation and beauty of community.

My Last Birthday

October 15, 2017

"What do you want for your birthday?" It's a reasonable question to ask someone, and usually, I have a quick-fire answer as I have a running list in my brain of all the things I'd want. This year the question seemed impossible to answer. Not because there wasn't anything I wanted, sure I could think of a few things here and there, but because this birthday may be the last birthday I will have on this Earth. Clothes, shoes, makeup, all the things I would have wanted seeming almost pointless. I found myself wondering what mattered to me the most for my last birthday.

It came down to quality time with the people that I love. I longed to be in fellowship with my family and friends. All I wanted was to enjoy spending time with them. So how was my last birthday?

It was a wonderful night spent with friends and family. But it had a unique feeling for me as I had the filter in my mind of, "this is it, you'll never have another birthday here on Earth again." It made every moment more special, yet it also forced me to have a cry in the bathroom. I wondered silently to myself what my birthday next year would look like? Would people be crying and mourning? Would they try to make it a celebration and reflect on all the memories we shared? Would they just get through the day doing their best not to think about it? Part of me likes the image of everyone celebrating my life and making it a happy day; the other part of me understands that it could be a tough day. But whether it's a celebration or a time of mourning, the best image is that of everyone thanking God for the 24 beautiful birthdays I had on Earth. Whether it's in the form of gratitude or lament, I would hope everyone could say a little prayer to God and say a little something to me.

One of the best gifts I received was a pile of letters that my sister gathered from people that I love. I stayed up late in the night crying and laughing as I read what people had to say to me on my last birthday. Some shared memories, some told me what I've meant to them, some had no words, and some praised God for my life. It was one of the most meaningful things that could have happened on my last birthday. It got me thinking, as someone who has the rare opportunity to be aware that my life is ending, I can tell you guys what not to miss out on. Some of you won't know when your last birthday will be. So let me give you some

One of the best gifts I received was a pile of letters that my sister gathered from people that I love. I stayed up late in the night crying and laughing as I read what people had to say to me on my last birthday.

advice. Get the clothes and shoes and tools and games that you want, those things aren't bad, but don't let that be the center, the epitome of your birthday. I challenge you to spend your next birthday with the people that you love. And for those of you celebrating someone's birthday, leave NOTHING unsaid. Tell them why they are important to you, share your favorite memory with them, write them a card so they can keep your words forever because you never know what tomorrow will bring, don't waste a day.

Planning My Funeral

November 3, 2017

~~~~~~~~~~

I've been having kind of a "dry" couple of weeks. And by dry, if I'm honest, I mean I've been trying to ignore God. I've been staying distracted and really kind of lazy. Spiritually I haven't wanted to grow, or be convicted, or put in the effort with God. I've been hiding behind the simple distractions in life and the excuse of being weary from cancer. Ah, but God won't let you stay there, no sir. That tugging at your heart, that conviction you feel when you are looking to Netflix to comfort you when you know you should crack open your bible. It's more work, it's not instantly mind-numbing or gratifying, but it's the better way.

It's hard for me during this season of cancer. I'm doing chemo, and while it's buying me time, it's not curing me. It's palliative. It's a stepping stone before my death. The cycle is difficult to navigate. You get chemo and it makes you sick for the first two weeks, then you have a one week window when your tumors are smaller and you don't have the side effects of chemo so you feel almost normal, then bam, tumors are hard and angry and growing again and you are reminded of your permanent state to come once the chemo stops working. Which could be any day now. Once chemo stops working, that's it, outside of a miracle. So it's been strange and, and I have tried to numb the confusion and anxiety of it all by distracting myself and staying in a form of denial.

Here's the reality:

Last week, I planned my funeral. Literally. Adam and I went to the funeral home, and I picked out a coffin, I picked out a funeral package, I answered questions like, "Do you want to be refrigerated or embalmed?" "Do you want a viewing?" "Do you want to be buried or cremated?". I even went outside to pick out a plot of land that I will eventually be buried at. Heck, I even picked out what kind of design I want on my gravestone. I planned my funeral.

Now, most of you will never plan your funeral. For some of you, it will be because you had an unexpected death, some of you will just avoid going altogether. It seems gruesome, it sounds depressing, and it seems unnatural. That's not exactly wrong. I sat there staring at the various coffins on the wall and as I walked outside past "Here lies dear old dad" and "Our Angel," I stopped at the little plot of land under the tree. I stared at the blank space that will eventually say "Hayden Palm." I imagined my loved ones coming to lay flowers on the gravestone that I picked out. I imagined the tears that would fall on the stone, I imagined Adam standing under the shade of the tree telling me about his life, but most of all, I imagined the despair and sickness I would feel if I stared at that plot of land and thought, "this is it." All that I would end up being after 24 years of life would be a pile of bones under a gravestone near a tree. What a bleak and bitter end. What hopelessness, and how depressing. I too would avoid planning my funeral if I was just planning on becoming dirt. Instead, I have a greater hope that this is far beyond it. That plot of land is not my forever home. My home to come is far better than anything I will ever be able to imagine. And because of that I was able to stand there, under the shade of the tree, next to my grave, and thank Jesus.

Last week, I planned my funeral. Literally. Adam and I went to the funeral home, and I picked out a coffin,... I even went outside to pick out a plot of land that I will eventually be buried at. Heck, I even picked out what kind of design I want on my gravestone. I planned my funeral.

Hayden Crebbin-Palm

Obituary

On November 7, 2017, Hayden Crebbin-Palm died at her child-hood home in Klamath Falls, Oregon. She was 24. The brevity of her life is mourned by all who knew her; her life though was a gift to all who knew her.

Hayden Crebbin was born on October 12, 1993, to Robert and Alisha Crebbin, their first child. After Hayden, followed another daughter, Chandler, on July 2, 1995.

Hayden attended Shasta Elementary, Henley Middle School, Triad and graduated with a 4.0 from Great Basin. After high school, she moved to Stuttgart, Germany, to work as an au pair for a family with a young boy. While in Europe, she backpacked around 15 countries with her mom, sister, and other friends accompanying her at various times. She then returned to Klamath Falls before she moved to Spokane, Washington, to attend Moody Bible Institute in 2014.

During her year at Moody, she started a photo-journalism project, called "Humans of Moody." She interviewed more than 200 students about their lives. Her desire in doing this was to foster a sense of community among the students at the school as well as use her talents for photography and writing. It became quite popular and was carried on by others after she was unable to return to school because of her cancer diagnosis on June 26, 2015.

Hayden was 21 when she was diagnosed with a rare and aggressive form of skin cancer called Merkel Cell Carcinoma. The day she was told she had cancer, she started a blog that at her death had reached tens of thousands of people all over the world. Through that blog, she met her husband, Adam Palm.

He wrote to her to encourage her after seeing an article about her in the Moody Bible Institute newspaper. On a return trip to Spokane in October of 2015, she went to the same church that Adam attended and after the service he introduced himself. They wrote, texted and called for a few months before Adam told her he wanted to date her. Hayden thought she would never get married and yet after eight months of dating, Adam and she were married on August 27, 2016, in the backyard of her childhood home.

Hayden battled cancer for two years and five months before she died. Throughout her entire battle, she faced all the fears and tears, the countless surgeries, the many failed treatments that worked for so many others, the death of so many dreams for her life, with a grace and grit that many admired and drew strength from, including her family. She wrote openly, poetically, clearly and rawly about her trials and triumphs in cancer. She charmed and encouraged thousands with her beauty (inside and out), honesty, her indefatigable spirit, her kindness, her goodness, and her love for all she met.

Hayden never lost sight of God's goodness to her through her trials. She trusted in Him; she leaned on Him, she longed to tell others about the hope that she had because of Jesus and her deep and abiding relationship with Him. It is without a doubt that her life and influence was disproportionate to the years God gave to her.

She has left a lasting legacy of triumph over tragedy through her faith in the God who loved her and gave himself up for her. It is no understatement to say that her life and God's use of her trials were truly awesome in its scope and span as she touched and continues to touch thousands who hear about her life and read her blog.

Hayden was known by her family as the "one percent (1%) girl." She seemed to have a knack for always having what seemed to be the worst of the worst situations happen to her. Her getting a rare form of cancer, that usually only white males over 64 get, is a case in point. Yet, she will be remembered by her family and friends as the "1% girl" for many other reasons. She truly was special. She brightened everything she was a part of with her laughter, wit, and humility. She was the best gift giver and always seemed to know what others wanted. She listened and cared about everyone she met. Many people who only met her once were moved by her spirit and thoughtfulness. Hayden always put others before herself. She will always be missed because of the love she gave to all.

It is with a firm hope in a future resurrection that her family grieves her passing. All of them look forward to the day when they will be reunited with her in heaven.

(Written by Hayden's loving husband, Adam Palm)

Letters From The *Family*

Dad's Letter

Thank you for supporting Hayden and our family through this cancer trial, ministry, and book. I hope that her words inspired, challenged, and caused you to think more deeply about the most important things in life and in death. I know her words, wisdom, advice, faith, and hope greatly affected thousands upon thousands of people and will continue though Hayden's race is finished. I also know, as her father, God used her in significant ways to help me love more deeply, forgive more readily, live more intentionally, and give God more Glory through this tough time. I was responsible for leading, nurturing, and loving my family through Hayden's and our family's battle. It was the most difficult thing I've ever faced.

Any dads reading this may God bless you as you lead through struggles, accidents, illnesses, and deaths. Never stop serving others. Don't try to think about the "right" thing to say, listen ten times more than you speak, if you are an external thinker find a listening ear – I'd suggest God as He has suffered all things and knows exactly what we are going through. Love your wife well, as many marriages break up after the death of a child. Hold tight to Christ. Finally, you can't fix some things so don't try—you just have to ride out the storm however rough and lead through it. Then as it calms, you'll be better prepared for the next one—which is coming sooner than you expect.

As Hayden fought her battle, she determined that even if her battle ended in death, it would not be a sad, woe is me, feel sorry for me story. If you read her blog or this book, you know that she certainly had moments of lamentation, but mostly she was vulnerable, raw, and honest with what was going on with her, but she still had hope and usually was other focused and not self-absorbed in her own trial.

I hope you took the time to think on the advice Hayden gave us throughout her blog about treatment of those around you and seeing another person's perspective. I also hope this helped improve and grow your relationships with others. Above all, I hope that you were led to a deeper understanding of how God prepares His children – Christians, to face the most difficult circumstances, suffering and death with grace, hope, and love.

Hayden was praised throughout her cancer battle with having great hope. We were praised with raising her to be courageous, brave, and hopeful. We can't take credit as our strength and hope through all of this was a direct gift from God and only comes through Him. From the first tear-filled, cracking voice, it is cancer phone call we all grew exponentially. We began weak, ignorant, fearful, and powerless. Any human prop holding us up was removed, and the varied gifts from God and His blessings were rained down upon us as His beloved children. All credit for how we made it through the difficulties associated with Hayden's cancer battle can be to God alone. Our confident hope is in Him. Many poor people dream up false hope in all sorts of ways when faced with difficulties relationally, physically, emotionally, and spiritually. We were inundated with advice in all the aforementioned areas attempting to help us cope. Yet potions, elixirs, crystals, positive thoughts, visualization, medicine men, rosary, pilgrimages, and the like failed at every turn to give us the lasting, and confident hope that only God can give—I hope you read that in page after page of this book – hope in life and death. Hayden was granted the gift of grace by repenting and placing faith in Jesus Christ to save her from the consequences of sin and giving her the guaranteed hope of Heaven forever in life and in death so she could confidently face anything that happened to come her way during her life on earth. Can you confidently assert the same? Have you considered what awaits you when you die? Will you be 'good' enough to be pardoned for your sin and be lovingly ushered into Heaven? The only hope that you can count on is hope from God. All other hope is false and will fail you in the end. Why did Hayden have such hope and strength, and bravery, and courage, and faith, and love? Each one is a gift from God to those who repent of their sin and place their present and future life in the hands of the One that died for the penalty of our sin, that rose from the grave on the third day, and was seen, heard, and touched by hundreds, then ascended to Heaven where He reigns and rules at the right hand of the Father. He will fulfill His promise to send you the Holy Spirit as He has countless others through history if you bow your knee to the One that has power over life and death. The One who gave Hayden hope, faith, and love. Won't you come to Him now as He has gently, and loving called to you through the pages of this book and given us the witness of the Bible to have a hope that defeats death?

Mom's Letter

Hello there. I have been praying for you, asking the Holy Spirit to give me His wisdom as you read this letter. Death is hard. The death of your child is harder. But as much as we don't like it, death is part of the human condition. We must examine this truth, remembering that God is good, only and always. He is good all the time.

I am Hayden's mom, and though there are many things I would love to share with you about my awesome daughter, her wonderful life and painful death, my focus for this letter is - Storms.

As you are reading this, one thing I know to be true; you are in the middle of a storm, you are heading out of a storm, or hold on tight my friend, because you are heading in.

Now, this shouldn't take us by surprise because God tells us in His Word that storms are a part of life. This is promised to everyone, whether you are a believer in Jesus or not, trials are coming.

"In the world you will have tribulation. But take heart;
I have overcome the world" (John 16:33).

When Hayden was diagnosed with cancer, not only cancer, but a rare and aggressive form of cancer, I felt like I had been tossed into a little boat against my will, and set out to rough sea. At times, the boat felt more like a flimsy child's blowup raft. Nothing to grab hold of, unstable and no protection of any kind from the storm.

Why God? How could this be your plan and how on earth could I survive this storm on a floaty?

There were times I felt like my boat was stuck on the shore. Like I was shipwrecked on a deserted island with no one around to offer a hand or help of any kind. These were lonely times, feeling stuck in the blazing hot sands of adversity, and no matter what I did, my boat wasn't going anywhere. These were dry and weary times with God.

Then suddenly, it seemed the waves would come crashing in and carry me out to deep waters with 50-foot swells. There were times I felt helpless, scared, and at the mercy of the tide, and distress was my constant companion. Then, just when I thought the pain in my heart would kill me, I found myself on still waters, and I felt the peace of God that surpasses all understanding, and I would rest.

Still, I wondered, where was God in all of this mess? Had He abandoned me, us, Hayden? Couldn't He hear our frantic cries and see our desperation? How could God be loving if He had the power to stop this and yet did not? I was tempted to think that God did not care, but I knew this couldn't be true. He had to be bigger than my storm because He is God over the winds and rains and He alone controls them.

> *"The LORD HURLED a great wind on the sea and there was a great storm on the sea so that the ship was about to break up" (Jonah 1:4).*

He is a Sovereign God, completely in control of all that He allows into our lives. Knowing this, I would fight. I would fight in the dry times, the calm times, and in the waves to trust God, to feel God, to find peace. There were many times that the only prayer I could whisper was "help me," and I would hear:

> *"Be strong and courageous. Do not be afraid or terrified because of them, for the Lord your God goes with you; he will never leave you nor forsake you" (Deuteronomy 31:6).*

> *"So do not fear, for I am with you; do not be dismayed, for I am your God. I will strengthen you and help you; I will uphold you with my righteous right hand" (Isaiah 41:10).*

> *"Peace I leave with you; my peace I give you. I do not give to you as the world gives. Do not let your hearts be troubled and do not be afraid" (John 14:27).*

I had to speak the truth from God's Word to my heart and mind over and over again and remind myself that God is only FOR me. He is not against me. He is with me in my trials and that He will never leave me or forsake me. You must do the same. No matter your situation or circumstances, you must fight your storm with the most effective tools—God's Word and prayer. Read it, say it, sing it.

And that is how I continue to get through the storms and the death of Hayden.

So where do you find yourself today? Financial difficulties? Divorce, wayward children, health issues, or perhaps dealing with death? It doesn't matter the storm you find yourself, and if you are on a boat, a raft, or the Titanic—cling tight. Dig your splintered, ragged nails in deep and hold on. God is there, and He has got this. He is sovereign over your storm. Not because I say so, but because the King of the Universe promises.

Your storm may last for days or years. The point is that God is using it to change you, to grow you, and to teach you. If you are a Christian, God is using your trials to help make you look more like Jesus before you leave the planet. Do not lose hope my friend, God is using this for your good and His Glory. Stay the course and show yourself patience and remember God's grace. Give yourself time to mourn and grieve. Lament and cry out to God, telling him about everything you feel. He gets it. He knows, and He has been there. God is not in a hurry, and He will be with you every step of the way.

> *"As I was with Moses, so I will be with you; I will never leave you nor forsake you" (Joshua 1:5)*

Do not focus on the storm, but fix your eyes on Christ, our living hope. Whether you are stranded in the blistering heat of the shore, bouncing around in the rapids or trying to survive a twenty-foot swell, fight. Fight to cling to Christ, and you will find that He is holding on to you, and Jesus will never let go of you.

> *"And He got up and rebuked the wind and said to the sea, "Hush, be still." And the wind died down, and it became perfectly calm. And He said to them, "Why are you afraid? Do you still have no faith?" They became very much afraid and said to one another, "Who then is this, that even the wind and the sea obey Him?" (Mark4:39-41).*

Adam's Letter

Dear Reader,

As I write this, I am sitting on the front steps of a Presbyterian church in Virginia. I just walked through the cemetery that rests to the side of the church. It's a peaceful spot. It makes my heart ache, though.

Death and suffering are terrible things we all must face. The people in the graves at the cemetery were all once filled with life. One lived to be ninety; another young man of 22 was killed in the Civil War. My wife's life was ended by cancer at 24.

I don't know why you read the book or the particulars of your life circumstances but I am glad you did. I hope Hayden's wit and wisdom encouraged you and perhaps challenged you in whatever you find yourself facing. I know it's been a cherished gift of mine to be able to read the words of my wife as I struggle through grief. She never intended or thought about it I am sure but she still counsels me today. Who might I ask, gets that? Sometimes, just like when she was alive, I know she is right, but I don't want to follow her advice. I do try though. Her words are a gift for which I am grateful.

Suffering can make a person wise. It can expand the soul. It did that to Hayden. One of my greatest longings was to live till we were old. In the year and two months of marriage that we richly enjoyed, Hayden was transformed. She was always a wonderful woman, why do you think I married her, yet in the last few months of her life, her beauty of spirit was its brightest. She, despite the fear and turmoil of facing death, lived for others so well. She became even more thoughtful and caring than she had been. She was peaceful and enjoyed each day. I wish I could have enjoyed her and life with her more.

We tend towards myopia more than ever today. We live distracted and restless lives. I wonder how many of us have any time to consider the length of our days and gain the heart of wisdom the psalmists refers to. Wisdom, I might add, that we desperately need these days. My hope is that Hayden's story would cause you to think more and reflect more on your life and its trajectory. This type of self reflection is painful, yet necessary.

When suffering enters our lives we are quick to ask how we can get out of it. It's much harder to ask, "How can I be transformed by this?" Believe me when I tell you that I would rather escape my grief most days than face it. The quickest way to the sunrise though is to chase the sun through the night so embracing our suffering and entering into it is the best way to work our way through it. That's frightening and most of us don't want to do it. But not doing it may be in the end the worst of both choices because more often than not our circumstances won't change. All that can change is us and as W.H. Auden once wrote, "We would rather be ruined than changed." Change takes work but it is worth it.

C.S. Lewis once wrote that, "Pain is God's megaphone to rouse a deaf world." What are we deaf to is a good question to ask, I think. I hope in whatever you face that you might ask that question and you might just find what your heart is truly looking for. Hayden and I would tell you that you are looking for God. A famous Christian theologian, St. Augustine, wrote that our hearts are restless till they rest in God. So, I want to encourage you reader that perhaps the purpose of your suffering is finally and fully to find the rest you long for in God.

It's hard though. Hayden and I both learned quickly that suffering can do one of two things. It can push you towards God or away from God. We have the choice. Could it be, dear reader, that the suffering you face could be God's way of seeking your attention? I think so and I think that is a very great thing, far greater than you or I often think.

What if my wife's suffering and writing was intended, in part, to be a way in which you for the first time wanted to know God? Hade and I would both agree that's a very good thing. Every night we went to bed when she was home we would pray using a book called, *The Songs of Jesus.* It's a devotional on the Psalms by Tim and Kathy Keller and some nights when we prayed, we would pray for people who may not know God that through our story they might come to know Him. I can't help but think that if you don't know God and you are reading this book that may be the start of an answered prayer.

Hayden's last blog post on planning her funeral ended with the words, "Thank Jesus." I have always found this so fitting. I preached from John 11 at Hade's funeral because it captures the full hope that we have in Christ. Jesus' good friend Lazarus was sick. Jesus had demonstrated to his followers that he could heal the sick so when they saw that he knew Lazarus was sick I assume they thought he would leave immediately to heal him. Instead Jesus waited two days before he went to Bethany where Lazarus lived. By the time Jesus reached Bethany, Lazarus had been dead for four days. One of the sisters of Lazarus, came to Jesus and told him that if he had come earlier Lazarus would not have died. Jesus looks at Martha and tells her that anyone who believes in Him even though he dies yet will he live. Then Jesus walked to the tomb, had them open the tomb, and called out to Lazarus. Lazarus gets up after being dead for four days and walks out. Jesus had just demonstrated to

Martha and all who followed him that he had power even over death itself. The story though doesn't end there. Jesus himself was killed soon after and was buried. Three days later, Jesus rose from the tomb and demonstrated that death was forever defeated for all those who trust in him. The writer of Hebrews, a letter in the New Testament put it this way, "he (Jesus) also became a human being, so that by going through death as a man he might destroy him who had the power of death, that is, the devil; and might also set free those who lived their whole lives a prey to the fear of death." This is why Hade thanked Jesus because he came and died in her place so that she might no longer fear death because for someone who has believed in Christ death is now gain.

What a great hope for anyone to have in the face of suffering. If all of that seems unbelievable for you as someone who does not believe in Christ or even knows much about Christianity may I encourage you to pursue learning all that you can about the claims of Christianity. If Jesus really did rise from the dead and offers salvation and eternal life to all who trust in His name, don't you think it's worth the trouble to investigate the truth of His claims? I for one think so.[1]

Finally, to all my brothers and sisters in Christ, I hope your faith is strengthened by my wife's faith in God through her trial. I hope you are encouraged to know that death does not have the final victory over us. Christ has conquered the grave and our deaths, really our final home-comings, are precious in His sight. May we who have lost loved ones in life be encouraged to know that one day the dead in Christ will rise first when Christ returns and we who are still alive will be caught up with them. Then we will be with the Lord forever. Let's encourage one another with these words.[2]

May God bless you,

Adam Palm

---

1. Some great resources for investigating the Christian faith are:
   - *The Reason for God* by Tim Keller
   - *Basic Christianity* by John Stott
   - *The Case for Christ* by Lee Strobel

2. Two book recommendations for anyone going through suffering:
   - *Walking with God through Pain and Suffering* by Tim Keller
   - *A Grace Disguised* by Jerry Sittser

Chandler's Letter

~~~~~~~

There are moments in time that change you. They take you by the shoulders and gently shake you to get your attention. These moments have only good intentions. They want to change you for the better, like hearing Johnny Cash's 'Hurt' for the first time. Or the moment when you look at a picture of your mom from ten years ago and notice just how silently and slowly time has left its mark on her, and you remember to love her better than you had before.

Then there are the others.

The moments that take you and shake you, and don't stop. You beg and plead, but these moments are not as forgiving. These moments want to do more than get your attention, they want to break you into a million small pieces. Like the moment you're shopping with your sister and she tells you through tears that she won't buy anything. She only has five months left, so why bother? Or the moment you call her because, somewhere buried in the deepest corners of your soul, you know that will be the last phone call you share.

Or the moment of writing this letter.

These 'other moments' are the ones that leave their deep scars all over you.

I have always liked things wrapped in ornate paper and tied up in a handmade bow. For the past four years I have been chasing down every possible simple explanation for these 'other moments'. Maybe a list of 'top ten things I learned from my sister dying' or 'how to get through a trial 101'.

But, after spending too many hours of contemplation and sob fests in the bathtub, I do finally have some sort of messy grasp on the 'why' of these past four years.

My family always called me 'another girl looks-on' which is a very long story that basically means I was always in the background, observing others before I experienced something myself. Hade was the oldest. She was the first to ride the bus alone, the first to drive, first to get a job, first to travel solo. She was the bold one. She would always say "Sissy, you're so lucky that I am always the one to go first!" she would then go on to explain the good parts, pitfalls to avoid, and guide me through every situation as to ensure my painless passage through every scenario.

June of 2015 was when this way of life changed for us. The first time we had to do and any 'firsts' together.

When Hade got diagnosed, she couldn't tell me how to react. She couldn't tell me, "Watch out Sis, this part right here, when the doctors say the diagnosis, that part is going to hurt a lot."

Oh, how I wish just for once, that I could switch places with my sweet Hade. That I could go first.

But that's not how our story goes. God equipped Hayden for these 'go first' moments. He made her able to look her fear in the face, nod, and keep moving.

I can't say that I have had some grand revelation and understand all the intricacies of life. That I now understand suffering and the role it plays in every one of our stories. I can say though, that I know why this was the script written for my sister. That she used her story to grab ahold of thousands of hearts and remind us all of the bigger picture. The one with vibrant colors and intricate details. The one where we love each other deeper. The one where we see God for the mighty savior and protector He truly is. The bigger picture where, in the midst of millions of books, you were meant to read this one.

From one sister's heart to yours, dear reader.

Chandler

Alec's Letter

~~~~~~~~

Dear reader,
   You have just explored a story of life and joy interrupted by suffering and death. The story of Hayden ended in a strange way that you may be wrestling to believe. You may think that this story's ending is a nice way to avoid feeling sad for an incredible loss. You may also think that this ending is absolutely true and there is a man who's life made is possible for Hayden to live on. And you may be anywhere in between.
   This story is a small piece of a much larger and more wonderful story of how this life we live and joy we experience is not meant to end, but is interrupted and corrupted by evil in our world. Hayden's life was redeemed by Jesus's life, death, and resurrection. Hayden chose to direct her life after this reality that Jesus lived and died for her. It is Jesus's life that makes this ending not a sad story. This same man's life and death is the climax of the larger story of suffering, evil and, death being destroyed and love, peace, and joy to start filling in the holes left by it. This story is not meant to be read and left alone. It is meant to be dealt with and thought through carefully. This story calls for a decision: can this really be true or not?
   I challenge you to take some time to wrestle with this question. Jesus is the hinge to this story's sequel. You also are invited by Jesus to take part in this sequel. This Jesus loves you and knows you, and I hope you will take this challenge seriously as Hayden did.

                              Alec

(I was fortunate enough to meet Hayden and Chandler the summer of 2015 at Camp Redwood Glen where all of us were working for the summer. I met Hade that summer and was able to talk with her about her life before this story began. Chandler and I met later that summer at a Camp Redwood Glen bonfire and immediately fell in love. Chandler and I were able to share 2016 with Hade and Adam as the year of engagements and wedding celebrations. Hayden and Adam married in August of 2016 and Chandler and I married in December of 2016 at the same camp where we met. God was truly gracious to us that year and blessed us tremendously.)

JB's Letter

Dear Reader,

I am writing this letter to give you a glimpse into Hayden's world, as well as share a bit about the way that my story was and still is being impacted by knowing her.

My name is JB. I am a Jesus follower, nurse, wannabe surfer, summer camp enthusiast, and lover of ice cream. Perhaps most relevant to this letter however, I am one of Hayden's older cousins.

If you didn't already know, Hayden and I come from a large, rather loud, and tight-knit family. With a slew of just over 30 cousins on our maternal side, holidays are big, traditions are strong, and nicknames are plenty. Falling somewhere in the middle of the bunch as a whole, I am the eldest of a cluster of five girls born one after the other. Hayden was next in the line-up, followed by Jessica, then Macaela Rose, and lastly Chandler (Sis) the baby of the bunch.

I've heard it said (probably on a Pinterest board) that *Grandma's house is where cousins go to become best friends.* I laugh because its cheesy, but this could not be truer of our childhood. Grandma Daisy was so intentional in helping foster close relationships among us girls. Growing up with only brothers, this was so special to me because I found sisterhood in this group of cousins.

Summer camp, like grandma's house, is a shared and sacred space for us cousins. In fact (spoiler alert), the summer Hayden was diagnosed we were working together at Camp Redwood Glen. I had just taken a full-time job there, so Hade, with a few of our other cousins had decided to join me as summer staff. Hard for me to comprehend that those early days of summer were the last time I saw Hade healthy.

The days since Hayden's diagnosis have been my darkest. Over the course of the next two years I watched as my cousin, sister and friend lost a heart wrenching battle to cancer. I spent those years in denial of the diagnosis, hoping that my lack of acknowledgement would strip away any power it had to take her from me. But our miracle never came, and on a grey Tuesday in biology lab the call came that it was time to say goodbye. With her gone, regret still lingers in the quiet, wishing I would have taken her illness more seriously. Oh to go back and soak in every moment we had together, holding each one a bit tighter.

When Hade died, I felt the inadequacies of my coping through-out her cancer battle weigh heavy. Since I felt I didn't get it right while she was alive, I wanted to honor her by grieving her well after death. I searched the scriptures for an example, I thought maybe I should weep like Jesus; or sit in sack cloth like Job; perhaps dust myself off, shower, and eat like King David. I was sure the sorrow would be brief if I could just grieve properly.

It has been two years now of learning to do life without Hade and I still am uncertain most days. Two long years of grief, which like the changing ocean tide still comes in waves. Some days the sorrow billows and crashes over me, destroying everything in its path. Other days, like a calm lapping of the sea against the shore grief is constant but bearable. Does this mean I'm still doing it all wrong?

I began this letter to you with hopes that I could share something useful, a simple thought to encourage and uplift you. I wish I could lay out for you my step by step process for living intentional when those around you are suffering, or how to mourn the "proper" and holy way. But the truth is, I'm still in the middle of it.

Perhaps however, if Hayden's blog has taught me anything, it is the value of the middle. After all, that is where Hayden invited us into her story isn't it? In the midst of uncharted territory, uncertain of the ending, she opened her computer and invited us all to join her. With each post she shared, Hade showed us that it is here, in the middle, where grace and beauty can be found.

My prayer for both you and for me, is that we would learn to value to middle, to search for the treasures hidden only here. I pray this book, this letter, and these sacred stories are part of the beauty you find.

With Grace & Peace,

Your Friend JB

Beauty from Ashes

Hayden's Courage Award

Before Hayden died, a local business came to her about starting a scholarship. I remember her coming home that day, sitting in our rocking chair, and telling me this really cool story about a lady that felt compelled by God to contact Hayden and give her some money to start a scholarship. Hayden gave it a lot of thought, and although she was honored by the offer, she knew she did not want to start a traditional scholarship. "Nothing against a scholarship or college, Mom, but I would like to do something different for kids that might not be heading to college or kids that need a different kind of help." We began to talk about different ideas, but time passed, and she died before we could plan anything.

Hayden loved people, community, mysteries, and she was brave. Hayden demonstrated great courage at times in her life, and she continued to grow braver, especially in her cancer journey. Although covered in painful tumors, and having a hard time breathing and walking, Hayden took her husband Adam on a five-hour drive to attend a Lecrae concert in Sacramento just two days before she passed away. Hayden would not let cancer dictate what she wanted to do. They had such a great time, got to meet Lecrae, and tell him what his music had meant to them, and they even got to snap a picture with the star. They got home early in the morning on November 6th, and Hayden died on the morning of November 7th.

COACH CREBBIN

As many of you know, my husband has been a football coach for many years. He's super gifted at what God has created him to do, and he has impacted hundreds of young men's lives. I love and adore this about him, and many parents and football players have taken the time to tell Rob, (Coach Crebbin), the influence he has had on their lives. Anyway, after Hayden died, the coaches and the team got together and started Hayden's Courage Award to honor the courageous way Hayden fought cancer, lived her life, and to honor her dad as well. It took us by complete surprise when they introduced Hayden's Courage Award and the recipient at the end of the football award ceremony, and the tears flowed that night.

Henley High School also added Hayden's Courage Award in their graduation ceremony which is only one of three awards allowed to be recognized at the event. Thus, the recipient is recognized by classmates, parents, and hundreds of other people as someone that has shown grit, courage and determination through difficult life trials.

Isn't that just like God? He used the coaches and team to accomplish what Hayden wasn't able to.

NOW IN FOUR SCHOOLS

Hayden's Courage Award has become so popular that it is now in four local schools. Shasta Elementary, Henley Middle School, Crosspoint, and Henley High School.

WHAT IS THE AWARD?

Hayden's Courage Award is a cash award given to a deserving student to use as they choose. There are no strings attached. The student is chosen by the school staff and administration and presented at the end of the school year.

WHY THE COURAGE AWARD?

Courage is lacking in our culture. Suicide is the second leading cause of death for people age 10 to 40 years old. We want to send the message to young people that you are not alone when hard things happen to you. Other people have gone before you and faced challenging situations too, and they persevered. They chose to be courageous in life and to not give up. You can choose courage and be strong and brave in your trials, just like Hayden and the other young people that have come after her.

If you would like to support Hayden's Courage Award you may send a check to:

The People Mender
1906 Madison St.
Klamath Falls, OR 97603

or visit our website:
www.thepeoplemender.com

Thank You

Thank you, my baby gal, Chandler Bobbitt, for the many hours you have spent listening to me lament over this project, the hours of prayer, and for designing the book cover, videos, and a beautiful website to make Hayden's story and book available. You are a gifted creative, and I love you with all that I am.

Thank you, my darling husband, Rob, for being the leader, listener and lover of God you are for me and our family. There are just no words. I love you forever.

Thank you to Gina McCuiston and Chadwick Mahanna for helping us edit this book. Thank you for loving the difficult English language, especially the grammar part—I don't care if I ever see another comma or quotation mark!

Thank **you**. Yes **you**, the thousands of kind folks that have been faithful in prayer, encouragement, support, financial gifts, fundraisers, hugs, food, and given so much love to our family. This book is for you, and our hearts could never express enough gratitude. Hayden wrote her blog with you in mind, and this book is a continuation of that desire to help the hurting and lost, and encourage you in the truth of Jesus Christ.

Thank you, Gary, at Maverick Publications, for being a kind light when my path was dark in the printing world, and to Jody for making Hade's book look beautiful. Also, to Josefine for reproducing Hade's tattoo art for use in the book.

Thank you to the community I adore—Klamath Falls, Oregon. For being the hands and feet of Jesus to our lives and providing love and support just when we needed it. We love you.

Thank you, Grandma Daisy, Mame, Grampa Sam, our brothers and sisters and families, Kathy, Char, Holly, Syd & Bill, Ed & Camp Redwood Glen, Traci, The Myrons, Kayla & Lisa, Glen & Janet, Alex Stork & the Henley Community.... If I mentioned every person I want to, I would never get this off to the printer.

Thank you, GOD – and if not, you are still good.

THE PEOPLE MENDER

Fo For more information please contact us at:
ThePeopleMender.com
ThePeopleMender@gmail.com

Please like and follow us on Facebook and Instagram:
@Alisha Shaw-Crebbin
@ThePeopleMender